The Popular Policeman

The Popular Policeman and Other Cases

Psychological Perspectives on Legal Evidence

Willem Albert Wagenaar
Hans Crombag

Amsterdam University Press

Some of the chapters in this book were written when the first author was a fellow of the Netherlands Institute for Advanced Study in the Humanities and Social Sciences (NIAS) in Wassenaar. The hospitality and support offered by NIAS and its staff are gratefully acknowledged.

Cover illustration: W.A. Wagenaar
Cover design: Sabine Mannel, NAP, Amsterdam
Lay-out: Het Steen Typografie, Maarssen

ISBN 90 5356 763 1 (paperback)
ISBN 90 5356 770 4 (hardcover)
NUR 824/770

Contents

Foreword 7

1 Illegal Gambling or the Victory Travel Club 9

2 On Causal Reasoning or Death in the Warmoesstraat 25

3 Consumer Confusion or Potato Chips and Olive Oil 43

4 Fiction and Reality of 'the Average Individual' or the Case of Old Mr. Lane 57

5 Case Histories and Scientific Proof or the Case of JR 71

6 Not a Good Story or the Disappearance of Maddy and Vicky 93

7 Conflicting Scenarios or the Case of the Man Who Needed a Companion 109

8 Two Processes Obstructing the Accuracy of Long-Term Memory or the Case of the Stolen Mercedes 123

9 Confessions after Repeated Interrogation or the Putten Murder Case 143

10 Collaborative Storytelling or the Artist's Models and an Angry Neighbourhood 161

11 Allegation of Sexual Child Abuse in a Case of Disputed Visitation or Cindy's Story 177

12 Psychogenic Amnesia or the Case of the Amnesic Strangler 195

13 Obeying Reflexes or Death on the Climbing Wall 211

14 Visual Acuity or Shooting Mimi the Cat 227

15 Sexual Semiotics or the Case of the Popular Policeman 235

Postscript: Psychological Expertise and the Law 251

Bibliography 263

Name Index 279

Subject Index 284

Foreword

The domain of *Psychology and Law* belongs more to psychology than to law. Typical studies and publications in the field are psychological in nature, as they are applications of psychology within a legal context. Such studies may influence the practice of law and even legislation, but they are based on the research logic and methodology of psychologists. In general, this is the methodology for empirical research into basic psychological faculties such as perception and memory, automatic and controlled behaviour, logical thinking and problem solving, the formation of complex judgements and decision making. Such empirical studies always involve human subjects and are therefore limited by ethical constraints. Although such constraints by themselves do not seriously hamper the research process, they often constitute a problem when we try to apply the results in a context in which deceit, fraud, theft, robbery, drug trafficking, sexual abuse, rape, torture, and murder are the common themes. For ethical reasons, that context cannot be replicated in the psychological laboratory. It is difficult to create a research design in which human subjects are made to witness or to become victims of a serious crime in an ethically acceptable way. For this reason, the link between psychological research and its application in legal practice is never simple and straightforward.

The parties involved in civil or criminal cases know only too well that their cases are primarily decided on their legal merits. Psychological insights may play a role, but only if there is legal precedent, and in so far as they have clearly demonstrable relevance for the cases at hand. This may explain why the field of psychology and law has developed mainly in the context of actual legal trials; it is based on psychological questions raised in court, the expert testimony presented, and the acceptance or rejection of such testimony by judges and juries. It is virtually impossible for researchers in this field to make significant progress without experience as expert witnesses in actual trials.

One might expect that the progress in the field of psychology and law is achieved by collecting in-depth descriptions of applications in actual trials. But this is not so. Often the scientific literature does not refer to any case in particular; at best it refers only obliquely to cases that the reader is supposed to recognise. Representative case collections that may be used for the training of our students, both in the faculties of law and of psychology, are rare. The few existing collections of case descriptions are almost without exception of American origin, which may be less useful for students in other countries with different legal systems. Another and more troublesome limitation is that most of the research in the field, and consequently of its application in the courtroom, is limited to a relatively small number of traditional topics, such as person identification through face recognition, the reliability of the memories of eyewitnesses, and false confessions. There are very few case descriptions involving the psychological aspects of automatic behaviour, consumer confusion, illegal gambling, causal reasoning, judicial decision making, and risky courtship behaviour. The reason for this paucity is apparently that psychologists are not thought to possess relevant information about these topics. Consequently, in these domains the expert opinion of psychologists is only rarely sought, even when such issues are raised in courtrooms.

This book is an attempt to fill some of these gaps. It discusses a number of often neglected issues in the field of psychology and law. The form chosen for these discussions is that of an extensive exposition of a case in which the issue arose and in which often one of the authors acted as an expert, appointed by the court or at the initiative of one of the parties involved in the case. The state of affairs with respect to scientific knowledge about the issue is then described in a succinct manner, with references to the relevant research literature. In the various chapters we describe how the psychological insights were introduced into the framework of predominantly legal reasoning, and what the courts did, or did not, do with our psychological knowledge. In this way, the book will not only be useful to those who wish to learn about the less frequently presented research on particular topics, but also, and particularly, about its application in legal practice.

It would have been impossible to describe and discuss such a variety of cases in sufficient detail without us having been involved in them as expert witnesses. Somewhat unfortunately, however, this means that almost all cases occurred in our own country and were thus decided within the framework of Dutch law and legal practice, with its sometimes surprising peculiarities. In our descriptions of the cases, we have attempted to leave out of consideration details that have no wider implication outside the Dutch context, and to concentrate on aspects of universal significance. It is our hope that teachers and students in the field of psychology and law will find this approach useful, and that some cases, in spite of their sometimes dramatic qualities, may occasionally elicit a smile.

CHAPTER 1

Illegal Gambling or the Victory Travel Club

In most countries gambling is regulated by the state, usually through legislation that forbids the commercial organisation of gambling activities, or through legislation that subjects commercial gambling operations to a licensing system. Legislation on gambling must contain a definition of what constitutes gambling. Which games are subject to the legislation, and which ones are exempt because they are considered games of skill? Such definitions are always problematic, because in reality there is no clear dichotomy of gambling games versus non-gambling games. Instead, there is a continuous scale with clear cases, like lotteries and roulette, at one end, and highly skilled games, like tennis or chess, at the other. The legally interesting cases are those in the middle, where there is uncertainty about the true nature of the game. There we find cases like blackjack and poker, in which professional players may earn considerable sums of money, which implies that skill is relevant, whereas beginners often lose because, lacking the relevant skills, they gamble. The dependence of the outcomes on the way in which individual players play leads almost automatically to a definition of gambling not in terms of the formal characteristics of the game, but in terms of how it is actually played. In that case, legislation on gambling should define the class of behaviours that constitute gambling, which almost inevitably leads to the involvement of psychological insights and concepts. As the case of the Victory Travel Club, discussed in this chapter, was tried in the Netherlands, it will be helpful to look at the definition of gambling according to Dutch law.

Dutch gambling legislation distinguishes between games of chance and games of skill. A game of chance is a game in which the large majority of the players do not have a decisive influence on the outcome upon which the winning of a prize is contingent[1]. There are two vague elements in this definition: *large majority* and *decisive influence*. Which proportion of players qualifies as a large majority, and how should

1 Article 1 of the Dutch Gambling Law (Wet op de Kansspelen).

the proportion of these unskilled players be measured in an actual case? And what constitutes a decisive influence? Decisive in what sense?

Both problems may be exemplified by the so-called 'card counters' in the game of blackjack. Card counting was first described by Thorp (1966). It consists of memorising the cards that have been played and, on the basis of this, evaluating the composition of the remaining deck. The betting strategy is varied according to whether the remaining deck is 'rich' in ten-point cards and aces, or 'poor'. Ten-point cards are disadvantageous for the bank, because the bank is required to buy cards until a total of seventeen points is reached. When there are still many tens in the deck, the bank risks 'going bust' when a total of twelve to sixteen points is reached, because the bank *must* buy an extra card. The player can anticipate on this by standing on – twelve to sixteen points, which is in principle a losing hand unless the bank busts. This is very likely with a 'rich' deck; hence, it is a good strategy for the counter to place a high bet when the deck is rich. Card counting is not difficult to learn and may turn the advantage slightly in the direction of the counter. Usually, the advantage of the card counter over the bank amounts to no more than 0.5-1.0 percent of the betting amount, which means that the card counter only wins in the long run, not in every single game. Nevertheless, casino owners consider card counting highly undesirable. When spotted, card counters are often asked to leave, or are counteracted in various other ways. More details are provided in Wagenaar (1988c) and Keren & Wagenaar (1985). The questions that concern us here are: is the influence of a card counter on the outcome of the game decisive, and how many card counters must be present to make blackjack a game of skill?

The first of these questions leads us directly into philosophical problems, because it is not clear what the 'outcome of the game' is. Is it the way in which the cards come out which determines whether an individual game is won by the player or the dealer? Clearly, the card counter has no influence on the sequence of the cards in the deck. Is it the number of times a player wins? This is only marginally influenced by the card counter's playing strategy. The real advantage of card counting is that, on average, higher bets were placed in those rounds in which the player wins, with the result that even when the counter does not win more often, his winnings will exceed his losses. If the financial gain or loss is considered to constitute the 'outcome of the game', it is clear that the outcome in the long run will be decisive in the eyes of the casino owner, even though it is negligible in a single hand. From earlier court decisions it is not clear what the legal meaning of 'outcome' is. In some cases those accused of organising illegal gambling were convicted simply because the large majority of the players lost, or merely because playing cards were used.

The second question leads us into even bigger problems. Let us assume that card counting is recognised as a skill. Then, if seven card counters find themselves at the same blackjack table, there is definitely an absolute majority of skilled players. Does this mean that the nature of blackjack changes with the composition of the group of players at the table, so that in one and the same casino blackjack may be a skilled game at one table, and a game of chance at another? This problem is even further aggravated by the phenomenon of 'following the card counter'. It often happens that the other players at a blackjack table spot the card counter, and begin to follow his betting pattern: high when the deck is rich, low when the deck is poor. In that manner all the players succeed in influencing the outcome of their bets, without possessing any relevant skill apart from spotting the card counter. They all depend on the skill of the card counter. In the long run, though, they all have a decisive influence on the financial outcome, a result that is even more feared by casino owners than the isolated activity of a single card counter. This effect of decisive influence is obtained even when only one out of seven players applies the skill of card counting, which clearly is not a majority.

These and similar problems have caused complicated legal procedures all over the world, concerning roulette-type games, blackjack, poker and, most relevant for the present chapter, pyramid games. In many of such procedures, psychologists have been asked to testify about the nature of the supposed skills that players might employ. Do such skills really exist? How many players may possess them and to what extent? How difficult are they to acquire and how large an effect might they have on the outcome of the game?

Why should gambling be prosecuted?

It is apparently *communis opinio* in our society that gambling is bad, that in principle it should not be done and that, in any case, unlicensed commercial gambling organisations must be prosecuted. But why is gambling bad? Historically, a wide variety of reasons has been offered. One of them is linked to religion. Gambling may result in a significant change of one's destiny, at a time determined by the gambler. Some religious people believe that man's destiny is in God's hands only, and that a gambler forces God to take a decision at a time not chosen by the deity himself. Such contempt of God's sovereign and mysterious ways constitutes a moral ground for rejecting gambling. Quite famous in this context is William Hogarth's 1747 engraving of the apprentice Thomas Idle, gambling in the graveyard during church service (Shesgreen, 1973; plate 62). Ironically though, the Christian churches have a long tradition of collecting funds through the organisation of lotteries. This tradition originated in the Middle Ages within the Catholic church, and was copied without critical consideration by the Reformed churches (Fokker, 1862).

A second religion-related reason may be that man is destined to toil 'by the sweat of his brow'. Acquiring wealth through gambling would be in violation of this old commandment. But again, the systematic organisation of gambling events by the churches appears to contradict this, and the argument may therefore be deemed a reason of little importance. A related argument, more social than religious in nature, may be more relevant. The option of earning an income through gambling may prevent people from doing their share of honest work. Gamblers, however, must lose in the long run, because the odds are inevitably against them. Thus, in the long run, gamblers will fall into beggary and crime, which is of course unacceptable to society. Significantly, Hogarth's character Thomas Idle ends up as a murderer, hanged at Tyburn. Related to this argument is the economical consideration that gambling is not productive; it is no more than a redistribution of money, to no societal advantage. Gamblers are freeloaders sponging on the work of others.

A third reason may be that some forms of gambling are highly addictive. Among the addictions, gambling has the highest rate of relapse after treatment. The effect of this addiction on the direct social environment of gamblers is often dramatic, because they will do almost anything to go on gambling. They will lie, cheat, steal, and may even turn to violent crime (Van 't Veer *et al.*, 1993; also Lesieur & Rosenthal, 1991). The commercial organisation of gambling can therefore be considered a provocation of addiction and criminality originating from it, which is the reason why gambling should at least be regulated and controlled. A licensing system may achieve this goal, which in turn implies that the organisation of gambling without a license must be prosecuted. This is a valid argument, although it ignores the obvious fact that in practice, licensing does not do anything to prevent a gambling addiction.

A fourth reason for a strict control of gambling is that commercial gambling organisations may offer a convenient way to whitewash money obtained by criminal means (Van 't Veer *et al.*, 1993). One can easily claim to have won a huge sum of money through gambling, unless gambling transactions are closely monitored and recorded. This requires a licensing system that includes rules to prevent whitewash operations and the prosecution of those who dodge these rules.

A fifth reason is that gambling operations are highly competitive. Every commercial organiser of gambling would love to have the monopoly in a certain region, during a certain period of time, and for a certain type of game. This argument played a role in church-organised gambling, and also in gambling organised by civil authorities, such as in state lotteries or state-owned casinos. Fokker (1862) describes how the city of Amsterdam established a monopoly by forbidding other cities in the province of Holland to organise lotteries during a period of two years surrounding big lotteries in Amsterdam. In 1726 this monopoly system was adopted by the Estates General when the Governmental Lottery was founded, the oldest state lottery in Europe. A direct consequence of this monopoly was, of course, that it needed to be enforced through the prosecution of invaders.

A final reason and perhaps the one that is closest to the current prosecution practice in the Western world is that commercially organised gambling must of necessity be fraudulent, in order to be profitable for the organisers. The basic rule of commercial gambling is that the odds must be in favour of the organiser, and thus against the individual player. This is, however, not the message that is communicated to the potential clients. On the contrary, the client is led to believe that gambling will lead to instantaneous and easily obtained wealth. The advertisements speak about winning, winners, amounts won, the joy of winning, and the things you can do when you have won. They suggest that people may control the process, that it is a matter of skill, and that through practice one can learn to improve one's performance. Just one example of the creation of such illusions is the electronic display at the roulette tables showing the numbers that were drawn in previous rounds, suggesting that this is useful information. Which, of course, it is not. A similar form of memory support is not provided at the blackjack table, although there it would be very helpful. Here, in reality, casinos employ the opposite strategy by strictly forbidding the recording of cards that have been removed from the deck in previous rounds. So, the clients in commercially organised gambling are misled about what they can achieve and what will happen. The truth about gambling is the law of large numbers: the more you gamble, the more the unfavourable odds will be reflected in your net result. It is this aspect of fraud that constitutes the rationale for the prosecution of illegal gambling in the United States, which implies, however, that licence holders are allowed to run a fraudulent operation.

The Dutch law, focussing on the absence of influence on the outcome, may be interpreted as reflecting the same argument because, as argued by Wagenaar (1988c), it is precisely this aspect that is misconstrued by habitual and addicted gamblers. Ideally, the key question in the prosecution of illegal gambling should be whether the gamblers are allowed complete understanding not only of the mechanism, the odds and their limited ability to influence the outcome, but also of what in practice happens to participants. In other words, to what extent are prospective gamblers misled about the reality of the game? In the remaining part of this chapter we will assume that the aspect of misleading the players is the true basis for prosecuting illegal gambling. In this context pyramid schemes constitute a prime example of a misleading mechanism for the redistribution of wealth.

Pyramid schemes

The best-known form of a pyramid scheme is the chain letter. At level 1[2] of the scheme, a person sends letters to a number of other people – say ten – who consti-

2 The numbering of the levels in the pyramid starts at the top.

tute level 2. Each of these ten persons sends letters to ten others, who together constitute the 100 participants at level 3; and so on. In the chain letter, the receivers are asked to do two things: send ten letters to persons at the next level of the scheme, and pay a certain amount of money to a person several levels higher up in the organisation. A person at level 7 may be asked to pay to one person at level 5. That person will receive payments from 100 players. In general, when every player indeed sends out the a required letters, and the payment is made to players x levels higher, then the total amount of money received by every player will be a^x. The system breaks down when new recipients of the letters refuse to participate. Then it will happen that players at the two lowest levels of the pyramid make their payments to players at a higher level, but do not receive payments themselves because the population of prospective players is exhausted.

In the legal sense, such a scheme may be considered a form of illegal gambling because the players have no decisive influence on the recruitment of new players x levels below them. This will especially be the case when x exceeds 2, because generally one does not know the persons recruited by one's own recruits, and *a fortiori* by the recruits of those recruits. Because of the exponential increase of the number of participants on the successive levels of the pyramidal structure, the group of losers will always constitute a large majority. For them, there are no potential new players, and whatever they do, they will fail and lose their investment. Hence, they have no 'decisive influence' on the outcome of the game. According to the Dutch legal definition of gambling, pyramid games are thus forms of gambling. In the American notion, the organisation of pyramid games constitutes fraud, because the majority of players are misled about the fact that they are destined to lose.

An exceptionally harmful form of the pyramid scheme is the so-called Ponzi scheme, named after Charles Ponzi, a racketeer active in the 1920s. The scheme is very simple: people are asked to lend money to the organiser against an extremely attractive interest rate. The money is not invested and the interest is not paid from any profit, but exclusively from new loans. So long as the number of money lenders keeps increasing exponentially, the system works very well. But as soon as the population of potential lenders is exhausted, it becomes impossible for the organiser to pay the interest. Even worse: the original investment of the majority of contributors has been used to pay interest to the minority of early participants. But even these early contributors will lose when the racketeer disappears with whatever money is left, which of course he will. It was in this manner that a substantial part of the Romanian population was robbed of its savings in 1993; this was repeated in 1997 with a substantial proportion of the Albanian population.

Ponzi schemes and multilevel marketing

Ponzi schemes illustrate that it may be extremely difficult to capture in a legal definition the dividing line between normal business practices and criminal behaviour. Lending money to a bank is usually based on the belief that the bank will invest the money and pay the interest from the profits thus made. But the lender has no influence on the investments. In fact, he does not receive any promise about the type of investment or, more generally, about the source from which the interest will be obtained. The lender has no influence on the bank's financial performance and is not insured against a sudden breakdown of the bank's solvency. The same can be said about buying shares in a commercial enterprise: the buyer of shares is speculating on the outcome of a probabilistic process on which he or she has no influence whatsoever. Is this gambling? Should it be deemed illegal?

Even more disturbing is the similarity between pyramid games and the well-known and widely accepted system of multilevel marketing (MLM). The idea here is that a manufacturer of, for instance, a health product does not distribute the products market-wide in health shops himself but recruits a number of level-1 individual distributors. These distributors buy the products from the manufacturer and sell them on their own account. Often the level-1 distributors recruit level-2 distributors, who buy their products through the level-1 distributors and pay a cut of their profits to the level-1 distributor by whom they were recruited. These level-2 distributors in turn may enlist level-3 distributors, and so on. In this way each distributor will sell the health product directly, hopefully with some profit, but may also act as an entrepreneur who employs a number of salespeople.

The biggest MLM scheme in the world is the Amway company, with bases in a vast number of countries. Amway produces a large variety of household goods, which are sold through the pyramidal structure of recruited private entrepreneurs, called Independent Business Owners (IBOs). In 2004, Amway has recruited 3 million IBOs worldwide, with sales worth US$ 6 billion (www.amway.com). Still, the Skeptic's Dictionary (www.skeptic.com) alleges that, in the year 2000, the average Amway IBO earned an average of US$ 700, but spent about US$ 1.000 on Amway products.

Amway has often been prosecuted for organising an illegal and deceptive gambling system. The landmark trial was in 1978-79, when it was decided by the American Federal Trade Commission[3] that MLM in this form is acceptable, provided that certain rules are observed. Most prominent were three rules already in use with Amway: the 'buy-back rule', the '70 percent rule', and the 'ten customers

3 93 F.T.C. 618, 716-17 (1979) ; see also the web site <mlmlegal.com/amway.html>.

rule'. The 'buy-back rule' specifies that an IBO must purchase any unused, marketable products back upon request from an IBO hierarchically ordered below him in the pyramid. This prevents IBOs at the top of a (sub)pyramid forcing participants below them to buy unrealistically large supplies. The '70 percent rule' provides that IBOs must sell at least 70 percent of the products received in one month in order to get a performance bonus. This prevents the unwanted accumulation of goods with certain IBOs. The '10 customers rule' states that each IBO must make sales at retail to at least ten different customers every month. This makes it impossible for IBOs to become nothing more but employers of other IBOs who do the real work. A fundamental attack on the whole idea of MLM was launched by Fitzpatrick & Reynolds (1997), who argue that, notwithstanding the FTC decision in the Amway case, MLM is in essence a pyramid scheme that cannot work because it would soon exhaust the population of individuals willing to serve at the lower levels. But since Amway and many other MLM organisations are successfully operating throughout the world without exhausting their markets even after several decades, this allegation is at least debatable; we do not really know how well the Amway IBOs are doing. The question of the success rate among the millions of Amway IBOs is important, since the key issue in the prosecution of illegal gambling is the question of whether these 'players' are, or are not, misled. In Amway's information to potential new IBOs, there is nothing about the probability of losing money, or the proportion of IBOs who actually do lose money, or the number of other IBOs one must recruit in order to make any money at all. The three important rules imposed by the FTC have nothing to do with fair and complete information to potential 'players'. There is no fundamental reason why the Amway scheme cannot work, and there is no clear information that in practice it does not work. But, since the use of deception and fraud is the key issue in the prosecution of organisations that employ pyramid schemes, it is surprising that the relevant information about how well the distribution system works in practice is not provided by Amway.

The problem of framing MLM as a form of illegal gambling becomes even more complicated when it is realised that the rather general criterion of not being able to influence the outcome of a game that is in essence probabilistic applies to many other commercial activities. The author of a book may try to produce an attractive and well-selling product, but the actual sale of the book is always quite uncertain and in the hands of publishers and booksellers. Moreover, the population of actual buyers is limited, and may become exhausted fairly soon. Publishing companies might therefore be construed as organisations that recruit authors to write books, but without allowing them a reasonable influence on the financial outcome of their enterprise. In fact, as we know from personal experience, the writing of scientific books is often very much like being an Amway distributor who spends 1000 dollars in order to win 700. Once in a while a science book becomes a bestseller, but this is altogether unpredictable. Would it be fair to prosecute the world's renowned scientific publishing houses for illegally organising a gambling racket?

Legal definition of pyramid games

In the Netherlands several trials against the organisers of commercial pyramid games have been held. A landmark trial was that against the club *Coin Liberté*, in which one of us served as a psychological expert, testifying on the amount of influence that the members had on the recruitment of novices. Since it was an essential feature of the scheme offered by *Coin Liberté* that one person could simultaneously act at many different levels of the pyramid, the possible exhaustion of the population was not a problem. The same people could be recruited again and again, and in actual practice indeed the majority of participants were active at various levels of the pyramid. The result was that the growth of the membership was linear rather than exponential. The growth rate was far below the autonomous growth rate of the Dutch population. It could therefore be argued that the group of potential new members was increasing, rather than decreasing. *Coin Liberté* won its case, but went bankrupt when its bookkeeper ran off with the cash. As a reaction to the outcome of this case, the legislator concluded that the general definition of games of chance needed to be supplemented with the explicit mention of pyramid schemes. Hence Article 1a was added to the Gambling Law as a *lex specialis*, specifying that pyramid games are games of chance. Since then the critical legal issue about pyramid schemes is not the decisive influence of the players, but simply whether a commercially offered scheme conforms to the legal definition of a pyramid game. In the same Article 1a, pyramid games are defined as games in which the gain of the participant is entirely or partially dependent on the surrender of any good (read: payment) or the acceptance of any obligation by later participants. We will see that this definition causes new problems, as it also covers almost any canvassing activity, and would also definitely outlaw the Amway-type sales system, which is operating rather successfully also in the Netherlands (see their website www.amway.nl).

The Victory Travel Club

Mr. Evans is a prolific salesman. He sells Victory Travel Club memberships at specially arranged mass meetings, attended by hundreds of potential buyers. His presentation is like stand-up comedy that is greatly enjoyed by the audience, even by those who do not in the end decide to become members. The audience consists of people who are already members and their guests. The membership fee is a one-off € 3350, which is not cheap. But consider what you get! Firstly, the Victory Travel

Club offers considerable reductions on a long list of travel arrangements. Since the Dutch make holiday travelling an almost sacred yearly event, the membership fee may be earned back through these reductions within a few years. The club also offers discounts on luxury products and services. In this respect, there is no difference between the Victory Travel Club and thousands of other cooperative consumer associations. But Victory offers more: a monetary bonus for the recruitment of new members. The payment schedule is simple. A member starts as an 'associate' of the travel club and is guided by an 'executive associate'. When the associate has recruited two new members, the guidance by the executive ends, and the associate himself becomes an executive associate. From then on, all new members recruited by this person start as his or her associates. Associates who recruit a new member receive € 550, which is taken out of the new member's entrance fee. The associate's executive associate receives € 850, which is also taken out of the new member's entrance fee. The remaining € 1950 is for the travel club. Executive associates who recruit a new member receive the total reward of € 550 + € 850 = € 1400. Thus, executives have two sources of income: directly from recruiting new associates, and indirectly from the first two recruitments made by their associates.

The interesting aspect of this structure is that the members have a considerable influence on their profits. A member who recruits four new members will receive 2 x € 550 as an associate, plus 2 x € 1.400 as an executive, amounting to a total of € 3900, which already exceeds his own membership fee. Hence, the initial investment may be earned back without the help of other associates. There is no particular reason to classify this section of the scheme as a pyramid game. There is also no multi-layered pyramidal structure, only an organisation with two levels: executive associates and mere associates, while the promotion to the level of executive may be rapid. Even if the two-tier structure should be seen as a pyramid, there is considerable control by the executives, since they recruit their associates personally. On top of this, the members are not actually expected to recruit new members all on their own, they are only asked to bring potential new buyers to Mr. Evans's wonderful show. The recruiting is done by him, with spectacular results. His most convincing story is about a member of the Victoria Travel Club who goes to the Caribbean on a reduced ticket, gets free massage sessions, and pays for his luxurious dinner from the € 550 paid out to him on that very day because he recruited a new member. It appears that the legal definition of a pyramid game – others, lower in the pyramid, must provide the income for those higher up – does not apply to the Victory Travel Club. According to this definition, the system of associates and executive associates does not constitute a pyramid, which leads directly to the conclusion that membership of the Club is not a form of gambling. When Mr. Evans was tried in a court of law, he should have been acquitted.

Exponential growth?

The recruitment system of the Victory Travel Club, however, has something in common with the typical structure of pyramid games: the number of participants must increase exponentially if all associate members want to become executives by recruiting two newcomers. It must grow even faster if all players want to recover the whole of their initial fees through the recruitment of at least four new members. In principle, this aspect of exponential growth will lead to saturation or exhaustion of the market. Mr. Evans never discussed this problem in his entertaining presentations and might therefore be accused of fraud. Such an accusation would definitively be the American approach. How urgent is this problem?

The argument of exponential growth that will cause the system to collapse is based on the assumed ambitions of the members. Unfortunately, nothing is known about these ambitions. When it was decided that Mr. Evans should be tried for running his operation, the prosecution did not collect information about the gains or losses of individual members, nor on how fast the membership had grown. Possibly, the majority of members were satisfied with the reductions and services offered by the travel club. Travelling can be expensive, but anyone who has compared the various prices of flight tickets knows that considerable reductions can often be obtained. The problem is to find out about them. The services offered by the travel club at reduced rates include physical therapy, massage, psychotherapy, and legal assistance. It is not unrealistic for prospective members to expect that they would soon be able to recover their membership fee through these reductions alone. Mr. Evans was also very explicit in his communication that the recruitment of new members is only an extra option and does not constitute the main part of Victory's activities. This consideration leads to two conclusions. The first of these is that it is not clear which proportion of the members will actually engage in recruiting new members, and secondly, that even if the market becomes exhausted, the members can still profit from the reductions. So long as we do not know how many members engage in recruitment, we cannot compute if or when the market will become saturated.

Let us look at the problem from Mr. Evans's perspective. Evans is the sole owner of the Victory Travel Club, although he has some hired assistants helping him with the organisation of his recruitment sessions. The activities of the associates and executive associates are administered by a computer programme. The reductions offered by the travel club are obtained through the mass purchase of services, and do not constitute an expense on the club's budget. Let us assume that Mr. Evans' ambition is to earn an income of, say, € 500,000 per year. With organising costs and other expenses, the total desired turnover of the club would then amount to € 750,000 per year. Since the club receives € 1.950 for each new member, a total of 400 new members per year would suffice. From this perspective no exponential growth is needed, just a steady yearly inflow of 400 new members. In a country like the Netherlands, with over 16 million inhabitants, this should be easy to achieve, especially when it is realised that about 200,000 new adults enter the market each year. The recruitment of new members is essential, because the fee provides for a lifelong membership. Therefore, the bonus system is a logical extension, as it relieves Mr. Evans from the task of finding new candidates himself. He leaves that to others, concentrating on the proper recruitment during his presentations. That is where his real talent resides. There is nothing fishy or mysterious about this organisation, and there is no reason to assume that Mr. Evans intends to mislead his members, as in the case of real pyramid schemes. There is no compelling reason for exponential growth of the travel club membership.

The only possible complication may be the as-yet-unknown ambitions of associates trying to recover their fee through the recruitment of new members. Such an ambition might ruin the whole set-up of the travel club because, indeed, Mr. Evans did not tell his associates that an explosion of new members will eventually lead to saturation of the market. Let us therefore try to compute whether saturation may occur under hypothesised, but not unreasonable conditions. We assume then that there are 400 members in the first year. One hundred of those are satisfied with the use of Victory's services as such, without any additional wish to collect recruitment fees. Of the remaining 300, 100 recruit one new member per year, 100 recruit two new members, and 100 recruit four new members. As soon as members have recruited four new members, they have recovered their fee and stop their recruiting activity. The division into four groups of equal size is maintained within the new recruitment. In this scheme the number of new members is 700 in the second year, and increasing with a factor of about 2.18 each successive year. In the ninth year the entire national supply of new young adults would be recruited and in the tenth year that would not be enough.

Like Amway, the Victory Travel Club might try to spread its wings by entering the international market, but even that will not prevent exhaustion: in the twentieth year of its existence almost a billion new members would be needed. It is obvious that even with limited ambitions of the members, the risk of exhaustion is real. In order not to mislead the members with unrealistic promises, Mr. Evans should de-emphasise the recruitment option or, if after a number of years the growth has been too rapid, make both membership and recruitment less attractive by lowering the recruitment rewards. The rules of the travel club might contain a statement, not unlike the three major rules of Amway, that the number of new members per year is limited to a maximum. At present there is no such rule, which makes Mr. Evans vulnerable for an accusation of creating false expectations.

There is yet another snag in the travel club scheme, about which the members are not properly informed. Mr. Evans may eventually retire or die, which in principle would terminate the activities of the club. Reductions will not be extended, and the fees for the recruitment of new members will no longer be paid out. In that case, obviously, the newest members would suffer most. Because of the exponential growth of the membership, this group of new members would constitute a significant majority, since about 90 percent would have been recruited in the last three years. Is it unethical and misleading not to inform the members about this problem? Or is it a matter of common sense that all businesses are finite?

Chance and luck

The critical element in games of chance is the illusion that unfavourable odds may be overcome by skill or luck or both. It is this illusion against which the general public must be protected by the legislator, and which leads to the prosecution of those who desire to exploit the gullibility of their fellow man. The major paradox of gambling behaviour is that this illusion is almost never shattered by a rational analysis of the situation, nor by experience. For this, the common lottery may serve as an obvious example. Lotteries are clearly profitable for those who organise them. In turn, this must mean that on the whole the players lose. This analysis is simple, and if this insight does not come immediately, one would expect that experience would help to remedy it. In practice though, it appears that about half of the Dutch population takes part in commercial lotteries of any kind on a regular basis, with an unavoidable loss of billions of euros for the players. Why are the simple laws of chance so difficult to fathom, or why do so many people believe that these laws do not apply to them? Surely, they cannot believe that lotteries involve any sort of skill which may turn the odds in their favour?

According to Wagenaar & Keren (1988), the problem is caused by the difference between chance and luck. Chance describes the outcome of mechanical processes like drawing lots, rolling dice, throwing balls in a roulette bowl, or the dealing of cards. But the outcome of gambling is not really determined by such events, but by a *coincidence* between chance events and a wilful action of the gambler. Winning in roulette is not determined by the mechanical selection of a number by the roulette machine, but by the coincidence of the winning number and the placement of bets by the gambler. Obviously, the roulette player has no influence on the ball, but the placements of bets is entirely his own choice. Many a gambler believes that this choice is guided by relevant factors. Wagenaar (1988c) described in chapter 4 of his book why roulette players hope to win. They think it is because they are skilled in placing the right amount on the right numbers. An important part of this skill has to do with luck. Luck has a very simple effect: with luck you win, without it you lose. Everybody gets his or her share of luck, and it is believed that good luck and bad luck alternate in a periodical manner. The art is to gamble in a period of good luck, and not in a period of bad luck. The fact that the odds are in favour of the house and against the gambler is easily overcome in a period of luck, and this conviction is repeatedly – but not continuously – confirmed by the outcome of the game. In the perception of the gambler, guided by the gambler's fallacy, there are systematic streaks of winning and losing, which cannot be explained by the rules of chance alone. Such streaks are perceived as being caused by the periodical fluctuation of fortune. The gambler's fallacy entails the subjective belief that winning and losing should quickly alternate if controlled by chance alone. Longer periods of consistent winning or losing cannot occur by chance and must therefore be caused by the persistence of good or bad luck (cf. also Wagenaar, 1970). Because of this illusion, the inevitable overall loss in the long run is not explained in terms of the unfavourable odds, but in terms of not being sensitive enough to the periodical change of good and bad luck. It is exactly this belief that the organisers of commercial gambling promote and reinforce in their communications. Winning is emphasised, for instance by placing hundreds of slot machines together in one playing hall. The disappearance of money into the machines is a silent and little noticeable event. The payment of money to winning players makes a conspicuously loud noise of metal on metal. In a hall with hundreds of slot machines the noise of rattling money is ever present, which creates the illusion that players are constantly winning. Casino owners know that the slot machines are especially lucrative when placed with hundreds together in one hall. Winning is emphasised and especially the fact that the winners are ordinary people, without any particular skill, so that it is easy to identify with them. Being lucky is constantly accentuated as the cause of winning, not being smart. You may not think yourself as smart as some others, but most people believe that they may well be as lucky as everybody else. The success of games like lotteries and roulettes is based on the fact that luck, instead of a highly developed skill as in chess or billiards, is considered to determine the outcome. Most people know that they stand no chance in a chess competition, but at the same time they believe that they may well get lucky in a lottery or a roulette game. The truth is, however, that for an addicted roulette player, it is equally as unlikely to make an overall profit at the roulette table as it is to win a chess championship.

The systematic promotion of luck against the laws of chance constitutes the most fraudulent element of the gambling industry. It needs to be prosecuted if the law intends to protect individuals against exploitation. This is true not only for illegal gambling by private organisations but also – or even more so – for licensed, legalised and state-operated gambling operations. Current gambling laws regulate licensing but not the deceptive practices of those who receive a licence. Mr. Evans was prosecuted not because he deceived his clientele per se, but because he was alleged to deceive them without a licence. Was Mr. Evans indeed suggesting that the recruitment of new members might be favoured by an unrealistic amount of luck? Not at all, in our opinion. There is no comparison between Mr. Evans's humorous description of the happy club member on holiday in the Caribbean on the one hand and the frequent misrepresentation of the opportunities in the government-owned state lottery in our nationwide television programmes on the other.

How the case ended

Mr. Evans was convicted of violating Dutch gambling laws, first by the lower courts and, subsequently on appeal, by the Supreme Court. The Victory Travel Club contains two levels of associates which, for the courts, was sufficient to classify his operation as a pyramid game. Mr. Evans is now considering submitting the case to the European Court.

CHAPTER 2

On Causal Reasoning or Death in the Warmoesstraat

At about 4:30 PM on 22 September 1997, a homeless, alcoholic man, whom we will call Van Eck, entered the police station in the Warmoesstraat in Amsterdam, loudly demanding that he be allowed to use the telephone to call someone. At first, police officer Abrams (a pseudonym) thought that Van Eck was drunk: he appeared 'unstable on his feet', but then his breath did not smell noticeably of alcohol. Officer Abrams pointed out that there was a public telephone booth nearby, but then Van Eck demanded a meal and a bed for the night in one of the detention cells. Officer Abrams told Van Eck that this was not possible and asked him to leave, which he refused. Abrams and his fellow officer Barends used ' mild force' to persuade Van Eck to leave (the passages in quotation marks are quotes from an interrogation of Abrams, as reported in the affidavit of that interrogation). Once outside, Van Eck took a step forward and let himself fall forward on the sidewalk, but he pulled himself up and walked away.

At about 7:45 PM on that same day, officer Abrams and a colleague, on patrol in the neighbourhood, saw Van Eck leave a café and walk away with unstable gait, presumably intoxicated. At about 8:15 PM Van Eck again entered the police station, demanding food and shelter for the night, which was again refused. And again officer Abrams and a colleague led Van Eck out the door of the police station. Once outside he again let himself fall forward, pulled himself up and walked away. Not for long though; a few minutes later he was back inside the police station. After an agitated exchange, officers Abrams and Barends each took hold of one of his arms and led the struggling Van Eck with some force out the door. Once outside, Van Eck stood on the sloping wooden ramp in front of the door, facing the street. He turned around, obviously intending to re-enter, but by standing in the narrow doorway officer Abrams prevented this. Loudly arguing, Van Eck kept trying to push his way back in, but Abrams resisted his pushing. Suddenly Van Eck appeared to give up and let himself fall again, backward this time. He fell like a log, without apparent signs of trying to stay upright or breaking his fall. With a sickening thud his head hit the stones of the sidewalk, where he remained lying with his eyes closed, motionless, but audibly breathing. Abrams returned inside the station and left Van Eck lying on the sidewalk. A few minutes later another police officer came out, moved Van Eck from where he had fallen to a position parallel with the front of the building and called for an ambulance, which arrived shortly afterwards and took Van Eck to a nearby hospital. At about 1 AM that night Van Eck died.

Witnesses

The description of the events so far is based on officer Abrams's testimony, given on 27 September, five days after the event. His description differs on an important point from the testimony given by witnesses who happened to walk past the police station at the time. Only one of these witnesses was on his own (witness 5 in table 1), the others were in a group of four, i.e., two couples on their way to a restaurant (witnesses 1 to 4 in table 1), and in a group of three consisting of two men and a woman (witnesses 6 to 8 in table 1). So there were eight witnesses altogether. When weeks later the police organised a reconstruction with some of the witnesses, there appeared to have been a ninth witness who had not been interrogated right away after that fateful night. After having witnessed the incident, they all went their way, and only became involved when the next day the media reported that the police had started an investigation into Van Eck's death and called for witnesses to report to the police to be interviewed.

First, officers Abrams and Barends were questioned, and within a period of nine days following Van Eck's death, the eight witnesses who had reported to the police were also questioned. They had all witnessed at least part of the incident. Table 1 contains an overview of what they said about four key parts of the incident: the manner in which officer Abrams had been in bodily contact with Van Eck at the moment he began to fall, the apparent force of the shove given by officer Abrams, the way Van Eck fell, and what it sounded like when Van Eck's head hit the pavement.

Only four out of the eight witnesses testified that they had observed that officer Abrams was in bodily contact with Van Eck at the moment he began to fall. As mentioned before, this was denied by officer Abrams himself; according to him at the moment Van Eck began to fall he was no longer in any way in contact with Van Eck's body. These four witnesses do not agree on the precise manner of the bodily contact. Witnesses 1 and 2 testified that both of officer Abrams's hands were on the front of Van Eck's body at the time, witnesses 6 and 7 say something different from witnesses 1 and 2, and also from each other. Since all of the witnesses saw Van Eck from behind, one wonders whether his body had not blocked their view, which may explain why four witnesses (3, 4, 5 and 8) stated that they had not seen if, and if so,

Table 1 ***Key parts of the testimony of eight witnesses***

Witness	Contact	Push	Way of falling	Sound
1	2 hands on front	Hard push	Backward	Very audible
2	2 hands on front	Forceful thrust & lost contact with ground	No statement	Real thud
3	Not seen	Not seen	Saw man lying	Not heard
4	Not seen	Not seen	Saw something flying through the air	Not heard
5	Not seen	Shove with full force	No attempt to break fall	Dull thud
6	Chin & shoulder	Pushed with force	Backward like a log	Loud thud, twice
7	Neck & chin	Forceful	Backward throwing	Thud
8	Not seen	Pushed	Backward, attempt to break fall	Head hit pavement

how officer Abrams had held Van Eck when he began to fall. During the later reconstruction of the incident, it was confirmed that if the witnesses had in fact been in the position they indicated during the reconstruction, they almost certainly could not have seen whether officer Abrams had been in bodily contact with Van Eck at the time.

Five witnesses testified that officer Abrams pushed Van Eck backward with considerable force, and again one wonders whether one can actually see how hard a push is. Probably the witnesses' judgment of the force exerted on Van Eck's body was based on the way he fell: backward like a log. If only for this reason, that would make these statements inferences, rather than observations. Witness 4 said she did not see the push itself, but had seen 'something fly through the air', implying that the push had been so forceful that Van Eck had lost contact with the ground, which appears quite unlikely. Nevertheless, during the reconstruction weeks later witness 2 confirmed such loss of contact, although she had not said so on first questioning. When asked explicitly on that same occasion, her husband, witness 1, denied that Van Eck had lost contact with the ground.

Four witnesses said they saw Van Eck fall backward like a log, his arms straight alongside his body and with no obvious attempt to stay upright or break his fall. Witness 8 disagreed; according to her, Van Eck was standing on the sloping wooden ramp in front of the door and, after being pushed by officer Abrams, took one or two steps backward and unsuccessfully tried not to fall. She called his fall 'unlucky'. When interviewed by a newspaper reporter (Bagijn, 2000), she called the incident 'an accident', this in sharp contrast with some of the other witnesses who testified in court that Van Eck had been thrown to the ground 'like a piece of dirt' and that 'you would not treat a dog like this'. Here perhaps it should be mentioned that the ninth witness, who was not questioned right away but took part in the later reconstruction, testified that he had the impression that Van Eck had let himself fall deliberately in protest. He thought that rather surprising, but his surprise would have been less if he had known of two other witnesses whom we will introduce later.

Five witnesses said that Van Eck's head had hit the pavement with a sickening thud. One of those five, witness 6, heard a second thud after his head had bounced up after the first impact. According to all witnesses, after his fall Van Eck lay motionless on the pavement, eyes closed, but audibly breathing. During the reconstruction they were all asked where he had lain, and, surprisingly, no two witnesses agreed on the precise spot; this, however, was of little importance. They also differed markedly as to the physical appearance of the pushing officer. Some described him as tall and broad shouldered, others as short and fat. In fact, officer Abrams is dark-haired, not very tall and by no means broad shouldered. Some said his hair was blond and that he had no facial hair, others that he was dark-haired and had a moustache. None of the witnesses identified officer Abrams in a photo lineup, but since he himself never denied that he had been the person who had stood in the doorway when Van Eck fell, this caused no problem for the prosecution.

The prosecution

In his affidavit, officer Abrams said that at the moment of the fall, he was no longer in bodily contact with Van Eck. Which raises the question of why Van Eck fell in the way he did. In officer Abrams's perception, Van Eck let himself fall deliberately. This corresponds with the impression of the ninth witness. From the fact that the district attorney decided to prosecute officer Abrams for the death of Van Eck, it is clear that he did not believe officer Abrams's rendition of the events. He believed that officer Abrams had pushed Van Eck in such a way that he had caused Van Eck's death later that night, and he had the testimony of enough witnesses to back this up.

At first, the reasoning of the prosecuting attorney appears straightforward: there simply must have been a powerful push, why else did Van Eck fall in the peculiar way described by the witnesses? Furthermore, since the witnesses heard a loud thud when Van Eck's head hit the pavement and since Van Eck died not long afterwards, there appears to be a straightforward causal chain from officer Abrams's behaviour to Van Eck's death. The causal chain assumed by the prosecutor consists of three links:

a. officer Abrams's push caused Van Eck to fall; implying that without the push Van Eck would not have fallen, at least not in this particular manner, i.e., backward like a log;
b. the fall caused Van Eck to incur a serious closed head injury;
c. the head injury incurred by the fall caused Van Eck to die sometime later.

Of these three, link (a) is the most important for the prosecution's case and also the most troublesome. Officer Abrams says that link (a) cannot be true because when Van Eck began to fall there was no longer bodily contact between them. But let us assume, if only for the sake of argument, that there *was* bodily contact. Then it is still questionable whether the push was forceful enough to make Van Eck fall the way he did. Well, five witnesses say it was very forceful. Why not believe them? The problem with this is that the witnesses only testified after they had come to know that Van Eck had died. Why this is a problem we intend to explain next, after having first mentioned that even if we believe these witnesses, there may have been other contributing causes to Van Eck's fall, in particular the fact that Van Eck was not standing on a level surface but on a ramp and that Van Eck was not very steady on his feet, possibly due to alcohol intoxication or for some other reason. The logical problems of multiple causation will be discussed further in the last section of this chapter.

Four basic tenets of causal explanation

Establishing a causal relation between two events is never a matter of simple perception. We cannot see what causes what; causal explanation is always a matter of interpretation of events and therefore an inference. Let us begin with summing up a few basic tenets of causal explanation.

(i) *Every event has a cause; in the physical world there is no such thing as an uncaused or self-initiating event. There are, however, events for which we cannot possibly think of a probable cause, which we therefore call coincidences.*

Coincidences only exist in the psychological world. For reasons of psychological convenience we tend to divide the world into parts or separate causal fields (Einhorn & Hogarth, 1985, p. 5). Within each of these fields we usually feel confident to infer the causes of what we observe and to foresee consequences because we know, or think we know, how things work within them. If we are not specialists in a particular field, we may do with an intuitive theory of it. For the field of moving objects we have an intuitive theory of mechanics, which more or less explains how moving objects interact and why. For the field of human behaviour we have folk psychology, explaining most of the time why people behave in the way they do, and allowing us to foresee how they will act under given circumstances. In a similar way most people have intuitive theories of economics, animal behaviour, politics, the weather and many other things. When we observe an event and ask ourselves what caused it, we choose intuitively, but by no means randomly, the appropriate causal field in which we expect to find the probable cause for it. During this process we may be wrong; we become aware of this because we cannot find an acceptable cause within the chosen causal field or, on closer inspection, come to realise that the probable cause is to be found in another causal field, than the one chosen spontaneously.

In everyday life the questions of why something has happened and what will happen in the future rarely rise into consciousness as long as the events we observe remain within their obvious causal field. Our intuitive theory of that field effortlessly explains it and we are not in the least surprised. But sometimes we are, and then we need to think hard about a cause. Then we first look for a probable cause inside the causal field that we deem the appropriate one. If we cannot think of an acceptable cause within that field, i.e., a cause that fits with our intuitive theory of that field, its cause may be found in another causal field, a field that most people would not spontaneously choose for that particular event. In that case, for most people the real cause has low subjective probability. This is what we call a coincidence (see: Von Kries, 1889; Kohnstamm, 1949).

(ii) *The more an event meets our expectations, the less we worry about its cause* (Hastie, 1984; Weiner, 1985).

For most everyday events the question of their causes is never raised because we think that we know their causes. In this we are often mistaken. For instance, psychological research has taught us that a good deal of the folk psychology we use to explain our own behaviour and that of others is quite misguided (cf. Wegner, 2002; Wilson, 2002). Similarly, professional meteorologists will be rather critical of the weather forecasts to which sailors and farmers are prone.

(iii) *Causal explanation critically depends on our presumed knowledge of the physical and social world* (cf. Read, 1987).

Most of our knowledge of the world consists of intuitive theories. Only in causal fields in which we have become specialists through training and experience do we 'know better'.

(iv) *Causal reasoning often proceeds regressively: we reason backward from effects to probable causes. Whenever we observe some event and ask ourselves what caused it, we engage in this kind of backward reasoning or postdiction.*

When postdicting causes from effects, people are prone to commit what John Stuart Mill has called 'the most deeply rooted fallacy in causal reasoning', that is, 'the prejudice that conditions of a phenomenon must resemble the phenomenon' (Mill, 1974/1843), which, in Mill's own words, means that we tend to think that 'great events ought to have great causes, complex events ought to have complex causes, and emotional events ought to have emotionally relevant causes' (Nisbett & Ross, 1980, p. 116).

Causal analysis of the Warmoesstraat case

Looking again now at the Warmoesstraat case, our first conclusion must be that what the witnesses said about the forcefulness of the push – if there was a push – cannot have been the result of straightforward observation. What they were saying was an interpretation of what they remembered having seen (see tenet i). This interpretation was based on their knowledge of the physical world, in particular that part of their knowledge that is concerned with the way in which a force is transmitted from one physical object (officer Abrams) to another (Van Eck), the causal field of their intuitive theory of mechanics (tenet iii).[1] But the witnesses probably regarded this interpretation as a straightforward observation, as something they had actually seen and on which they only needed to report as faithfully as possible. Also, the police and the prosecution probably took their reports as factual evidence. How this can come about was aptly demonstrated by a recent experiment by Hannigan and Reinitz (2001). They showed subjects a series of slides of a woman shopping in a supermarket and at one point picking up an orange off the floor. How the orange had got there was not shown, but an obvious explanation was that the woman had dropped it first. That indeed was what the experimental subjects thought, because in a subsequent recognition test most of them also picked a slide depicting the woman dropping the orange as one they had seen earlier, thus recognising an inference as something they had actually seen.

The causal field of intuitive mechanics was studied experimentally some time ago by Albert Michotte (1954). He showed his experimental subjects images of circles of different sizes moving at varying speeds over a surface and occasionally coming into contact with each other. The images looked like a billiard table with

1 We will have to amend this later on.

moving balls seen from above. Depending on the size and speed of the 'balls' when they came into contact with each other, his subjects concluded whether or not one 'ball' caused another 'ball' to move (see tenet iv). Thus Michotte experimentally demonstrated, among many other things, that small 'balls' cannot cause large 'balls' to move, because in the minds of his subjects a small ball is not big enough to cause a big ball to move. Big effects must have big causes. That is what our intuitive theory of mechanics usually dictates.

When Van Eck fell backward on that fateful night in the way he did, the cause must have been that officer Abrams pushed him because, according to our intuitive theory of mechanics, people do not normally fall backward on their own. The pressure exerted by officer Abrams on the front of Van Eck's body – if there was any – must have been more than just counterpressure to prevent Van Eck from re-entering the police station, because it not only stopped Van Eck moving forward, it made him move backward. The force exerted on his body must have been sudden and very forceful to make him fall like a log and to make his head hit the pavement with such a loud thud, a thud that may have been even louder than they originally estimated, since Van Eck died later that night from the head injury he apparently incurred from it.

For these reasons we think that the testimony of the majority of the witnesses about the forcefulness of the push should not be taken at face value without further examination. Corroboration of this scepticism may be found in the statement of witness 8. She was a young woman of German nationality, in Amsterdam for a brief visit. According to her, Van Eck did not fall backward in the manner described by the other witnesses. Although she too thought that officer Abrams had pushed Van Eck, whom, moreover, she thought to be intoxicated, she reported that he had stumbled, had unsuccessfully tried to stay upright and had fallen in an unfortunate manner. Nothing in her original testimony indicated that she thought that the push by officer Abrams had been particularly forceful. When she testified soon after that night, she probably did not know that Van Eck had died; because she was German, she could not read the newspapers or watch the television news. Not knowing that Van Eck had died, which all the other witnesses did know when they testified, may have given her less reason to adapt her evaluation of the cause of Van Eck's fall to the seriousness of the consequence. When weeks later she also took part in the reconstruction organised by the police, she said that the push had been forceful, but then of course she had also learned that Van Eck had died.

Some experimental support

One of our students, Caroline Remijn, tried to test empirically the theory explained in the preceding paragraph (Remijn, 2004). On the basis of the videotaped reconstruction of the events in the Warmoesstraat made by the police during the investigation, she created a 42-second-long video showing two men in front of the entrance of a Maastricht police station. A shabbily dressed man stands in front of the entrance of the station and tries to push his way in, while a uniformed police officer prevents this by putting both of his hands on the front of the other man's body. While the police officer stretches his arms the position of the man trying to enter changes from leaning forward to upright. Next the man appears to stagger and begins to fall backward. Whether the police officer is still pushing at that particular moment or simply loses contact with the victim's body remains unclear, or at least was meant to remain unclear. For obvious reasons, the fall itself is not shown. The final images show the man, lying on his back on the sidewalk.

As a simulation of the real events in the Warmoesstraat, the video used in the experiment was fairly crude. In contrast to what the real witnesses in this case could have seen, the video clearly established the presence and manner of bodily contact between the police officer and the victim. Moreover, the particular way in which Van Eck had fallen could not be shown in the video, and neither could the thud of the victim's head hitting the ground be heard. More serious is the fact that the experimental subjects in the study knew that the two protagonists in the video were only play-acting.

After watching the video, half of the 87 experimental subjects (65 of whom were women) read a (fictional) newspaper clipping with the heading 'INVESTIGATION INTO THE DEATH OF AN EVICTED HOMELESS MAN' (the 'death condition') , while the other half read a clipping with the heading 'COMPLAINT BY HOMELESS MAN AFTER EVICTION' (the 'complaint condition'). After reading the clipping, the subjects were asked to answer some questions about what they had seen. The pertinent question read as follows:

> Give your best possible judgement as to whether the police officer pushed the tramp. In particular, we want to know how hard the officer pushed at the moment that the tramp began to fall. In this case, 0 means that the officer simply prevented the tramp from entering, and 100 means that the officer pushed the tramp as hard as he possibly could.

The answer to this question was given by marking a point on a rating scale running from 0 to 100. The expectation was that the subjects in the death condition would rate the force of the push significantly larger than those in the complaint condition. This turned out not to be the case: the mean score in the death condition was 39.4 (SD = 18.5), and in the complaint condition 38.2 (SD = 22.3); the difference (F (1,85) = .08; p = .78) was insignificant.

The answers to another question may shed more light on this disappointing out-

come. After having rated the forcefulness of the push, the subjects were asked the open question:
'Do you think that the police officer is to blame for the tramp's fall? Please explain your response.'

Seven subjects could not be scored either yes or no on the basis of their answers to this question. The results of the remaining 80 subjects are given in Table 2.

Table 2 ***Number of subjects scoring 'yes' or 'no' in both experimental conditions***

	Officer to blame	**Officer not to blame**	**Total**
Death condition	23 (59%)	16 (41%)	39
Complaint condition	12 (29%)	29 (71%)	41
Total	35	45	80

Significantly more subjects in the death condition believed that the police officer was to blame for causing the fall of the tramp than in the complaint condition (Chi-square (df=1) = 7.17; p< .01). Hence the experimental manipulation had a significant effect, not on the judgment of the force of the push, but on the attribution of blame. It appears that the experimental subjects, looking for a cause of the victim's fall, did not choose to look for it in the causal field of intuitive mechanics, to which the question about the force of the push was intended to steer them. Instead, they chose the causal field of folk psychology, and blame attribution in particular. When two people are seen interacting and something bad happens to one of them, the first question that apparently comes to mind is: who is to blame for it?

Asking ourselves why this would be the case, we were reminded of Robert Zajonc's thesis that people observing an event first have a nearly instant emotional evaluation of it and only then reason about it (Zajonc, 1980). In Zajonc's own words: 'Affective judgments may be fairly independent of, and precede in time, the sorts of perceptions and cognitive operations commonly assumed to be the basis of these affective judgments'. Sixteen years later Joseph LeDoux (1996) confirmed that perceptions are affectively evaluated instantaneously, i.e., within 0.25 seconds. Assuming that the attribution of blame is an affective judgement, it may well have been that, although the question about the force of the push was asked first, in the minds of the respondents the attribution of guilt had already been decided. Although logically the push as the cause of the fall precedes the attribution of blame for it, the participants' first reaction must have been who was to blame. If that is indeed what happened, it is not unreasonable to assume that only for those who deemed the police officer guilty of Van Eck's fall, in either experimental condition, did the question about the force of the push have any relevance. This is confirmed by the empirical data: those observers who accepted the push as the physical cause of the tramp's fall judged the force of the push to be significantly stronger: 52.0 (SD = 16.3) versus 28.3 (SD = 16.5); $F(1,78) = 41.31, p < .001$).

Other empirical support for the major-event major-cause heuristic

Since the results of the experiment described in the preceding section may not be taken to support straightforwardly that people tend to think that major consequences must have major causes, it is relevant to scan the literature for direct empirical support for this hypothesis. An experiment by Leman (2003) is a case in point. He presented his experimental subjects with what looked like a clipping from a newspaper, in which an assault on the president of a fictional country was reported. Four groups of subjects received four different versions of the story:

a. the president was said to have been shot and killed;
b. the president was said to have been shot and survived;
c. the president was shot and died of a heart attack later on; and
d. a shot was fired at the president, but it missed.

The subjects were then asked whether they thought it probable that the gunman acted alone, or if there might have been a conspiracy to assassinate the president (the second possibility, of course, having more serious political implications). As it turned out, if the fictional president had died after the shooting, even if not directly from the gunshot wound (as in condition c), the readers of the report were much more likely to believe that the gunman was part of a conspiracy.

In a related experiment, subjects were shown a brief film of a speeding police car (Kebbell *et al.*, 2002). Half of them were next shown a picture of a crashed car of the same type, the other half a picture of the same type of car in pristine condition. The subjects were asked to estimate the speed of the car in the film. The participants in the crashed car condition gave significantly higher speed estimates than those in the non-crashed condition. Again, this result demonstrates that in the minds of witnesses, bigger effects require bigger causes. The results in this study were relatively ambivalent, because when the police car in the film was replaced by a civilian car, the subjects in the crashed-car condition did not estimate the speed of the car significantly higher than those in the non-crashed condition. The explanation given by the authors of the study is that the subjects probably assumed that police officers are highly skilled drivers, and when they crash despite their skills, it must be due to their speed, while civilian drivers may crash because they are poor drivers, irrespective of their speed. It therefore appears that, in the two versions of the experiment, the subjects spontaneously chose different causal fields in their search for a cause.

Choosing a probable cause from among possible alternatives

While witnessing an event – in particular an unexpected negative event – and asking ourselves what might have caused it, not just any possible cause will do. So the next question is how we make a choice from among possible alternatives. Which heuristics are used in making this choice?

Various authors have spoken to this issue. Einhorn and Hogarth (1986, p. 4)[2] sum up five 'cues to causality', i.e., criteria that, if met in a given situation, lead people to choose something as the cause of a particular incident:

a. precedence, i.e., a chosen cause precedes the effect which it is taken to cause;
b. covariation, i.e., causes and effects are (almost) always together;
c. contiguity in time and space, i.e., causes and effects are close in time and space;
d. congruity, i.e., causes and effects are similar in strength and length;
e. few alternative explanations for an event are available.

These five criteria are indeed heuristics: they may help to identify the probable cause of a particular event, but they are not foolproof. On occasion they may be definitely misleading, as already demonstrated in the foregoing with respect to criterion (d), congruity. It is probably true that often an effect resembles its cause in strength and/or length, but it is by no means certain: little mistakes may lead to major disasters, and very big mistakes may have happy endings.

In the Warmoesstraat case the supposed cause, a push by officer Abrams, and its supposed effect, Van Eck's fall and subsequent death, straightforwardly meet (a) and (c) of the above given criteria. Criterion (d) is problematic in this case, because while judging the force of officer Abrams' push from the way Van Eck fell, all but one of the witnesses had the post hoc information of Van Eck's subsequent death. Also criterion (b) is problematic: although a push may well make someone fall, most pushes do not make people fall, and not all falling people were pushed. The causal field of intuitive mechanics, telling us that upon contact a force may be transmitted from one object to another, makes it seductive to attribute Van Eck's

2 A somewhat different list of criteria was given by Nisbett & Ross (1980), p. 113.

fall to a push by officer Abrams. And this is particularly so because criterion (e) applies: for these witnesses there was no apparent other explanation for Van Eck's fall.[3] In the preceding sentence the words 'for these witnesses' are important, because it was different for the prosecuting attorney. When he decided to prosecute, he must have been aware of the statements of two witnesses in the case file, whose testimony did offer an alternative explanation.

The first of these witnesses was the manager of a hostel for the homeless in some other town. In his establishment one could stay the night, either in one of the beds in a large hall or in one of a small number of private rooms. One day in the early evening Van Eck came to this hostel and was promised a bed in one of the private rooms, on the condition that he would not be drunk, upon his return. When he came back, Van Eck was obviously drunk and the manager told him he could not have one of the private rooms. This made Van Eck very angry. He ran out the door, with the manager in pursuit, and then was observed to let himself fall on the sidewalk in a manner quite similar to how he fell in front of the Amsterdam police station, i.e., backward. And also that time, according to the hostel manager, Van Eck's head had hit the pavement with a loud thud.

The other extra witness was Van Eck's daughter, who described a similar incident at a time when she did not let her father have his way at her house. She declared that her father made it a habit to let himself fall suddenly when he became angry and frustrated about something. On the basis of these two testimonies, available in the case file in the form of affidavits, one can speculate that maybe officer Abrams was right when he surmised that Van Eck had let himself fall down on his own, although this time once too often. For the witnesses present in the Warmoesstraat, however, this explanation was almost impossible to surmise because it lies outside the obviously applicable causal field.

We mentioned before that the causal chain in this case contains three links. Until now we have restricted our commentary to the first link, the fall. What about the other two links? Was it indeed the fall that caused Van Eck's head injury, and was it closed head injury that caused his subsequent death? We know that his physical condition was very poor, due to his nomadic way of living and his alcoholism. Perhaps Van Eck died of something else. The doctor who signed his death certificate attributed his death to closed head injury. We do not know from the case file how thorough the doctor was in his examination of the cause of death. Perhaps to him the cause of death was obvious after he was told about what had happened earlier

3 Perhaps there was: the sloping ramp on which Van Eck was standing, but that detail may not have been very prominent. That Van Eck was also not very stable on his feet may not have been obvious to all the witnesses.

that night in the Warmoesstraat. Did he consider alternative possibilities? We do not know this, and neither did the court.

How the case ended

What happened when the case went to court? Having read the case file containing the affidavits of all the witnesses mentioned before, the Amsterdam court wrote in its verdict:

> The physical condition of the victim, his diminished reaction capacity and the position in which he found himself (i.e., his standing on a sloping ramp) together constituted such an unfavourable combination of factors that the backward push by the suspect created the not insignificant chance that the victim would lose his footing, fall and hit the ground in an unfortunate manner. Although, behaving in this manner, the suspect did not intentionally cause the victim's death, nor did he intentionally cause severe bodily harm to the victim, his behaviour was nevertheless seriously negligent, and in this manner he caused the victim's death.

So, officer Abrams was convicted of accidental manslaughter, with the aggravating circumstance that it was committed in the line of duty, and was sentenced to 140 hours of community service. Why? Was the court not aware of the complexities and pitfalls of causal reasoning? Yes it was, because one of us had explained these in a written expert opinion that had become part of the case file. Did the court not know about the two witnesses whose testimony suggested an alternative causal explanation for Van Eck's fall? Yes it did, because affidavits of their testimony were also part of the case file. So, what made the court so certain that a push by officer Abrams caused Van Eck to fall and die of his injuries later on? Perhaps also the court could not resist the appeal of the hazardous big effect-big cause heuristic.

Are we certain then that the court made the wrong decision? No, we are not. Maybe the court got it right.

Multiple causation

A complicating factor, also apparent from the court's verdict, is that events may not be the result of a single cause, but rather of a coincidence of several causes, each of which constitutes a necessary condition. The ferry *Herald of Free Enterprise* (see chapter 13) capsized near the Belgian coast because the boatswain left the bow doors open, *and* because the captain made a fatal manoeuvre shortly after his ship had left the harbour. Neither of the two would have sufficed to sink the ship, but still both the boatswain and the captain might be held responsible for their contribution to the disaster in which 250 people died. Accidents, unlike premeditated crimes, are typically characterised by a complex interaction among a substantial number of causal influences. Wagenaar & Groeneweg (1987) found that accidents at sea are usually caused by between ten to twenty necessary precursors. The accidents would not have happened if only one of these precursors had been absent. The same was found for the occurrence of police shooting incidents in which people were accidentally injured (Groeneweg & Wagenaar, 1989). The death of Van Eck in front of the police station in the Warmoesstraat can probably best be characterised as an accident, and was caused by the coincidence of at least three factors: the push by officer Abrams, the sloping ramp on which he was standing, and Van Eck's psychological and physical condition, including his peculiar habit of letting himself fall on occasions when he did not get his way. So one may well ask why officer Abrams alone should be held responsible for the entire event.

Although single individuals often may not be responsible for each and every cause in a multiple-cause event, they may still be held responsible for their own contribution to that event, and may therefore be liable under criminal or tort law. Three criteria may underlie such a judgement. The first criterion may be called the *fatal blow* criterion, which is related to the time order of events. According to this criterion, the last contribution of giving the fatal blow is seen as the decisive cause and therefore the one for which the responsible actor should be held liable. It is this rationale that gives all credit to the soccer player who scores the goal, and in a multiple person fight imposes the heaviest punishment on the participant whose action actually killed the victim. This criterion is also called *causa proxima.*

Closely related to the *fatal blow* criterion is the criterion of *discarded insight.* Under this criterion those individuals who had the most complete insight in the causal forces, but still continued their contribution to the disaster scenario are held responsible. This may coincide with the first criterion, because the person who gave the fatal blow is often also in the best position to oversee all contributing factors.

The third criterion, *culpability*, holds responsible any person in the scenario with a clear intention to do harm, even when the causal configuration is not entirely clear to him.

What do these three principles reveal when applied to the death of Van Eck? Do they suggest that officer Abrams was indeed liable for his contribution to the accident scenario? For the sake of argument, let us assume that officer Abrams was in fact in bodily contact with Van Eck briefly before the fall, and also that officer Abrams exerted at least some pressure on Van Eck's chest. Next, Van Eck lost his equilibrium on the sloping ramp and fell, possibly by his own doing. The first criterion, *fatal blow*, does not seem applicable to this scenario. There is too much time between officer Abrams's alleged push and Van Eck's movement on the ramp, his fall and his head hitting the pavement. From what we know, the *culpability* criterion does not apply either, since it was obviously not officer Abrams' intention to cause harm. That leaves the second criterion: *discarded insight.* Did Abrams have enough insight into the multiple causes of the accident to realise what might happen? Officer Abrams must (or at least could) have been aware that Van Eck stood on a sloping ramp. He probably did not know that Van Eck had a habit of letting himself fall deliberately, although he had witnessed this twice before on that very day. But, in any case, he knew of Van Eck's physical and psychological condition. According to the file, officer Abrams had already noticed that Van Eck looked drunk in the afternoon. He had also seen that Van Eck walked with an unstable gait, and may have concluded that he was intoxicated. Knowing about Van Eck's condition and the sloping ramp, we could conclude that Abrams had sufficient information to foresee the possibility of a serious accident. It's best not to push an intoxicated individual off a sloping ramp; not gently and certainly not forcefully.

If officer Abrams indeed pushed Van Eck, he may be held legally responsible for the latter's death on the basis of the criterion of *discarded insight*, even though the push itself may not be considered a sufficient cause of the accident. The advantage of this analysis is that it removes the necessity of assessing the force of officer Abrams' push, or of the extent to which the push can be taken as the only and sufficient cause of Van Eck's fall. Probably, awareness of the sloping ramp and Van Eck's condition should have convinced officer Abrams that Van Eck could better be left inside the police station, or should only be removed in a very different manner. And that is precisely how we can read the court's verdict:

> The physical condition of the victim, (...) and the position in which he found himself (...) constituted such an unfavourable combination of factors, that the backward push (...) created the by-no-means-neglible chance that the victim would lose his footing, fall, and hit the ground in an unfortunate manner.

In its opinion, the court obviously assumed that officer Abrams was, in fact, aware of all the contributing factors in a multiple-causation risk, and negligently ignored this awareness by pushing Van Eck down the sloping ramp. Van Eck's death was not simply caused by officer Abrams's push, but rather by his neglect of a clearly noticeable risk.

This still leaves us with the question of whether officer Abrams pushed Van Eck at all. This 'fact', assumed by the court, was possibly based on nothing more than the inference of a cause by witnesses who had actually observed only the outcome of the event. It is possible that the witnesses did not realise that multiple causes contributed to Van Eck's fall. Hence we end with the intriguing paradox that the court held officer Abrams responsible for not being aware of the multiple-causation structure of the risk in which he engaged. At the same time, witnesses were not required to take this structure into account when reporting what they had seen, as if their simplistic causal attribution might not also create a severe risk to others, in particular to officer Abrams.

CHAPTER 3

Consumer Confusion or Potato Chips and Olive Oil

Manufacturers of consumer goods have a legal obligation to inform the consumer accurately about the nature and the origin of their products. Company B should not create the suggestion that its products are manufactured by Company A, and should also not suggest that its products have certain properties which, in fact, they do not. Litigation about such issues is of considerable importance to almost every large national and multinational industry. Many have a specialised legal department involved in watching and, if necessary, prosecuting competitors who allegedly invade their rights.

The basic issue in the thousands of lawsuits every year is the allegation that consumers are confused by the suggestive or blatantly untrue statements by competitors. Such confusion may lead consumers either to buy products manufactured by company B believing that they are produced by A or to buy products in the false belief that they have certain properties.

The legal issue is how a court or jury can decide that the average consumer of a certain product will in fact be confused. The simplest way for judges and juries to decide such matters is to consider whether they themselves would be confused. If so, they may reason that others will be equally confused and decide accordingly. In many cases the litigating parties do not dare to rely on the uncertain outcome of such subjective judgements in multi-million cases. Instead, they offer the results of empirical investigations based on samples from the consumer population, demonstrating that these sample consumers actually were, or were not, confused. Often the marketing researchers who conduct these studies are asked to testify in court, while others are asked to comment on these studies as counter-experts. One of us has served as an expert witness in a considerable number of such cases (see: Verkade & Wagenaar, 2002). Monahan & Walker in their 'cases and materials' book provide a brief overview of such cases litigated in the United States of America (Monahan & Walker, 2002). Apart from the predominantly legal literature, there is almost nothing published about the European situation, which is shaped mainly by the decisions of the Court of the European Union in Luxemburg, and for the

Netherlands by those of the Benelux Court for Trademarks.

The European and American trademark statutes and litigation differ considerably. To mention but one point: following the landmark case about Zippo cigarette lighters (Zippo v. Rogers Imports, 1963[1]), the U.S. courts have adopted the basic position that claims about the invasion of trademark rights need to be supported by survey research. The Court of the European Union on the other hand still maintains that courts in the member states may decide about trademark infringements on the basis of their own subjective evaluations. Empirical research may be offered but is not required, and is definitely not encouraged.

Another difference is the European doctrine of the *reasonably well-informed and reasonably observant and circumspect consumer*, which holds that confusion must be established not for your average rather uncritical, inattentive and hurried buyer of a product, but for consumers who attentively study the information provided to them on the package or in separate instructions.[2] The case of *Gut Springenheide* was about eggs that were advertised as laid by chickens fed a six-grain mixture. In fact, the chicken feed was made up of 60 percent six-grain mixture and 40 percent 'other' feed. This was clearly labelled on the packaging of the eggs. The complaint was that consumers would be misled by the slogan, and would believe that the chickens were fed exclusively on a six-grain mixture. The Court of the European Union decided, however, that precise information about the composition of the product was given on the label of *Gut Springenheide* and that the observant and circumspect consumer could and would consult this information instead of naively trusting a slogan. The far-reaching consequence of this doctrine for empirical research on consumer confusion will be explained below.

Different experimental designs for the measurement of consumer confusion

Several experimental designs for the measurement of consumer confusion have been proposed. Each design has advantages and disadvantages, and none of them is ideal. It has never been attempted to develop an optimal design that might be adopted as a standard for litigation in Europe.

The most direct way in which consumer confusion about the origin of a product is measured is the so-called *exit study*. Consumers are interviewed upon leaving a

---

1 Zippo Manufacturing Co. v. Rogers Imports, Inc. United States District Court, Southern District of New York, 1963. 216 F.Supp. 670.

2 Court of Justice of the European Communities, Case C-342/97, 22 June 1999 (*Lloyd/Klijsen*); Case C–210/96, 16 July 1998 (*Gut Springenheide).*

shop or supermarket and asked: 'Which brands of products did you buy?' Next the contents of their shopping bags are inspected. If they say they have bought the well-established brand A, but turn out to have the newly introduced product of brand B in their shopping bag, it is fair to assume that the new product B does create confusion. This design has several drawbacks. The first is that it cannot be applied if brand B is not yet available in the shops. This is a problem because much research on consumer confusion is done before the actual introduction of products into the market. This is done because convictions after the introduction of a new product may result in considerable financial loss. Another drawback is that the criterion of the *reasonably observant and circumspect* consumer is not automatically met by the random sampling of respondents in exit interviews. It is possible and even probable that, in practice, the majority of consumers are not very observant and circumspect, and as a result, randomly sampled consumers may not be deemed relevant for the court's decision. A third drawback is that exit studies may be very time consuming, because it is likely that only a minority of clients will have bought either product A or product B. Given that the average supermarket offers several thousand products and most consumers buy fewer than twenty per visit, it may well happen that less than one percent of all clients interviewed can be used for the sample. A final methodological problem with exit interviews is that confusion may not have occurred at the time of selecting a particular product from the shelves, but may be a result of memory failure: upon leaving the shop, consumers may have forgotten which brand they bought and, when asked, simply mention the first brand that springs to mind, i.e., the familiar brand A. Thus, they may answer that they bought brand A, while in fact they bought B. At the time when they actually picked B from the shelf, they may not have been confused about its origin. In practice, exit studies are rarely done.

A more efficient technique is the *shopping list method.* Subjects are sent into the shop with a shopping list. The list may contain ten to twenty different items, one of which is the product of brand A. If the subjects return with brand B in their baskets, they are apparently confused about the true origin of B. Ideally, the shop would be a real shop with a familiar assortment of products. If brand B has not yet been introduced into the market but is only being considered for possible introduction, specimens of brand B can be temporarily added for the purpose of the study. This method solves a number of problems in the exit method, but introduces a new one in that the subjects are not unsuspecting consumers, but participants in a study of which they are aware. This may lead to a so-called demand characteristic, which means that the experiment's setting affects the behaviour to be studied. The participants may, for instance, be more cautious and not become as easily confused as would occur under ordinary circumstances. One could argue that these demand characteristics have the desired effect of turning the experimental subjects into the observant and circumspect consumers required by the courts, but such arbitrary considerations will only serve to make the courts more suspicious of empirical research. McCarthy (1984) noted that it is 'notoriously easy for one survey expert to appear to tear apart the methodology of a survey taken by another'. One of the reasons is that, almost without exception, survey subjects are exposed to demand characteristics that may distort their natural reactions.

A further step to a more controlled experimental design is the construction of an *artificial shop*. Again, subjects are sent in with a shopping list, but this time the shop consists of only a few shelves with carefully selected products, for instance two brands of each product on the list. Obviously, in such a set-up the demand characteristics are even higher. The limited choice for each product makes the subjects aware of the fact that they can make a right or a wrong choice, and that the purpose of the study is to measure their accuracy. Especially when there is only one unfamiliar brand, they will be acutely aware of the fact that the focus is on the difference between the two brands. This will almost certainly result in an underestimation of consumer confusion, which is to the advantage of the manufacturer of the unfamiliar brand. Another disadvantage, inherent in the testing of products before they appear on the market, is that the advertisement campaign is missing, which is normally used for the introduction of new products. Introductory campaigns serve to make consumers familiar with the nature and outer appearance of new products, hopefully with the result that confusion with already existing products is diminished. The absence of such a publicity campaign may result in an overestimation of consumer confusion. On the whole, the artificial shop method may be said to result in both underestimation and overestimation of consumer confusion, resulting in battles of experts that may only confuse the courts. In that sense this sort of empirical research may fail to meet the third Dyas criterion (see Dyas v. United States, 1977[3]) that the state of the art should permit a reasonable opinion to be asserted even by an expert.

Still further away from a realistic shop situation is the method that is called the *guess the maker* method. The disputed product B is shown to respondents with the question: 'Who do you think manufactured this product?' If the response is manufacturer A, we may assume that the respondents are confused by the outer appearance of product B. The first problem with this method is that the name of the manufacturer is almost always clearly indicated on the package or even on the product itself. No truly observant and circumspect respondent should therefore mention A as the manufacturer of product B. In order to prevent such an effect, in studies like these the name of B is usually removed from the package and/or the product. Pre-

3 Dyas v. United States, D.C. App., 376 A.2d 827 (1977).

dictably, this creates an unrealistic situation; products are always labelled in an actual shopping situation. Thus, the researcher may be criticised for artificially creating confusion instead of just observing it. But even correctly naming the new product B is not very informative if the dispute is about two highly similar names, such as in the case of the fruit drinks Squirt and Quirst (The Squirt Company v. Seven Up, 1979[4]). Correctly naming 'Quirst' does not mean that it is distinguished from 'Squirt'. This can only be demonstrated when both drinks are shown and the respondents manage to name them both by their proper names. But simultaneously showing both disputed products again creates a demand characteristic because the explicit comparison suggests a difference that might remain unnoticed under everyday conditions. Further complications with the 'guess the maker' method arise when B has not yet been introduced into the market. How can respondents 'guess' the name of the manufacturer of a product that they have never seen before? Still, this method was used in a study on the possible confusion between baby foods manufactured by Nutricia and Danone, before the Nutricia baby food was introduced.

A truly fundamental problem of the 'guess the maker' methodology is the so-called *market leader effect.* Respondents are inclined to guess when they do not really know the correct answer. This guess will be guided by the frequency with which they have encountered names of similar products. This is called 'frequency gambling' (cf. Reason, 1994), and it leads to the result that when the name of the unfamiliar new product B is removed, it is often confused with the product of the market leader, who in many cases appears as the litigating party. A dispute about chocolate drinks may serve as an example. Market leader Chocomel sold its product with yellow labels on bottles or in yellow cartons. The new product, Choq, also came in a partly yellow packaging. The researchers working for Chocomel showed their respondents a piece of yellow paper with the question: 'Of which brand of chocolate drink does this colour remind you?' Ninety percent responded with 'Chocomel'. To check for the market leader effect, Choq had the study replicated with a piece of white paper. Again 90 percent named Chocomel, demonstrating that the respondents apparently did not respond to the colour, but simply came up with the best-known brand of chocolate drinks. It is sometimes difficult to control the market-leader effect, and it requires a control condition, which usually is not provided for in market research.

A final way of creating an artificial test situation is the *questionnaire method.* These questionnaires also employ 'guess the maker' questions, but this time with

4 The Squirt Company v. The Seven-Up Company. United States District Court, Eastern District of Missouri, 1979. 207 U.S. patent Quarterly 12.

the help of a preprinted list of choice alternatives. But a preprinted list also creates demand characteristics, because it suggests all possible answers. If B is an entirely new product, the respondents will learn about it for the first time from the questionnaire. It cannot be the objective of surveys to teach the interviewees possible responses of which they would have had no knowledge without the survey. If B is not well known and A is, it matters a great deal which other alternatives C, D, E, F, etc. are presented in the list. If these are also not well known, the market-leader effect of A may well have its full effect. However, if C, D, E, F, etc. are also well-known brands, the market-leader effect will be much smaller. Although the selection of the choice alternatives is thus important, there is no clear prescription for how this should be done. In practice, the choice of alternatives is often the source of considerable distortion in the responses. In a study involving soap powder, the researchers even went as far as to omit the correct choice of brand B from the list!

A specific example

A specific example of a survey study on trademark confusion may further illustrate some of its problems. ID&T is a company involved in organising pop concerts, dances and other mass events for young people. Now they are also offering subscriptions to a mobile phone system, hosted by Telfort. The system is called ID&T Mobile, which partly sounds like T-Mobile, the name of another mobile phone system hosted by Deutsche Telekom. T-Mobile goes to court arguing that consumers will confuse the two names and come to believe that ID&T Mobile is offered by T-Mobile. The claim is supported by survey data from 801 respondents. In Question 1 of the survey, the name of ID&T Mobile was presented in three different modalities to each of three subgroups. The three modalities were: auditory by way of a tape-recorded message 'ID&T Mobile'; in written form by way of presenting the name 'ID&T Mobile' on a sheet of paper; and by showing the ID&T Mobile logo. Respondents were asked which company used this name. In the auditory condition, 65 percent of the respondents named T-Mobile and 2 percent were unable to answer the question. In the two visual conditions, the percentages of respondents naming T-mobile were 11 percent and 10 percent respectively, but in these conditions 46 percent and 49 percent respectively, were unable to answer the question. To a lesser extent than in the auditory condition, the visual presentation of the name 'ID&T Mobile' or its logo also resulted in a significant amount of confusion about its origin. In Question 4 of the survey, the names of ID&T Mobile and T-Mobile were presented together, and the respondents were asked whether these names were used by one company or by two, and if one, by which company. Some 39 percent of the respondents in the auditory condition thought the two names belonged to one and the same company. The comparable scores for the two visual conditions were 39 percent and 31 percent, respectively. When asked about the name of this single company, 63 percent, 67 percent and 75 percent respectively, chose T-Mobile as the company of origin of the ID&T Mobile services.

The method employed in the ID&T Mobile/T-Mobile study resembles the 'guess the maker' method, but instead of showing products without a brand name, the brand name is shown without the product. The criticism may be the same, that is, that in the real world such an isolated and reduced confrontation will rarely occur. Potential customers considering a subscription to the ID&T Mobile services will receive more elaborate information and may also be expected to gather relevant information on their own. The number of subscribers opting for ID&T Mobile cum Telfort in the firm belief that they are buying a service from T-Mobile of Deutsche Telekom might be substantially smaller than suggested by the percentages found in the survey. It is not easy, though, to come up with a better method. Consumers who have actually decided to subscribe to ID&T Mobile may have taken their decision on the basis of a vague notion that there is a relation with the much better known T-Mobile. At a later time they may have discovered their mistake, so some sort of 'exit survey' would not demonstrate the same, if any, level of confusion. The case was won by T-Mobile, and the decision was largely based upon the empirical study.

In summary, we conclude that there is no optimal method for the empirical study of confusion among brand names or the outer appearance of products. All methods used to this end have serious drawbacks. This may be one of the reasons why the Court of the European Union is not particularly fond of survey data supporting or rebutting claims of trademark infringement.

Misleading information about the nature of products

Empirically establishing misleading effects of information about the nature of products is definitely not easier than measuring confusion about their origin. The major reason for this is that the spontaneous and natural interpretation of messages and slogans is artificially interrupted as soon as critical questions about their meaning are asked. Another complicating factor is the common understanding that advertisements usually exaggerate. The bottle of toilet cleaner does not really contain a fairy who cleans the toilet in the blink of an eye, as suggested in some television advertisements. The consumption of a coconut-filled chocolate bar does not really transport you instantly to the Seychelles. But what are the limits of acceptable exaggeration?

Let us, as an example, take the slogan from Specsavers, a chain of retail opticians. They advertise with the slogan 'Europe's best is cheaper'. Pearle, a competitor in the market, argued in a lawsuit that Specsavers was misleading the consumers on two counts. First, 'Europe's best' purportedly suggests that Specsavers has shops all over Europe, while in fact they only have shops in Ireland and the Netherlands. Second, the claim that they are cheaper suggests that all their products are cheaper than those in any other optician shop. In reality, some of their products are more expensive than Pearle's. The problem of these contentions is that Pearle's interpretation of the slogan is not necessarily correct. The decisive issue is what the consumer population thinks that the slogan means. One of us argued that the meaning of vague expressions like 'Europe's best' is dependent on the context in which it is used. Strictly speaking, one may claim to be Europe's best soccer team only after winning the European Championships, in which all European national teams take part. But nobody will honestly believe that Europe's best optician has won a European Opticians Championship. Ranshuysen's Bakery in Zutphen (in the east of the Netherlands) may advertise that they make the best cinnamon buns in Europe, but nobody will assume that these buns are offered in all European member states, or that there has been a European Cinnamon Bun Championship. Besides, it is not clear what is meant exactly when an optician claims to be 'Europe's best'. Does he offer better glasses? Is he representing the most fashionable manufacturers? Is he cheaper, or maybe faster? Does he provide better service in his shops? The claim is largely unspecified and thus not testable. The same is true with respect to the claim that Specsavers is cheaper. Is this on average, for some of its products or for all its products? Is this compared to other shops in the same locations as where Specsavers operates (Ireland and the Netherlands) or to all opticians in Europe? And finally, can it be expected that consumers will give the slogan the specific interpretation submitted by Pearle, or will they realise that this slogan is one more example of the usual exaggeration in advertisement? It was proposed to the court to investigate these linguistic problems in a survey study. Fortunately for Specsavers, the court decided in a very quick procedure that the meaning of such slogans is vague by definition, and that an outcome supporting Pearle's rather extravagant claim was highly unlikely. Without further ado the claim was rejected, and Specsavers was allowed to use the slogan.

In another case a manufacturer of toothpaste claimed that their product would 'restore receding gums'. A survey study revealed that consumers did not interpret this claim as the usual exaggeration, but really believed the false contention that toothpaste may have such a beneficial effect. The company was thereafter ordered to declare publicly, in newspapers and magazines and on nationwide television, that they had misled the general public. They were ordered to stop their campaign, to withdraw their product from the market, and to offer compensation to all those consumers who had bought the toothpaste in the belief that it would restore their gums. The total effect of the court's decision almost bankrupted the company, which illustrates that lawsuits of this type are not marginal events, but vital tactics in industrial competition. This makes the question of exactly how survey research on consumer confusion should be conducted a matter of some urgency.

The case of Lay's Mediterrãneas

The Smiths Food Group introduced a new type of potato chips under the name Lay's Mediterrãneas. There are three flavours: Tomato & Basil, Oregano, and Greek Feta. On the front of the packages these flavours are mentioned together with an artistic rendering of tomatoes and basil, oregano, or feta, and in all cases two life-sized olives and a nine-centimetre-high glass jar with the inscription 'Olio di Oliva'. The back of the package carries the following texts:

> THE MEDITERRANEAN LIFE
> Lay's Mediterrãneas brings the rich Mediterranean life into your home. The mild climate, the authentic culture, the quiet, and of course the pure and tasteful kitchen. In short, everything that makes Mediterranean life so special.
> OLIVE OIL
> Olive oil: an essential part of the Mediterranean kitchen. Lay's Mediterrãneas is also enriched with olive oil, so that you may enjoy its good qualities to the full.

The first paragraph of the description, saying what will happen when you eat Lay's potato chips, is obviously an exaggeration. But the damage is probably nil, as no one will honestly believe that his home will suddenly metamorphose into a Mediterranean residence just by buying and eating Lay's Tomato & Basil potato chips. The second paragraph is more problematic, because Lay's Mediterrãneas are not fried in olive oil, but in regular vegetable oil. The 'enrichment' with olive oil, mentioned on the front of the package, is achieved by sprinkling some olive oil over the already-fried chips, with the result that Lay's Mediterrãneas contain only 2 percent olive oil, as indicated in the obligatory list of ingredients, of a total of 34 percent vegetable oil also mentioned in the list of nutritional values. If consumers misinterpret the information in the second paragraph, it cannot so easily be excused as resulting from the usual exaggeration in product advertisements.

Smiths' competitor in the potato chips market is the Italian company San Carlo, which sells potato chips with tomato & basil flavour under the name of 'Trattoria, Chips all' Olio di Oliva'. The special feature of Trattoria chips is that they are indeed fried in pure olive oil. The list of ingredients mentions 34 percent of this rather expensive product. Understandably, this manufacturing process affects the price of Trattoria chips: San Carlo chips are far more expensive than Lay's chips. San Carlo accused Smiths of unfair competition by creating the false impression that the much cheaper Lay's Mediterrãneas are also fried in pure olive oil. This impression is allegedly created by the picture on the package of olives and a jar of olive oil, and by the passage quoted above. Moreover, San Carlo accused Smiths of imitating the design of their package of the tomato & basil flavoured chips: pictures of a tomato, basil leaves, and potato chips on an orange background.

Smiths' defence against the first accusation rested on the simple assertion that the information on their packages does not say that Mediterrãneas are fried in olive oil, and that the true state of affairs can be inferred easily from the list of ingredients printed on the back of the package. This defence does not exclude, however, the possibility that a substantial proportion of the consumers, by seeing the jar of olive oil and reading the suggestive text about enjoying the 'good qualities' of olive oil 'to the full', will come to believe that either the chips are fried in olive oil, or will have the beneficial health effects that olive oil is presumed to have, or at least will taste like olive oil. Smiths did not contest that each of these expectations would be mistaken. It was therefore decided to conduct a survey study on how the population of consumers interpret the information on the packages of Lay's Mediterrãneas. But how to conduct such a study?

Survey study

The simplest method for studying the consumers' interpretations of the information on Lay's Mediterrãneas would be to ask buyers in a shop to describe the product they just had bought. The problem, however, would be that many of these respondents would not necessarily be the observant and circumspect consumers required by the Court of the European Union. In the opinion of Smiths it is important that potential buyers not only look at the pictures and/or read the accompanying label text, but also consult the list of ingredients on the back side of the package, or the indication of the nutritional value of their product, as in the case of *Gut Springenheide* (see above).

It was therefore decided to run a less realistic study in which a sample group of consumers in supermarkets were shown the various pieces of information on the package in a preprogrammed order. As in the actual shop situation, all respondents were first confronted with the front side of the package, on which the picture of olives and a jar of olive oil can be seen. On the basis of this, they were asked to describe the nature of the product in the package. Then they were asked two more questions which were presented in two different orders: subgroup A received them in the order 2-3, subgroup B in the order 3-2. In Question 2, the written passages about Mediterranean life and olive oil were shown and the respondents were asked to indicate what this information implied about the potato chips. In Question 3 the list of ingredients was shown, again followed by the question what for the respondents the implications were for the product in the package. Group B is the one that best represents the observant and circumspect consumer who will not be led by slogans, but pays attention to the factual information on the package. The critical responses, reflecting a certain degree of confusion about the true nature of Lay's Mediterrãneas, are those that indicate that the chips are *fried in olive oil*, are *healthier through the use of olive oil*, or *taste like olive oil*. A distinction was made between consumers who had bought Lay's Mediterrãneas before (users) and could therefore respond from experience, and consumers who had never before bought these chips before (non-users).

In total, 240 consumers were interviewed: 120 users and 120 non-users. To marketing researchers this number may not seem very large, but even a sample of 100 respondents allows us to assess a proportion with a 95 percent confidence interval of less than 10 percent, which is sufficient to test San Carlo's contention that a *substantial* proportion of consumers will be confused.

On Question 1, the 240 respondents produced 358 different descriptive statements. Only nine respondents, or 4 percent, demonstrated some degree of confusion about olive oil. Seven of these responses were produced by non-users, and only two by users. The conclusion is that the proportion of consumers misled by the front of the package, as shown on the shelves in the shop, cannot be called 'considerable'.

On Question 2, 255 descriptive statements were produced. Group A, who got Question 2 first, produced 30 critical statements from a total of 120 respondents, or 25 percent. Only 11 respondents in this group, or 9 percent, thought that the chips were fried in olive oil. Group B, who got Question 3 first, produced 22 critical statements from a total of 120 respondents, or 18 percent. Only eight respondents, or 7 percent, believed that the chips were fried in olive oil. Smiths argued in court that none of these percentages comes close to San Carlo's alleged massive effect of misleading.

On Question 3, 258 different statements were produced. Only thirteen respondents, or 5 percent, produced a critical statement, four (or 3 percent) of which implied that the chips were fried in olive oil. This was interpreted to demonstrate that the factual information about the limited use of olive oil in Lay's Mediterrãneas had come across quite effectively. The number of thirteen respondents is too small to test any effect of question order.

What the court decided

The Utrecht District Court was asked for a temporary injunction, because of the urgent nature of the matter. The definitive ruling, if sought at all, would probably take years, by which time the market for Trattoria might already have disappeared. The court's decision reads as follows:

The preliminary judgement of this court is that the general population of consumers will not relate the mentioning of olive oil on the package to the manner in which the chips are prepared. It can be expected of the reasonably informed, observant, and circumspect normal consumer that he will not only consult the front, but also the back side of the package. There the consumer will not only find the list of ingredients, indicating that the chips contain much vegetable oil but only 2 percent olive oil, but also the information that the chips are 'enriched' with olive oil. From this the consumer should conclude that the chips were not fried in olive oil. Moreover, mentioning olive oil does not necessarily refer to the way in which the chips were manufactured (fried in olive oil). It is a fact of common knowledge that olive oil can be sprinkled over chips after they have been fried. A confirmation of this opinion is found in the empirical study submitted to this court. The study demonstrates that only a small proportion of the respondents related the olive oil mentioned to the way in which the chips are manufactured.

Similarity between packages

San Carlo did not support its other accusation that Smiths had copied the design of their packaging by any empirical study, nor was the accusation empirically falsified by Smiths. This is in the best European tradition that a court is believed to be able to adjudicate such an issue on the basis of its own impression. The ruling of the Utrecht Court is an apt illustration of a judge's personal perceptions and considerations. The first consideration was that San Carlo registered the design for the package of Trattoria only in black and white. The colour orange used in Smiths Tomato & Basil packages can therefore not be an infringement of any right established through proper registration. The second consideration was that the name 'Trattoria' is placed in a rectangular frame, while the Mediterrãneas layout has no such frame. The third consideration was that the depiction of a tomato, basil leaves, and potato chips follows directly from the nature of the product. The production of chips with tomato & basil flavour is in itself not protected. Consequently, a manufacturer may claim the right to depict those ingredients on its package, unless the representation is a blatant imitation of the competitor's design. There is, however, no question of imitation in the case of Lay's Mediterrãneas, for the following reasons:

- Trattoria placed the basil leaves to the right of the tomato; Lay's has the leaves to the left of the tomato.
- Trattoria shows only two potato chips, Lay's seven.
- Trattoria's chips are ribbed while Lay's chips are flat.
- Trattoria does not show a jar of olive oil, while Lay's does (this argument must have sounded somewhat cynical to San Carlo, as they objected to the presentation of the jar).

– Trattoria's picture is rather photographic, while Lay's picture is more like a painted impression.

The wisdom of Smiths's decision to subject this issue to the personal judgement of the trial judge instead of offering the outcome of a survey study is obvious. The strong similarity between the overall impressions of the two designs, which might well have been decisive for the consumers' sampled opinions, has entirely disappeared in the rather analytical approach taken by this particular judge.

Post hoc evaluation of the survey research

As said before, it is not difficult to criticise survey research on consumer confusion. Although San Carlo did not invite an expert for a critical counter opinion, it is easy to imagine what such an expert might say. The most obvious objection is that explicit questions about what consumers think implicitly when they buy such mundane products as potato chips will inevitably introduce demand characteristics. The association with olive oil, elicited by the picture of a jar of olive oil and the story about Mediterranean life and the Mediterranean cuisine, may well contribute significantly to the decision to buy one product rather than another, even when the buyers are not fully aware of their reasons for doing so. Answering questions about such associations will change their nature and thereby possibly also their meaning. The free association with Mediterranean life may disappear when one is requested to think critically about the possible effect of 2 percent olive oil against 32 percent other vegetable oil. The results of a questionnaire study may therefore not reflect the real reasons for an impulse purchase. At the basis of this objection lies, of course, the not-unreasonable argument that the distinction made by the European Court between the average consumer and the observant, circumspect consumer is highly artificial, runs the risk of neglecting the vast majority of buying situations, and should therefore not define the methods used in a survey. A third objection is that there is no normative basis for the judgement that 2 percent, 9 percent, 18 percent, 27 percent, or any other percentage does not constitute a significant infringement. In comparison with the limited market of Trattoria's luxury product, Smiths is a very big player in the potato chip market. If only 10 percent of Smiths' customers are misled about the meaning of the information on Lay's packages, the absolute number of people involved might well exceed by far the total number of consumers who buy Trattoria chips.

These objections do not mean that we intend to disqualify the survey, which was conducted by one of us. The problem lies not in the quality of the survey, but in the translation of its outcome into legally relevant facts. Until the case of the Zippo cigarette lighters in 1963, in the United States survey data were considered inadmissible hearsay evidence, the argument being that the respondents could have a variety of reasons for their responses and could not be cross-examined about them in court. In the Zippo case it was decided that survey responses constituted an exception to the hearsay rule because, the court argued, they are like 'present sense impressions'. A present sense impression of an event is a statement made by a witness not in court during testimony but during the experience of the event itself. For example, the exclamation made during an assault 'Oh God, it is my father', reported by a bystander, is admissible under the American federal rules of evidence as testimony for the fact that at that moment the victim thought she was assaulted by her father. Similarly, the perceptions of respondents in an interview are accepted as reliable indications of what these respondents experienced at that moment, as reported by the researcher. The logic of this ruling is not compelling, since the similarity between the two situations appears limited at best. Surveys are renowned for the influence of the exact wording of the questions, the order in which the questions are asked, and the unintentional influence of the interviewer posing them. It is extremely difficult to assess the balance between what a respondent perceived and the demand characteristics of the survey. It is obvious that few respondents were confused about the exact role of olive oil in the production of Lay's Mediterrãneas, once they were asked about it. But what did they think before those questions were posed? The discussion about this issue should not be shunned in court, but the only available discussants are experts solicited by one or the other party. The question of whether survey research and subsequent battles between experts provide the courts with better insights than their own subjective evaluation of the issues at hand remains unresolved. It is possible that courts may ultimately decide to reject survey research as evidence in disputes on consumer confusion.

CHAPTER 4

Fiction and Reality of 'the Average Individual' or the Case of Old Mr. Lane

Much of what the expert psychologist can tell a judge or a jury is related to research outcomes averaged over many individual subjects. There is even a tendency to value empirical evidence proportional to the number of subjects involved, and to disregard data based on few subjects, particularly evidence from single-subject designs. The rationale of using many subjects is, of course, that the outcome becomes less sensitive to the idiosyncrasies of one or a few participants in a small sample. Thus, the *reliability* of the results obtained in large samples is enhanced, which is the likelihood that other investigators repeating the study will obtain the same outcome. But the *validity* of the average for application to an individual case is less dependent upon the sample size than on the distance of that particular individual from the average.

Lawyers seem to be aware of this problem. It is not unusual for experts to be confronted with the question: 'This is all very well as far as your average subject is concerned, but how do you know that Mr. or Mrs. X (the witness, the suspect, or any other person under discussion) does not differ significantly from the group mean?' And what about the following question: 'Did you test the vision (or memory, or any other relevant aptitude or characteristic) of Mr. or Mrs. X?' The answer to the latter question is almost always negative because expert psychologists usually do not, and may not even be allowed to run tests on individuals featuring in a trial. A case in point is the identification of a suspect through recognition of their appearance. An identification expert is almost never allowed to test the vision or memory of the witnesses, particularly not if these witnesses are police officers. Another example is the reliability of the accuser in a sexual abuse case. Even though we know that in this type of case false accusations are by no means rare (cf. chapter 11), experts on issues of memory, who are often consulted in such cases, are seldom allowed to test the memory of the individual bringing such a charge.

In principle, the question about applicability of averages to individual cases can be answered in six different ways:

1. The expert agrees that he or she is only informing the court about the average person. Since the expert is not privy to any other pertinent information about the person under discussion, the court is left to use the information at its own discretion.
2. The expert explains that the reported group data are only offered to illustrate a possible alternative scenario, for instance a scenario that exonerates the accused. If it is demonstrated that such a scenario exists for the average person, the other side should provide a plausible argument that the actual person or persons in the case are significantly different from the average.
3. The expert not only reports averages but also standard deviations (or other measures of dispersion), which indicate the probability that a particular individual will fall inside or outside certain boundaries.
4. The expert may explain that in a particular case there is enough information about the person under review to place her or him in the distribution of empirical outcomes.
5. The expert may claim that the reported averages are characteristic for almost everyone in the relevant population and must therefore almost certainly also apply to the individual under discussion.
6. The expert may propose to administer psychological tests to the person under discussion, in order to establish how close he or she is to the average subject in the empirical study.

These various answers will be discussed below, using the case of Mr. Lane as an illustration.

The case of Mr. Lane

At the advanced age of 98, Mr. Lane married his nurse Mrs. McCarty, age 43 at the time. The marriage was meant to be a mere business deal: Mrs. McCarty would take care of the old man until his death, which could not be far off, and upon his death Mr. Lane would leave Mrs. McCarty a substantial fortune. As it turned out, Mrs. McCarty was unable to keep her side of the deal, because two years into the marriage, her husband developed severe dementia, which made 24-hour care mandatory. This meant that he had to be placed in a nursing home. The screening for admission to the nursing home included the MMSE ('mini mental state examination') test for dementia (Folstein *et al.*, 1975), on which he obtained a score of nine on a scale ranging from zero to 30. Two weeks after the screening, Mr. Lane died, and Mrs. McCarty expected to inherit his estate. But then it transpired that the childless Mr. Lane's nephew contested the marriage contract on the argument that his uncle had already been suffering from dementia when he agreed to the marriage. In his opinion, Mr. Lane was forced by the nurse into marrying her, with the sole objective of securing the inheritance.

The nephew produced an expert psychiatrist who explained that senile dementia causes, on average, a yearly loss of four points on the MMSE scale. Hence he concluded that, at the time of the marriage two years earlier, Mr. Lane would have scored no more than seventeen points on the MMSE scale. The literature on the normalisation of MMSE scores (Crum *et al.*, 1993) shows that a score below 24 points indicates a significant loss of intellectual capacities, which would exclude a well-considered decision to get married.

The problem with this case is that Mr. Lane was not actually tested when he decided to marry his nurse. The registrar, who conducted the marriage proceedings, testified that Mr. Lane had appeared intellectually capable and had been aware of the rationale of marrying at such an advanced age. But a registrar is not an expert on dementia. Perhaps Mr. Lane had simply been instructed to say the right things. The condition of Mr. Lane's intellectual powers at the time of the wedding is therefore a matter of dispute, unless the progression of the disease is the same in all dementia patients, without much variation. One reason to doubt this is that there are at least two main types of senile dementia: one is Alzheimer's disease; the other is known as vascular dementia and is caused by problems of blood circulation in the brain. The most common form of vascular dementia is called multi-infarct dementia (MID), which is caused by a number of small strokes or ministrokes, also called TIAs, transient ischemic attacks. According to the literature, the progression of MID is faster than the progression of Alzheimer's-type dementia. The average decrease of four test points per year is calculated across all types of dementia and therefore not necessarily typical for MID. More specifically, if Mr. Lane suffered from MID, it is not impossible that his mental powers were unimpaired when he decided to marry. Unfortunately, which type of dementia Mr. Lane had suffered from was never established.

We will now try to use Mr. Lane's case to illustrate the six different answers to the problem of how to deal with information about the average person.

Option 1: Leave it to the court's own discretion

The expert in Mr. Lane's case might have restricted himself to presenting information about the average progression of dementia, or about the progression in the various types of dementia, without drawing a conclusion with respect to Mr. Lane's condition two years earlier. The court would have been helped further by the information that about 15 percent of all dementia cases are of the MID type (for a general review, see: Choi *et al.*, 1993). On the basis of this information, the court might have reached the conclusion that, although the nephew's assertion might be true, there was a reasonable chance that Mr. Lane had been intellectually fit when he decided to marry. Even without the exact percentages, general information about the existence of various types of dementia would have led the court to the insight that nothing could be concluded about Mr. Lane's state of mind as long as the causes of his illness had not properly been diagnosed.

This illustrates that general information, not applied to a specific individual, can still be helpful in the court's decision making. It is not surprising that in many American courts, experimental psychologists acting as expert witnesses are explicitly limited to providing general information and are prohibited from commenting on the case under consideration. Application of the general insight that dementia is a symptom of a variety of substantially different diseases would clearly have made it undesirable to attempt an estimation of Mr. Lane's cognitive abilities at a particular time in the past.

There may, however, be instances in which judges or juries want to apply expert knowledge to a particular case at hand. In the case of Mr. Lane, the court might have learned only about the average loss of four points a year on the MMSE scale. Would the court be willing to apply this general knowledge to Mr. Lane, without the realisation that an average score is not descriptive for all individuals? There is not much information about the way in which non-experts like judges and jury members apply abstract expert knowledge to specific cases. But we are aware of a phenomenon called the 'representativeness heuristic', according to which people tend to believe that individual cases (or small samples) reflect the properties of the population to which they belong (Kahneman, Slovic, & Tversky, 1982; in particular, chapters 2-6). This heuristic could help to create the belief that the average yearly progression of four points in the population must be indicative of Mr. Lane's dementia at an earlier time. If such a bias is to be avoided, it would be advisable to ask the expert to explain in explicit terms how information about the average person can be applied in a specific case, and in particular what the limits of such an application are. This contention is based upon the strong belief that psychological expertise is not limited to averages, but that it includes knowledge about the various ways in which group averages can be applied to individual cases.

Our objection against the psychiatrist's expert testimony in the case of Mr. Lane is therefore not so much that he attempted to apply his knowledge to the individual case, but that he did not explain the limitations of his inferences, stemming from the fact that dementia is a symptom of various, significantly different diseases. He left it to the court to make this discovery, with the almost certain result that the judge remained ignorant about this.

One might argue that in this civil lawsuit both parties had equal opportunities for the use and misuse of expert testimony, and that from the clash of different opinions the court can 'gauge the full force of the argument' before rendering its decision (Fuller, 1968).[1] Since the information about the various types of dementia does not support the plaintiff's case, his expert might be excused when he leaves it to the defendant's expert to inform the court about this.[2] However, in this case the plaintiff's expert went further than that, since he drew a conclusion about an individual that was clearly based on an incomplete and therefore misleading presentation of the available scientific knowledge. We think that this sort of deception is beyond the bias that may be expected when the expert is asked to act for one of the parties in the litigation.

Option 2: Use averages only by way of example

In some situations, it will suffice to argue that group averages illustrate the mere possibility of a certain scenario. The average progression of dementia illustrates that the scenario in which Mr. Lane was already suffering from dementia when he married is not impossible, nor even unlikely. The assertion supports the plaintiff's case, and the plaintiff's expert fulfilled a useful role, even when he limited himself to the presentation of group averages. Whether the assertion about group averages is enough to decide the case depends on the legal situation; criminal law and civil law differ in this respect.

In the course of a civil trial contesting the validity of the marriage, it is not a priori obvious who must prove what, the nephew as the plaintiff or Mrs. McCarty as the defendant. In principle, the nephew who brought the suit by contesting the validity of the marriage must prove his assertions. As a starting point, the court may accept the testimony from various witnesses, including the registrar and the notary who drew up the marriage contract, that Mr. Lane had been sane. Consequently, it may request that the nephew proves the opposite. In that case, the group means are not good enough: it must also be shown that the group average provides an adequate estimate of Mr. Lane's mental deterioration.

On the other hand, the court may, as a starting point, agree with the plaintiff that the conditions under which the marriage took place are somewhat suspect; this is corroborated by the undisputed fact that Mr. Lane was suffering from severe dementia when he died, and by the expert testimony about the average progression of dementia. The court might decide that this information turns the scales against Mrs. McCarty and that it therefore would not be unreasonable to shift the burden of proof. Consequently, Mrs. McCarty would be ordered to prove that her late hus-

---

1 The quote refers to the English version of the French dictum: Du choc des opinions jaillit la vérité.

2 For discussions on this issue see: Loftus, E.F. (1986), and Wagenaar, W.A. (1988a).

band had been *compos mentis* at the time of their marriage. Again, the general information about various forms of dementia and their progression would not be good enough, since it *does not exclude* that Mr. Lane was indeed suffering from dementia when he agreed to the marriage. A positive assertion about his condition is required, which implies that information is needed at the level of the individual. In such a situation, Mrs. McCarty would be required to prove that the average is *not* representative of her husband's condition.

The preceding analysis shows that in a civil lawsuit, irrespective of which side is ordered to prove its case, when there is no specific information about Mr. Lane's individual condition, the general information about dementia will leave room for the arguments of the opposing side. The attempt to prove one's case will always fail because the expert cannot exclude the alternative scenario with sufficient certainty. The outcome of the case is not so much determined by the expert's opinion, but rather by the court's imposition of the *onus probandi*. Whoever is ordered to prove his or her claims will need information about the individual. The opposite side can successfully defend its position through reference to group averages; to them, option 2 is quite useful.

The situation is even clearer in the case of a criminal trial, in which Mrs. McCarthy is accused of fraud. Then the point of departure is Mrs. McCarty's presumed innocence. The prosecution must prove the opposite of that presumption, that is, that Mr. Lane was suffering from dementia at the time of the marriage. Clearly, the possibility that Mr. Lane had been relatively sane is sufficiently supported by the fact that 15 percent of those in the group with dementia suffers from a rapidly progressing disease. Thus, the expert's opinion would be decisive, even without application to the individual level. Therefore, we can say that because of the presumption of innocence, group data, when used as proposed in option 2, are highly relevant in criminal trials.

Option 3: Report measures of dispersion

It is not unusual for researchers to report the dispersion or variability of their results, or to report a variety of measures of central tendency, since the differences between these measures give an indication of the distribution of the scores among subjects. Let us assume that they report that the yearly loss on the MMSE scale is four points, with a standard deviation of 0.5. Provided that the distribution around the mean is more or less normal, in which case other measures of central tendency like the median and the mode should approximately coincide with the mean, this means that 95 percent of the members of the population has a loss of no less than three, and no more than five points. Applied to the case of Mr. Lane, this would mean that there is 97.5 percent chance that his score at the time of his marriage to Mrs. McCarty was no more than 19, which indeed implies a considerable level of mental deterioration. Similarly, there would be 99.9 percent chance that his score was no more than 20. Thus, there would be a high degree of certainty about Mr. Lane's mental condition at the time of his marriage, even though it was not actually investigated at the time. If, again by way of example, the empirical results had revealed a standard deviation of 2.0, there would have been about a 7 percent chance that Mr. Lane's score was above 23, and this number would have created at least some doubt about the validity of the plaintiff's argument.

However, in Mr. Lane's case the expert failed to report standard deviations, although he mentioned that the regression 'may vary considerably' and that it 'would be difficult to make exact calculations'. Other than these remarks, he only reported the group average. Why he did not report a standard deviation is understandable, as the literature reports considerable individual differences. The most authoritative study is the so-called Nun Study (Snowdon *et al.*, 1997), based on elderly nuns who had made themselves available for scientific research both before and after their deaths. On the basis of an autopsy, 61 percent of the participants were diagnosed as suffering from Alzheimer's disease. Their mean MMSE score was thirteen, with a 95 percent confidence interval ranging from four to twenty. The variability is even more striking when two types of cases are distinguished: Alzheimer's disease combined or not combined with a stroke. Combined with a stroke, the mean MMSE score was three, with a 95 percent confidence interval ranging from three to twelve. Without a stroke, the mean score was seventeen, with a confidence interval ranging from fourteen to twenty-one. If the autopsy did not reveal any neuro-pathologic signs of Alzheimer's disease (41 cases), the mean MMSE score was 26, and this was largely independent of the presence of a stroke. Thus, the debilitating effects of Alzheimer's disease and strokes are particularly pronounced when they occur together. This again emphasises the point that treating the patient group as homogeneous would not have been warranted.

Unfortunately, in the Nun Study the rate of progression over time was not reported. In another longitudinal study (Petersen *et al., 1999)* a relatively homogeneous group of 106 patients with an initially mild form of Alzheimer's disease was followed. The average initial MMSE score was 22, with a standard deviation of 0.4. This small dispersion was clearly the result of the selection of mild cases and is therefore not representative of Alzheimer's patients in the general population. The mean annual rate of change in MMSE scores was a loss of three points, with a standard deviation of 0.5 point. This progression is even slower than that reported by the expert in Mr. Lane's case, but it must be realised that the small individual variability may well have resulted from the initial selection of a homogeneous set of apparently mild cases. If Mr. Lane's MMSE score dropped approximately twenty points in two years, his case was definitely not a mild one, which means that the conclusions reached by Petersen *et al.* are not applicable to him. Some evidence for the rapid progression is obtained from the observation that his dementia appeared to worsen already some weeks into the marriage when he was hospitalised for a hip operation after a fall (see option 4).

The expert who testified in favour of Mr. Lane's nephew did not report the literature on individual differences. As a consequence, the court may have overestimated the validity of conclusions based on the application of group means. However, as a mitigating factor it must be realised that even knowledge of the standard deviations would not have made it possible to place Mr. Lane at a particular point in the population distribution with any degree of certainty. This is simply because too little indisputable information about him was available. But clearly, the information from the Nun Study would have illustrated the defendant's point, that, without a clear diagnosis of Mr. Lane's disease, there is no reliable rule for projecting the process of dementia backward in time.

Whenever research outcomes are to be applied to the specifics of a case on trial, it should be common practice for experts to report averages as well as measures of variability, whenever they are available. If they fail to do so, the courts should ask for them. If such data are not available, there is a good reason to disregard the expertise, or at least to ask the experts how their data are to be applied to a particular case in the absence of measures of variability.

Option 4: Seek additional individualised information

Additional information about an individual may be used to support the notion that the individual is not an outlier in the distribution around the mean, in order to relate the individual to a norm group. Often the expert can be instrumental in identifying or interpreting such information. In the case of Mr. Lane there was a wealth of additional information, even though not always consistent and certainly not undisputed.

Mrs. Craig and Dr. Owen, a psychiatric nurse and a gerontologist, visited Mr. Lane one month before the wedding, shortly after his first wife had died. Their mission was to form an opinion regarding the necessity of placing him in a nursing home. Their conclusion was that Mr. Lane did not understand his own condition. An example was that he had no idea of the financial arrangements that were made for him, which is remarkable considering his earlier career as a banker. In his testimony to the court two years later, Dr. Harris, the superior of the two women, concluded that it was logical that Mr. Lane must have been equally incapable of understanding the consequences of his marriage. It should be noted, however, that Dr. Harris never actually did meet with Mr. Lane and that, during Mrs. Craig's and Dr.

Owen's visit, the subject of a second marriage had not been broached.

To some extent, Dr. Harris' conclusion is contradicted by the observation by several witnesses that, after the visit by Mrs. Craig and Dr. Owen, Mr. Lane decided he did not wish to go to a nursing home, and that this had been the reason for his marrying his nurse. This would imply at least a minimal amount of comprehension of his situation. But these witnesses were all close friends of Mrs. McCarty.

Two video recordings had been made: one of Mr. Lane's discussion with the notary who drew up the marriage contract, and one of the wedding party. Mr. Lane is seen to engage in a number of discussions on the consequences of his wedding. Dr. Stutts, the gerontologist who administered the MMSE two weeks before Mr. Lane died, watched the video recordings and concluded that Mr. Lane had a 'clear consciousness' throughout but 'a distinct awareness of what was happening around him could not be demonstrated', whatever that means.

Dr. Stutts also indicated that Mr. Lane had suffered from temporary lapses in consciousness, due to TIAs. This suggests that his dementia was of the MID type, not of the more slowly progressing Alzheimer's type. Surprisingly, Dr. Stutts concluded that in Mr. Lane the general pattern was one of a slowly progressing Alzheimer's-type dementia. It must be noted that Dr. Stutts saw Mr. Lane only once, two weeks before his death. He therefore could not have any personal observations about the progression of the disease.

The registrar, Mr. Manning, stated that he visited Mr. Lane one week before the wedding. They talked for about an hour about various subjects, and he verified that Mr. Lane understood the rationale and the consequences of the marriage arrangement. Although Mrs. McCarty was present in the house, she did not take part in this conversation. Mr. Manning was not a gerontologist; nevertheless, his conclusion was that Mr. Lane was sufficiently aware of the consequences of his decision to remarry.

Shortly after his marriage to Mrs. McCarty, Mr. Lane accidentally fell. He broke his hipbone and was taken to the hospital for an operation. After the operation he appeared to be severely disoriented. He was visited by a social-psychiatric nurse, who concluded that he suffered from Alzheimer's-type dementia. The problem with this conclusion is that hospitalisation is a well-known factor that promotes disorientation, often producing long-lasting effects in very old people (Moller *et al.*, 1998). It is not clear how the nurse could differentiate between Alzheimer's disease and the effects of hospitalisation. Mr. Lane's physician, Dr. Wilson, stated that up to the time of the accident, Mr. Lane had suffered from no other symptoms than slight short-term memory problems. Obviously, understanding the rationale of the marriage had nothing to do with short-term memory.

Taken together, it appears that this individualised information does not lead to a clear conclusion about Mr. Lane's position in the distribution of elderly dementia patients. It is not clear whether he suffered from an Alzheimer's-type dementia or from MID. It is not clear whether his dementia was already present at the time of his marriage, or if it developed as a result of his later hospitalisation. It is not clear which functions, if any, were affected at the time of his marriage or, in particular, if the memory problems that presented themselves as the first symptoms of his disease were accompanied from the beginning by a diminished understanding of his situation. Hence it is unknown whether Mr. Lane may be considered as representative of the group of patients studied in MMSE normalisation studies.

Sometimes psychologists chart the relevance of certain easily assessable variables such as age, gender and level of education. Norm sheets, obtained through large-scale studies of norm groups, enable us to produce information that is more relevant for an individual case than a grand mean across the entire population. Crum *et al.* (1993) have produced such a norm sheet for MMSE scores, with age and education levels as entrance parameters. It shows that MMSE scores are positively related to level of education, and inversely related to age. The total range for unaffected subjects runs from 29 points for college-educated subjects between the ages of 18 to 24, to 19 points for subjects with up to a fourth-grade education who are older than 84 years of age. For Mr. Lane, the norm would have been 27 points. Unfortunately, there are no norms for the annual rate of performance loss due to the various dementia-causing diseases.

Option 5: Declare that all individuals are characterised by the group average

Sometimes psychologists obtain empirical results that are meant to be representative of all normal individuals, without exception. An example is the maximal visual acuity during daylight, which is limited by the density of cones in the retina (see also chapter 14). There is a slight variation in visual acuity, probably due to variations in cone density, but this effect is negligible since there are no individuals with, for example, three times as many cones as others. When the empirical finding is that the accurate perception of faces deteriorates rapidly beyond an observation distance of fifteen metres (Wagenaar & Van der Schrier, 1996), it is impossible that a particular observer has recognised a face at a distance of 50 metres.

A somewhat weaker position is to hold that a psychological law applies to all normal people unless the opposite is demonstrated. A normal person will have a considerable problem remembering the date on which some everyday event happened if it happened in the distant past. Exception would be an individual with a neurotic habit of storing and rehearsing dates, or when there was a special reason for remembering that particular date, for instance the day of the attacks on the World Trade Center towers in New York. Nevertheless, the general rule remains that people are not good at remembering dates. If a witness testifies that a certain event happened on 10 October 1995, he should be asked to supply further information that makes it credible that this particular date remains fixed in his mind.

In the case of Mr. Lane, the expert could have testified that dementia in elderly people is always progressive; there is no regression and (as yet) no cure. He could have argued further that orientation in place and time are among the first psychological functions affected by all types of dementia. It is also a general rule that, in the final stages of dementia, most or even all psychological functions are affected. It can also be stated that the MMSE has a zero rate of false-positives for persons with more than nine years of education (Anthony *et al.*, 1982). All these general rules are directly applicable to Mr. Lane. Unfortunately, there is no such 'psychological law' about the rate of progression, expressed in scoring points on the MMSE.

Option 6: Propose to administer individual tests to the person under discussion

Whenever there is doubt about the applicability of group data to an individual, testing the individual may be considered. For instance, in a case in which an individual witness claims to have seen the suspect at night and at a distance of more than fifteen metres, an expert might assess the eyesight of the witness under night conditions. The test would not definitely answer the question of whether the reported observation is correct, as there may be many reasons why even a person with exceptionally good eyesight could still be mistaken. But the test would allot to the witness a place in the group distribution, so that it can be judged to what extent group data are applicable to him.

There are limitations to this approach. The first is that not every 'psychological law' can be translated into individual tests. Consider the case in which it is claimed that imagery techniques may have changed the recollection of a suspect to such an extent that he confessed to a murder that he did not commit (cf. chapter 9). We do know that imagery techniques may have such an effect, although not on every individual. It will be difficult to prove in an individual test that the suspect is not only particularly sensitive to imagery techniques, but was also actually made to believe that he committed a murder.

A second limitation is that not everybody in a criminal trial can be obliged to submit to psychological tests; a suspect cannot be forced to incriminate himself. The same goes for some witnesses for a variety of legal reasons. Psychological tests cannot be administered against the will of the person to be tested, as most psychological tests are based on the assumption of cooperation. A special issue is the psychological testing of police officers. Their psychological abilities are often assumed but rarely tested, simply because the prosecution obstructs it, and sometimes because their identities are not revealed.

A third limitation is that individuals may become aware of the significance of test results in the context of the trial and may therefore unconsciously or deliberately try to influence the outcome of the test. A well-known example is the polygraph test, by which an individual may try to prove his innocence by not showing increased physiological reactions to certain test items. The realisation that the outcome will determine his fate may invalidate the test results (Lykken, 1998).

Notwithstanding all these problems, there are types of individual tests that are habitually administered to witnesses or suspects. We mention two of these: the personality assessment of a suspect, and the lineup test for the identification of a suspect. We will see that their usefulness is limited.

In many countries the personality assessment of a suspect is more or less routine for suspects of serious crimes like sexual assault and murder. To this purpose, it is not unusual in our country to institutionalise the suspect for a period of six weeks, during which a host of experts observe and test him. Cooperation with this procedure cannot be enforced, but a refusal may be interpreted as a confession of guilt, and the suspect is informed about this in no uncertain terms. Many submit to this procedure, only to learn that they have a low IQ score, or that they suffer from a narcissistic personality, or were themselves the victim of abuse in early childhood. What can courts do with this sort of information? Is there a general psychological law according to which narcissistic personalities are prone to commit arson, or swindle in the stock market? The problem seems to be that, apart from the low validity of such individual diagnoses, they cannot be linked with enough safety to group data describing their forensic implications. As a consequence, the assessment of a suspect's personality may produce highly suggestive results, and may become a dangerous instrument in the hands of judges and juries.

Witnesses often take part in identification tests that serve the dual purpose of assessing the general quality of the witness's memory, and of verifying whether the witness really recognises the suspect (Wagenaar, 1988b). This dual purpose is only achieved in properly organised lineups, but unfortunately procedural mistakes are often made (Wagenaar & Loftus, 1990). In the majority of cases, the result is that we learn nothing about the quality of the witnesses' perceptual powers or the quality of their memory, and consequently we cannot relate them to the distribution of subjects in our research outcomes. As a result, the vast body of general research findings on eyewitness identification cannot easily be applied to the situation in which an individual witness claims to recognise a suspect.

In the case of Mr. Lane, it is obvious that a test of his individual mental abilities at the time of his marriage would constitute the decisive argument in the case, if we could obtain this information; however, we cannot. Instead, the court was informed about the average progression of the disease, which gave rise to the problems described above.

Our actual testimony

1. Mr. Lane's decision to remarry at the age of 98 required a certain degree of insight into the consequences of his decision. It is not obvious that Mr. Lane's much-discussed memory problems would preclude his having such insight. It is also not clear that the MMSE testing of mental faculties relates to the ability to make such a decision.
2. Dementia is not a disease, but a symptom of various substantially different diseases. The progression rate of dementia depends on the disease causing it. None of the medical specialists who saw Mr. Lane in the last two years of his life specified from which disease he was assumed to suffer. Consequently, in his case it is not possible to apply a rule such as the four-point-reduction-per-year of the MMSE score.
3. Even with sufficient knowledge about the standard deviation of MMSE reduction in the population, and of Mr. Lane's position relative to the population of elderly people with dementia, the conclusion about his condition two years before he was actually tested would be probabilistic at best. The testifying expert should at least have indicated what the probability margins were.
4. Dr. Harris claimed that there had been a steady decline in Mr. Lane's cognitive abilities. This was based on one single observation (not even made by himself; see above). It is impossible to decide whether a decline had been steady or sudden, without having more than a single observation.
5. The plaintiff's expert told the court that MID is characterised by a decline in some cognitive faculties, while other faculties remain relatively unaffected. He mentioned memory as one of the areas that is most often affected. This might explain why some observers noticed a decline in Mr. Lane, whereas others concluded that he understood the rationale of his marriage quite well. MMSE relies heavily on the ability to remember things. A progressive dementia caused by MID would certainly cause a reduction in MMSE scores, even if the ability to take decisions was not affected.
6. The examinations of Mr. Lane by Mrs. Craig and Dr. Owen took place after his hip operation. They failed to indicate how they distinguished between the effects of the operation and hospitalisation and a general decline that might have set in even before his marriage. It is also not clear how these factors might be disentangled.

What the court decided

The court's decision[3] constitutes an apt illustration of the difficulties introduced by the dilemmas described above. The court reasoned that the plaintiff's expert was a specialist in the field of senile dementia, whereas our discussion of the risks of applying general statistics to the specifics of this case was not based on a clear specialisation in this particular field. This argument allowed the court to avoid a judgment about the applicability of the four-points-a-year rule. At first, it may seem that the court was dodging the issue. It should be understood, however, that the court had probably never before thought about this problem and was also not really in a position to judge whether it needed to be raised. Probably, judges do apply general statistics to individual cases all the time. Criminal courts would probably be at a loss if the jump from the general to the specific were made too problematic. The court's argument was that the plaintiff's expert could be trusted to have formed his opinion about Mr. Lane on the basis of his expertise. This adds a seventh option to our list of six options: *Claim that your expertise is a sufficient basis for going from the average to the individual, even without explaining how this is done.* We prefer not to include this option in our list.

3 Amsterdam District Court, case 128109/97.2273F, 17 October 2001.

CHAPTER 5

Case Histories and Scientific Proof or the Case of JR

Case histories are used to illustrate a scientific principle and often also to prove the validity of the principle. The history of psychology is particularly full of illustrious case histories; from Freud's Anna O. (cf. Freud, 1896) to Wilbur's Sybil (cf. Schreiber, 1973), Luria's Mnemonist (1987), Baddeley's Clive Wearing (1990), Woodruff's Tichborne Claimant (1957), and Wagenaar's Ivan the Terrible (1988b). There are huge differences with respect to the use of such case histories in scientific discourse. Freud used cases to prove his theory. They constitute the empirical evidence in support of his theory, as he offers no other, more systematic and prospective empirical research. Therefore, showing a case as historically false as, for instance, Israels (1999) did for the case of Anna O. simultaneously undermines Freud's theory. Baddeley's description of Clive Wearing, a man who lost his memory after encephalitis, is of a different type. The case is not meant to prove that meningitis can have this effect; we knew this already. Also, the case is not meant to prove that amnesia really exists; that too was already known. The case is meant to illustrate the horrors of living as an amnesiac. The film presents a vivid image of the affliction and is remarkably effective in demonstrating a few simple facts that cannot be imagined easily. Baddeley's case history, moreover, provides a number of empirical tests, admittedly in n=1 designs, but open to the same scrutiny as any empirical study. Other investigators may repeat these tests provided that similar patients can be found, which is not unlikely, because memory loss is becoming more frequent in the aging population of Western countries.

In legal discourse, cases are used in an entirely different manner. Especially in common-law countries, the decision of a single case may become a precedent applicable to new cases. A precedent, however, is not based on the facts of the case, but on the reasoning followed in it. The Miranda rights (1966) from the case Miranda v. Arizona have become general rules.[1] Their power does not come from the partic-

1 Miranda v. Arizona, 284 U.S. 436 (1966) 165.

ulars of the Miranda case, but from the rationale underlying them. The rationale was based on legal logic, not on empirical fact.

Psychological theory differs considerably from legal logic. In psychology, the facts of the case should prove the point. Psychology purports to describe some part of reality, and must therefore be tested empirically. The facts of case histories are supposed to provide such a test. We will argue that although a case history, if well researched and faithfully reported, is an empirical datum, it falls short of empirically supporting any scientific regularity. What good are case histories, then, for psychological theory?

Proof of existence and acceptance of scientific evidence

Sometimes a scientific debate centres around the question of whether a particular phenomenon really exists. Do witches exist? Finding a single, generally accepted example would answer the question. A reliable case history may serve this purpose. It would be nonsensical to argue that a single witch is not very convincing, that a single witch is not statistically significant, or that a single witch, being an exception to the rule, must be declared a *monstrum*, in the words of Lakatos (1976). The discussion was about the *possibility* of existence, not about the *size* of the witch population. Statistics have nothing to do with it, and the declaration of *monstra* is just the last step before a limited theory is replaced by a better one.

Simple as all this may seem, the critical element in defining proof of existence is that of a *reliable* case history. When is a case history reliable? Is it sufficient to be informed that a witch was discovered in Transylvania in 1878? Or that the District Court of Zutphen in the Netherlands convicted Mrs. Van B. of being a witch? Or that the Parapsychology Department of Duke University established empirically that Miss W. is a witch? When is scientific evidence really evidence?

There are a few criteria that are accepted by scientists in most disciplines. One of these is *public control*. The evidence should be open to inspection by the scientific community. Case histories do not always meet this criterion, sometimes simply because the information does not exist. In the Putten murder case (see chapter 9), we cannot know for sure whether the two defendants actually committed the murder. Therefore, we cannot conclude with certainty that their case proves the existence of coerced memory-based 'false' confessions. It is also possible that the investigator of a case history refuses to provide relevant information. The case of Jane Doe, described by Corwin & Olafson (1997) and critically analysed by Loftus & Guyer (2002), is a clear demonstration of this. Still, it is understandable that the people involved in a case demand protection of their privacy, making public control of the case findings impossible. In fact, in the domain of psychology it is the rule rather than the exception to not identify fully the people involved in a case. Sometimes this is overcome by stating that access to all relevant details will be given to serious investigators on demand, but this is rare.

A second criterion for the acceptance of scientific evidence is that the findings can be *replicated* by others. To that end, it is important to describe all relevant conditions and experimental manipulations minutely, so that identical situations can be created by other researchers. For several reasons, case histories will not easily meet this criterion. One reason is that the most characteristic feature of a case history is its uniqueness. Another reason is that experimental manipulations in case histories are rarely described with the precise detail that is customary in prospective experimental studies. Case studies of psychiatric treatment are often very vague concerning the details of the treatment given. Worse, often the description of experimental manipulations in case histories is deliberately incomplete, or even false. This was one of the major criticisms of Freud's use of case histories (cf. Crews, 1995). And even if all manipulations are carefully described, it is often questionable as to whether they can be replicated. Can a therapist replicate a Freud case simply by following his prescriptions?

A third criterion for the acceptability of scientific evidence is *generalisability*. This criterion is clearly not relevant when the case history is only supposed to provide proof of existence. But support for a scientific law or regularity, e.g., a cause-effect relationship, requires that the evidence is generalisable from the sample that was studied to a broader population. Such generalisations can be achieved on the basis of two methodologies: the selection of a representative sample, and the use of statistical methods. Neither can be applied to case histories.

A fourth criterion for the acceptability of scientific evidence is plausibility of *underlying assumptions*. Every empirical study presupposes that the recipient accepts a number of plausible facts. For instance, that the experimenter really conducted the experiment, and that the results were actually what was reported. An infamous exception may have been Sir Cyril Burt's much-discussed studies on identical twins and the heredity of intelligence (cf. Kamin, 1974; Gillie, 1976). Some of the tests that he reported may not have been conducted. His assistants and co-authors Jane Conway and Margaret Howard could not be traced and may not have existed at all.

There are less-conspicuous assumptions. One is that the human subjects partaking in the experiments will not cheat. It is surprising to see how naive some researchers are in this respect, and how easy it is to obtain desired responses from cheating subjects. A well-known example is the experiment on clairvoyance by Pratt and Pearce, in the famous school of parapsychology founded by J.B. Rhine at Duke University. The extraordinarily gifted subject, Pearce, was seated in a room of what is now the Social Sciences Building at Duke. He was asked to report on which of five figures the 'transmitter' was concentrating in another room in the same building. Hansel's study of the amazing results produced by Pearce revealed that the subject could easily have cheated, simply by briefly stepping out of the room and peeking through a window over the door into the transmitter's room (Hansel, 1989). Pratt, however, retorted that this had not happened, arguing that Pearce was a honest man, who later even became a church minister, that the reward of US$ 100 paid to him for his cooperation in the experiment would not have seduced a man like Pearce, that others undoubtedly would have noticed him crossing the hall, that there was insufficient time to go from one room to another, that Pratt was effectively shielding the figures on the desk with his body, etc. But the truth of the matter is that we are asked to *assume* these things, instead of rejecting the evidence for Pearce's clairvoyance. One wonders why the experiment was not properly controlled? And why was Pearce not retested in another environment and/or by different experimenters?

Even less conspicuous are the assumptions about undue influences, which may be difficult to detect. One kind of influence is the *demand characteristic* of an experimental test situation. The term refers to the fact that defining a task for a human subject may limit the response to such an extent that it reflects the expectations of the experimenter, rather than anything we wanted to learn about the subject of the study. The following questions in a marketing study can serve as an example:

1. Have you ever heard of the Dutch company AEX?
2. What do you think the letters AEX stand for?

AEX stands for Amsterdam Exchange and is the equivalent of the American Dow Jones Index. It is a concept with which many in the Dutch population are familiar. Therefore, Question 2 would have been rather silly if in Question 1 it was not suggested that AEX was also the name of a company. Combined, these questions make it rather compelling to answer that AEX is the name of the Amsterdam Stock Exchange, rather than the name of an index produced by the Amsterdam Stock Exchange, or the name of the department that produces the index.

Many demand characteristics are difficult to detect because they are defined by properties of the experimental situation that are not explicitly described in our publications. In the description of the case of JR, below, we will see that JR might have been put in a condition with the strong demand characteristic of telling his story within the framework of a recovered memory. The acceptance of this case as an illustration of a more general principle relies on the assumption that the narrative was not shaped by this or other demand characteristics.

A fifth criterion for the acceptance of scientific evidence is *consistency* with other known facts and established scientific theories. The allegation that someone was sexually molested after being abducted by aliens is less acceptable than testimony about sexual abuse by a family member. The narrative qualities of both statements may be identical, but they clearly differ in consistency with existing knowledge. The second assertion is consistent with our general awareness of familial abuse, whereas there is no generally accepted evidence of aliens visiting our planet.[2] The case of JR represents a situation in which the general theory to be confirmed by the case is highly controversial.

The latter criterion is, of course, somewhat problematic because it is not impossible that old theories must be rejected on the basis of new evidence. But some safeguards are needed before this is done. To overthrow an existing and generally accepted theory, the new evidence should meet the other criteria mentioned above, and moreover, the new theory must be better in that it also accounts for the already existing body of empirical knowledge. These safeguards almost by definition imply that existing theories cannot be rejected on the basis of one or a few case histories.

The case of JR

The case of JR was offered by Jonathan Schooler and his associates as proof that recovered memories may stem from real traumatic experiences (Schooler, Ambadar, & Bendiksen, 1997a, b). Some people claim that they suddenly remember psychological trauma, most often sexual abuse, which occurred earlier in their lives and of which they had been oblivious for many years. Opponents of these claims have argued that such a sudden return of memory is improbable to say the least, and that it is far more likely that such recovered memories are false, and elicited by suggestive therapeutic methods. The earlier discussions can be found in articles by Loftus (1993) and Lindsay & Read (1994), and in the Netherlands in a book by Crombag and Merckelbach (1996).

A later discussion of the full breadth of what is now known as 'The Memory Wars' can be found in the reports of a worldwide experts meeting held in 1996 (Read & Lindsay, 1997). At this meeting Schooler and his associates presented case histories that were purported to demonstrate that recovered memories may originate from actual trauma, and that such memories may reappear even without the intervention of any form of therapy or suggestion. Schooler *et al.* do not deny that suggestive forms of psychotherapy may generate false memories, they only mean to argue that not all recovered memories can be explained this way. It seems that there is no easy way to prove the disappearance and later recovery of memories of real and severe trauma in a prospective experimental design. Can proof of existence be

---

2 Although Harvard psychiatrist John Mack thinks differently. See: J.E. Mack (1994), *Abduction: Human Encounters with Aliens.* New York: Ballatine Books.

given by a study of case histories? Schooler *et al.* presented four cases. One of those four was the case of JR, which we will analyse in some detail. It might be argued that Schooler *et al.*'s proof of existence is only rebutted when all their four cases are analysed and rejected. Our answer to that argument is that the analysis of JR's case will disclose a number of objections against the use of case histories in general, which equally apply to the other three cases.

In the words of Schooler *et al.* the case of JR reads as follows:

> The first case was brought to our attention by a colleague of the first author. It involved JR, a 39-year-old male who at the age of 30 remembered being fondled by a parish priest when he was twelve years old. Subsequent to this initial recollection, JR recalled additional episodes of abuse spanning several years.

JR's experience of discovering a memory of having been abused by a priest occurred after he watched a movie in which the main character grapples with sexual abuse. He reported great shock at the discovery of the memory which occurred 'fairly suddenly' with great vividness. As JR described it 'I was stunned, I was somewhat confused you know, the memory was very vivid and yet... I didn't know one word about repressed memory'.

> JR was completely unambiguous in his account of his perceived awareness of the memory prior to discovery, observing: 'If you had done a survey of people walking into the movie theatre when I saw the movie... asking people about child and sexual abuse 'have you ever been, or do you know anybody who has ever been', I would have absolutely, flatly, unhesitatingly, said no!'
>
> In addition to JR's report that he confronted the priest who admitted the abuse, we also independently acquired corroborative evidence in the form of an interview with another individual. This individual reported that he had also been the victim of sexual advances by the priest (a memory which he reported he had never forgotten).
>
> A former therapist of JR's indicated that JR had discussed many other embarrassing experiences but had never mentioned being abused by a priest (note the issue of sexual abuse was never mentioned during therapy).

From another publication by Schooler *et al.* we learn even more about the case:

> Over the following six to ten months after the first memory was recovered, JR remembered at least ten other incidents of abuse by the same individual that he estimated occurred over the next several years, all of which were recalled as occurring while the two were on trips to different places.

> JR further believed that he forgot the memory of each episode of sexual abuse right after it happened so that when he woke up the next morning he did not have any sense of what had occurred the night before. JR suggested that his immediate forgetting of the incidents accounts for why he continued to willingly go on subsequent trips with the priest.
>
> JR reported that he directly confronted the priest regarding the prior molestation. According to JR, during confrontation, the priest acknowledged the molestation and tried to assuage him by indicating that he had sought treatment for sexually abusive clergy following an incident with another individual. JR also reported that several of his brothers also indicated that they had been approached by the priest.
>
> One possible argument against the authenticity of this case is that JR did ultimately attempt to press charges. Thus, sceptics might argue that JR's recovered memory report was simply a ruse to get past statute of limitation laws. However, it is important to note that at the time of his recovery (1986) there were no cases in which memory repression had been successfully used as an argument for overturning statute of limitation laws, and indeed it was such laws that ultimately prevented the prosecution of the case (p.266).

The main conclusion drawn by Schooler *et al.* from the four cases is that:

> A corroborative case study approach, grounded in an understanding of basic cognitive mechanisms, is likely to provide an important tool for furthering our understanding of how individuals can have the shocking experience of discovering memories of seemingly unknown trauma.

Thus, the claim seems to extend even beyond the sheer proof of existence: the case histories are said to further our general understanding of rediscovering memories of forgotten trauma. How this sort of generalisation can be achieved is not explained. But the authors add that scepticism may also be directed against the more traditional research in psychological laboratories:

> We note, however, that a priori beliefs might also lead to scepticism regarding the applicability of laboratory research to this issue. If one is highly doubtful that memories of abuse could be suggested, they might reasonably question the generalisability of suggested memory experiments...

The argument seems to be, in conformity with the Bayesian tradition, that everybody has prior beliefs, and that the power to convince someone of the truth of a hypothesis depends as much on prior beliefs as on the diagnostic value of the empirical evidence. This argument is assumed to hold equally for case studies as for experimental research. However, the argument should be, of course, that the power to convince depends not just on the presence of prior beliefs, but on the *prior probability* of these beliefs. Are the prior probabilities attached to assumptions underlying case histories of the same magnitude as in the case of experimental research? Our argument would be that the answer is negative. Formalised research methods, meeting the criteria defined above, are explicitly directed at minimising the influence of prior assumptions, or maximising the odds connected with the few assumptions that still have to be made. The use of case histories is not formalised in a similar way. Case histories do not convince through their methodical solidity, but through their narrative quality. There is, however, no special reason to assume that a good narrative is also a true one.

Anchoring narratives to implicit assumptions

A case history is first of all a narrative. It does not convince through reference to scientific literature or empirical data. The convincing argument is that the case represents life itself, in the shape of a strong narrative that adroitly illustrates the issue. But there is a latent conflict in this characteristic. Good narratives may convince simply because they are good narratives. Novels, short stories, movies, they all have the power to convince, even if the stories they tell are completely fictitious. But in science the authoritative power of case histories should stem from their links to reality, not from narrative quality.

Criteria for the 'goodness' of narratives were proposed by Bennett & Feldman (1981). They asked 58 students to tell a story; half of them were instructed to tell a true story, the other half to invent one. Every time a story had been told, the others were asked to assess whether this was a true or an invented story. These guesses turned out not to be better than chance, but stories that were accepted as true shared some properties which the other stories lacked. These properties were: a readily identifiable central action, and a context that provides an easy and natural explanation of why the actors behaved in the way they did.

This analysis was extended by Pennington & Hastie in a series of publications (1986, 1988, 1993). In their view good stories explain all human actions by three kinds of factors: physical conditions, psychological conditions, and goals. In one of their studies (1986) they presented over 200 prospective jurors with a filmed documentary of a criminal trial. The possible verdicts were first-degree murder, second-degree murder, manslaughter, and self-defence. On the basis of what was shown in the film, all these options were chosen by some number of subjects. They then asked their subjects to tell what they thought had really happened in this case. All story structures thus obtained conformed to the postulated story grammar, that is, to the rules for telling a 'good' story. The differences among the subjects were brought about mainly by *inferences* about what protagonists in the case supposedly had thought, felt, or wanted. Forty-five percent of all story components consisted of inferred facts that had not actually been present in the film.

The relevance of studies on the 'goodness' of narratives is, of course, that case histories are selected precisely with this quality in mind, in order to make them believable. Or, even worse, most facts describing the case are selected from a wider range of facts precisely to make a good story that people can easily grasp. The central action is presented in a prominent manner, and only those actions of the people involved are presented that are easily understood on the basis of physical and psychological conditions and goals. The end result may not be a fair representation of what actually happened, but of what can be readily understood. Elements that do not fit a 'good' narrative may be omitted, and such elements may well be the story's links to reality. If the story is 'good' in that it meets Pennington & Hastie's criteria, it may not strike the reader that essential anchors to reality are missing.

The concept of anchoring is more fully explained by Wagenaar, Van Koppen, & Crombag (1993). The basic idea is that each element of a narrative is linked to reality by a hierarchy of nested sub-narratives. Imagine that John is accused of killing his father in law. When John's marriage failed, his father-in-law came to John's house to pick up the property of his daughter, John's ex-wife Nancy. John objected to this, and there was a fight in which Nancy's father was killed. So far the story is good; there is a neat central action and everybody's behaviour is psychologically plausible because it is related to the theme of the failed marriage between John and Nancy. The evidence shows that John's fingerprints are on the handgun that probably was the murder weapon. There are two sub-stories, nested in the main story that John is guilty of killing his father in law: that there were fingerprints on the probable murder weapon, and that those fingerprints are John's. How do we know those facts? Because they are supported by sub-sub-stories. The weapon was found next to the victim's body and taken to a forensic laboratory, where a test showed that the bullets in the victim's body were fired from that gun. The fingerprints were compared to John's fingerprints by a forensic expert, who reported that they were identical. But what are the chances that these sub-sub-stories are wrong? To decide this, we need a series of sub-sub-sub-stories:

- The weapon was found by a police officer, who did not accidentally or intentionally switch it with another weapon.
- The bullets were taken from the body and were also not accidentally or intentionally switched with other bullets.
- Ballistic tests with the gun yield uncontroversial and 100 percent certain outcomes.
- The fingerprints were also not switched.

- Fingerprint experts make no mistakes, and their conclusions are drawn with (almost) absolute certainty.
- It is not possible that John's fingerprints were on the weapon for a totally innocent reason (like John wrestling the gun from the hands of the real murderer).
- Etc.

Do we accept all these sub-sub-sub-stories as true, or do we need evidence for each of them? It is possible that the police make mistakes or may have a motive to frame an innocent suspect (e.g., because John is a known drug dealer). The problem is that the string of sub-narratives may never end, unless a stop rule is applied. A reason to stop asking further questions and thereby digging deeper into the hierarchy of nested sub-stories is that a point is reached where everybody agrees that no further questions need to be asked. Perhaps we should all agree that experts on fingerprints and ballistics are competent and use sophisticated techniques that allow them to draw conclusions with virtual certainty. If that is what everybody believes, there is no point in digging any further. The problem is not so much that such 'golden rules', or 'common sense presumptions' as Cohen (1977) called them, on which almost everybody will agree, are rare. More problematic is that case histories fail to make the underlying assumptions explicit. As a consequence, it is difficult to realise that they too need to be anchored in generally accepted facts about the physical and social world.

Application to the case of JR

The difference between narrative quality on the one hand and proper anchoring onto generally accepted facts about reality on the other can be demonstrated by analysing JR's story more closely. The point that this case was meant to make is that the recovery of a lost memory can occur without the intervention of any sort of psychotherapy. The almost pictorial emblem is that of JR, who goes into sudden and deep shock immediately after watching a movie. The following morning he wakes up a different man: from a normal person he is turned into a victim of abuse. From a happy family man and friend to many, he becomes a deeply disturbed party in a lawsuit. It is almost a literary cliché: a man changes abruptly through a sudden twist of fate. The biblical figure Job, St. Paul on his way to Damascus, the Count of Monte Christo when thrown in jail, Hitler on 11 November 1918, they all conform to this narrative. Many a born-again Christian tells a similar story. JR's story is a good story, one that we easily recognise as such.

The main themes or first-order statements in JR's story are:

1. JR was abused.
2. The perpetrator was his parish priest.

3. The abuse occurred when JR was twelve years old.
4. JR forgot about the abuse for an extended period of time.
5. The recovered memory was elicited by seeing the movie.
6. The recovered memory is a reliable copy of the original events.

How do we know that these six statements are safely anchored onto facts that are generally accepted as true, or at least safe enough to accept the implied theory of the operation of human memory? Let us consider which presupposed truths are underlying these six statements.

Theme 1: JR was abused

The second-order statements supporting this theme are:
1.1 JR says that he remembers it.
1.2 JR's therapist affirms this.
1.3 JR has been telling the same story since 1990.
1.4 Once they have returned, recovered memories are and remain accurate.

We do not possess a transcript of JR's testimony. The only thing that we know is what Schooler *et al.* wrote about JR, after having interviewed JR nine years after he recovered the memory of his abuse. The claim that JR at the time that he recovered his memory had no knowledge of the recovered memory theory and could therefore not have been influenced by knowledge about it does not hold water because while testifying nine years later he must have been quite familiar with it. What we do know is what JR claimed to remember. The real issue is that JR's claim implies that he suffered from an – at best – rare memory disorder presumably related to the theme of sexual abuse. Why should we trust his memory report of nine years after the fact? The answer of Schooler *et al.* appears to be that JR told his therapist before telling Schooler. But we are also told that the therapist 'learned of the events of this case indirectly'. What does this mean and when did this happen? The therapist introduced Schooler to the case because of Schooler's known interest in recovered memories. This interest may well have shaped the therapist's story. The therapist is said to be 'a well-respected university professor' and 'a colleague of the first author', but that does not exclude that the therapist's perceptions and memories were shaped by his beliefs and expectations. Knowing about Schooler's interest in recovered memories, he may have reconstructed JR's story to fit the model. One wonders how Schooler was subsequently introduced to JR. 'Please meet Dr. Schooler, who is terribly interested in your recovered memories'? Such an introduction may have shaped JR's story or his recollection of the story after nine years. On second thought, the issue of the therapist's mediation is suspect. First, we are told that JR recovered his abuse memories without the interference of a psychotherapist, next we read that JR was in psychotherapy, and that the therapist was the first to tell Schooler about JR's claim that he recovered his memories independently. Why should we take this fairly complicated narrative at face value?

The acceptance of assumption 1.1 requires believing a considerable number of sub-sub-stories. In particular, we must believe that *after recovery of lost memories, the recollection of the recovery remains intact for a period of nine years (a)*. Another assumption underlying 1.1 is that JR is an honest person. What if his story is based on his intention to press charges? Schooler *et al.* merely tell us that a ruse to circumvent a statute of limitations problem is not likely. But that is not the point: JR actually did start a lawsuit, hence financial gain could have been a motive. The fact that it turned out that the statute of limitations in the end prevented him from succeeding in his suit cannot change that. We are thus asked to assume that JR is not at all led by a financial motive, and moreover that the therapist did not hope to improve his status in the therapeutic community. In general, we are asked to believe that *people will not tell lies about such things, even when in doing so they would profit from it financially or gain in status (b)*.

The therapist 'strongly discounts the possibility that JR could have invented all of the corroborating evidence that he reported in their numerous conversations' (Schooler *et al.*, 1997b, p. 266). We are not told what this evidence was, or whether the story was partially shaped by these 'numerous conversations', but apparently we are asked to believe that *psychotherapists can see with the naked eye when their patients are lying or telling the truth (c)*. If the therapist was also convinced by other symptoms than just JR's story, we are asked to believe that *psychotherapists are able to diagnose sexual abuse in someone's distant past on the basis of more recent psychological symptoms (d)*.

About assumption (c) we can say that the literature on distinguishing truth from falsehood is not encouraging (cf. Vrij, 2000). Assumption (d) is even less likely. There are indeed symptoms, like those of post-traumatic stress disorder (PTSD), that correspond with a limited validity to earlier trauma. But it has never been claimed that such specific symptoms are diagnostic for different types of trauma. What if JR's symptoms (the particulars of which we do not know) are caused by an entirely different trauma in his past?

The fact that JR's story has been consistent since 1990 could support the notion that the story must be true, but only if it were established that *consistency in the telling of stories is diagnostic for their truth (e)*. Such an assertion is not to be found in the scientific literature (cf. Candel, 2003). The art of lying depends largely on being consistent. It is not difficult to imagine that JR took care to be consistent precisely because of his charge against the priest in a criminal trial. He would lose credibility by changing his story along the way. This connects assumption (e) with assumption (b).

It is obvious that assumption 1.1 cannot easily be anchored onto generally shared beliefs. We know that memories of abuse can be the result of suggestive psychotherapeutic techniques. Even though Schooler *et al.* presented the case as a demonstration of recovered memories without the intervention of psychotherapy, to our surprise we learn that JR had been in psychotherapy during the critical period. We know nothing of the nature of the problems that led him to seek help from a therapist, nor of the type of therapy he received, nor of the beliefs of the therapist regarding recovered memories and recovered-memory therapy. The little that we do know about the therapist is that he discussed the abuse with JR and that he supports the notion that JR really lost and recovered true memories of abuse. The conclusion is almost inescapable that JR's therapist believes in the psychological mechanism of repression and in subsequent recovery of memories. Is it unlikely that he would have applied this insight in his therapy? So, one more assumption must be that *the therapist, even though he believed in repression and recovery of memories of early trauma, did not allow these beliefs to affect the way in which he conducted JR's therapy (f).*

Finally, we must assume that recovered memories are accurate. But since most memories, especially for things in the distant past, are known not to be very accurate, there must be a special reason why recovered memories are an exception to this rule. The operation of memory is usually divided into three stages: acquisition, retention and reproduction. The theory of recovered memories holds that traumatic memories are repressed and recovered after a retention period of many years. Tacitly it is assumed that repressed memories remain unaltered during the stage of repression. Constancy, however, is not typical for retention. On the contrary, all sorts of post-event information may alter the contents of the stored memories (see chapter 8). Usually this happens through a rehearsal of the event, during which new elements may be added or new interpretations from outside sources may be suggested. Repressed information may not take part in some sort of conscious rehearsal loop. But it is a good step further to assume that *repressed information is entirely immune to interference (g).*

An additional problem is that recovered memories typically do not return in one sudden gush. It usually takes weeks or months, beginning with flashbacks, isolated fragments like unrelated parts of an incomprehensible film. It takes considerable effort to assemble these into a coherent story. Memory being in any case a reconstructive rather than a reproductive process (cf. Bartlett, 1933), the type of active reconstruction required for recovering repressed memories, if there is such a thing, must be vulnerable to suggestive influences. Even if the patchy images were accurate representations of things in the past, their reconstruction into a coherent story may well place them in a mistaken context. Why should we assume that *the lengthy retrieval process typical of recovered memories always ends in a correct reconstruction of the past (h)?*

Theme 2: The perpetrator was his parish priest

The second-order arguments for this theme are:
2.1 JR says he remembers the abuse by the priest.
2.2 The story about the priest is corroborated by another victim.
2.3 JR has no motive to accuse the priest falsely.
2.4 The priest admitted the abuse.

This part of JR's memory is as questionable as 1.1. Given that stories about priests abusing boys are frequently reported in the media and are therefore well known, it is probable that JR was familiar with these stories. It is not at all impossible that these stories have created a false memory in JR during suggestive therapeutic treatment. Can we exclude the possibility that JR correctly recollects sexual abuse by some person, and that the priest as the perpetrator was a later intrusion into this memory? Are priests not more likely to intrude into vague recollections of abuse simply because they often figure as perpetrators in stories in the media? Must we assume that *memories are either entirely true, or entirely false (i)?* Moreover, it is possible that JR, knowing about the frequency of abuse by priests, reckoned that a priest would be an easy target in a suit for damages. Or that the therapist suggested the parish priest as the probable perpetrator because he or she also knew about the frequent media reports of such cases. The underlying assumptions are again that the therapist did not use suggestive techniques – not even inadvertently –, and also that JR is an honest person.

The story about the other victim is intriguing. This man came forward after he read in the newspaper about JR's case. It is assumed that this alleged victim did not simply want a share in the damages and fabricated a similar story for this purpose. But we do not know anything about this person: not whether he also filed a complaint, nor whether he had mentioned his abuse before he read about JR, nor whether he showed any symptoms of an abuse victim; nor do we know for certain if he was really abused. The only thing we do know for certain is that his testimony was not independent of JR's story, and therefore cannot be considered independent corroboration, unless we assume that *JR's story had no suggestive influence on this alleged victim (j),* and that *he had no financial motive (k).* The other victim's continuous memory is used as an argument for his credibility. The assumption appears to be that *continuous memories are more reliable than recovered memories (l).* There is nothing in the scientific literature to support this contention. Another supposition underlying the other-victim argument is that child abusers will almost always abuse more than one child: *if the second alleged victim was really abused, then the first alleged victim was almost certainly also abused (m)*. In reality we do not know how diagnostic the abuse of one child is for the abuse of another child.

The argument that JR has no motive to falsely accuse his former priest cannot possibly be verified. We know that false accusations of sexual abuse are not exceptional. They are made for a variety of reasons. There is no exhaustive list of possible motives. For JR we can think of at least two possible motives: the hope of financial gain, and a wish for revenge for ending their friendly relationship of seven years. We know that it ended, we do not know how or why. The assumptions are apparently that *hope for financial gain or the wish to take revenge are not sufficient motives for making a false accusation (n)*, and also that *false accusations are never made without an obvious motive (o)*.

The priest admitted the abuse, we are told, but there is no corroborating evidence in support of this information. It is what JR says, but there is no recorded admission, not even in the court record. Hence we are asked to assume that *an admission of abuse was really made whenever the victim says so (p)*. Even if JR is completely sincere about this, we cannot be sure that JR understood correctly what the priest said when confronted. 'I am sorry to hear this' is not the same as 'I am sorry for what I did to you'. Sometimes confessions are not what they appear to be, or statements are misinterpreted by someone who is not impartial about what is said. The guided imagery and guessing exercises practised in the Putten murder case (chapter 9) did not yield proper confessions, but the police and the courts took them as such. In JR's case, we really need a positive statement from the priest saying he confessed to sexually abusing JR. Moreover, we must assume that *admissions of abuse are never false (q)*. Could the priest have hoped that the amount of damages awarded would be reduced after a confession? The story is set in the United States, where plea bargaining is common. Chapter 9 describes more mechanisms that may lead to false confessions.

Theme 3: The abuse occurred when JR was twelve years old

The arguments supporting this theme are:

3.1 This is what JR tells us, and there is no reason to doubt his veracity.
3.2 This is the same period claimed by the other victim.

A peculiar thing about this claim is that JR had an intimate sexual relationship with the priest when he was about sixteen years old. Why would the abuse have stopped when JR was twelve? Why, following this, would JR have remained friendly with the priest? JR tells us that he forgot the abuse instantly each time it had occurred: the next morning he woke up without any sense of what had happened the night before. This must have been a rather exceptional type of repression, because it has not been reliably reported before. Usually, in stories of recovered memories, whatever their trustworthiness, the repression is said to have started after the abuse episode had ended. Moreover, JR's repression was exceptionally effective, because time and again he went on a new outing with the priest, without the slightest premonition of what was going to happen. The exact same conditions that had led to sexual abuse many times before apparently were ineffective as recall cues. We are to believe that *instances of sexual abuse can be repressed instantaneously and with a complete paralysis of the cueing potential of the circumstances (r)*. It is also puzzling that, according to JR, the priest stopped abusing him at a particular point in time, but continued his friendship with JR for another five years, which then again developed into a sexual relationship.

The localisation in time of the abuse by means of the other victim's statement is somewhat illogical. It is not unknown that the abuse of one victim stops when the perpetrator finds another victim. Hence the period indicated by the other victim was not necessarily contemporaneous with the period in which JR might have been abused. We are apparently supposed to believe that *abusers abuse all their victims in the same period (s)*. We see no reason why this would be true.

Theme 4: JR forgot about the abuse until he saw the movie

The arguments behind this assertion are:
4.1 JR says so.
4.2 JR was shocked by the sudden recollection.
4.3 JR disclosed other incidents to his therapist, but not the abuse.
4.4 Prior to seeing the movie, JR told nobody about the abuse.

'Knowing that one does not know' is a problem of metamemory. How did JR know what he did not know? Is he aware of the difference between not trying to activate some memories, and not having access to these memories? Let us assume that someone suffers from a psychological trauma in his childhood, and that he tries not to think of the events that caused the trauma. Can we be certain that the metamemory of such a person is not affected by this avoidance behaviour? Is it possible that the traumatic recollection pops up from time to time, but that such unwanted intrusions are subsequently forgotten? If repression is taken to occur for entire memories, why could rehearsal of those memories not also be subject to repression? We are asked to assume that *metamemory is immune from the alleged repression mechanism (t)*.

According to JR's story, seeing a movie about an abuse victim was a sufficient cue to start recovery. This is quite surprising if we realise that being repeatedly victimised by the same perpetrator in the same manner did not prove, according to JR, to be an effective retrieval cue. Apparently, there is an underlying theory saying that *there is a 'critical period' for recovery, and outside that critical period even repetition of the abuse itself is not a strong enough retrieval cue (u).* As far as we know, the theory of recovered memories does not mention or specify a critical period for recovery.

It is said that JR was deeply shocked by his recollection of abuse, which should indicate that the thought was entirely new to him. But the sudden reinterpretation of already-existing memories might also have been a tremendous shock for him. It does happen that people suddenly realise that they have been abused at some earlier time, but until then had not realised that what had happened to them is commonly called 'sexual abuse', even though the facts have always been known to them. This also applies to JR's statement that, up until watching the movie, he would have denied that he was a victim of sexual abuse. Thus, we are asked to assume that *victims can distinguish between the type of shock caused by recovery, and one caused by a reinterpretation of a never-forgotten experience (v).* To our knowledge, there is no scientific evidence to support this assertion.

The fact that JR did not spontaneously disclose the abuse to his therapist may mean a host of different things. First, if his memory of the abuse was the product of suggestion by the therapist, it is logical that JR did not disclose anything before the suggestion took effect. The same goes for the possibility that JR was just making it up. Secondly, we are asked to assume that *clients tell their therapist everything they know (w).* That, however, is not very likely. Thirdly, a reinterpretation scenario implies that there was nothing to tell, even though nothing was forgotten.

Apparently, JR did not tell anybody else about the abuse prior to seeing the movie. But how do we know this? This argument is itself the subject of a proof-of-existence problem. We cannot solve the problem by replacing one proof of existence with another. But at least there is an opportunity of some sort of control measure: did JR tell many others about the problems for which he sought psychiatric help? If he did not, the argument is void, because without some control observation we are being asked to assume that *people will almost always tell others about their problems, even if they are embarrassing (x),* which does not seem to be a safe assumption.

Theme 5: The recovery was suddenly elicited by seeing the movie

We only have JR's word for this; see also assumptions (a) and (b). There are no other anchors than JR's word. The 'good story' argument may, perhaps implicitly, be taken as a safe anchor: since the theme of the movie (we are not told which movie it was) was sexual abuse, it can be understood that it triggered JR's repressed abuse memories. But the movie did not have the same effect on the other spectators. Moreover, it can hardly be imagined that this is the first time in his life that JR saw something that might have reminded him of the possibility of sexual abuse. So again we are asked to believe that there is a critical period for the recall of repressed memories (assumption *u*).

Too many assumptions

We have seen that in order to accept JR's story, we need to make at least 24 assumptions. Perhaps they are not all necessary. For the proof of existence of recovered memories, it may be sufficient to support the notions that JR was indeed abused (theme 1), that for a considerable period of time he completely forgot the abuse (theme 4) and that the movie suddenly brought it all back to him (theme 5). But even then, we still need to accept the eleven assumptions underlying these three themes, and they are at least questionable. We administered a simple questionnaire about some of these assumptions to 100 trained psychologists at a professional conference. Here is a sample of the outcome:

85% rejected *(e)*: *that consistency in the telling of stories is diagnostic for their truth;*
78% rejected *(j)*: *that JR's story had no suggestive influence on the other corroborating victim;*
87% rejected *(l)*: *that continuous memories are more reliable than recovered memories;*
44% rejected *(o)*: *that false accusations are never made without any identifiable motive;*
71% rejected *(t)*: *that metamemory is not afflicted by the alleged repression mechanism;*
94% rejected *(x)*: *that people will always tell others about their sexual problems.*

The acceptance of JR's story, based on the combination of these assumptions, ought to be very low indeed, if the criterion for their anchoring is the general acceptance of these beliefs, instead of the narrative quality of JR's story. Nevertheless, the case of JR is offered to us as a prime example of recovered memory without the intervention of psychotherapy. As such, we do not think it succeeds.

Logical impossibilities

Is JR's case only one example of an incompletely told, and therefore inconclusive, case history? We think not. The same critical analysis can be applied to all other case histories that have served in the 'Memory Wars'; even those that are offered to prove the falsehood of recovered memories, such as those described by Loftus & Ketcham (1994). The basic problem is that without proper anchoring there are no facts. We believe that men have walked on the moon because that is what we have been told. We saw the photographs, the television broadcasts, and we believe that the authorities would not deceive us. Without anchoring onto that belief, the fact is not a fact at all. We may realise that Hollywood could make equally convincing photographs and films, as in the hilarious motion picture *Wag the Dog*, and that during the cold war governments produced far worse lies. For some, the case of JR proves that recovered memories really exist; to others that they are artefacts produced under the influence of therapists. The difference between these two groups lies in their prior beliefs. Case histories may only confirm what is already believed. It is for this reason that case histories do not offer a useful contribution to the debate.

The argument holds for case histories and empirical research alike. If we do not start with some belief, they will never produce facts. But the beliefs underlying case histories and empirical studies do make a difference. Case histories do not meet the two most important criteria for empirical research: public control and replicability. We cannot check most of the details of JR's story because his case, as is typical for case histories, was made anonymous: the people who provided most of the information cannot be questioned critically, the case files are inaccessible, making the story simply hearsay. This would not be too bad if the storyteller realised that dishonesty in telling the story could be detected through replication. But case histories cannot be replicated, not only because no two cases are identical, but also – and more importantly – because each case is an argument in itself, independent of possible replications. Finding a single witch proves the existence of witches, even if the case is never replicated. Case histories are by definition anchored onto unfalsifiable assumptions.

Consider how a case of recovered memories may be handled in a court of law. Imagine that the question arises as to whether the recollection was induced by psychotherapy. It is possible that the victim's narrative by itself will convince the judge or the jury that this was not the case. But it is also possible that the court relies on expert opinion that is based on the case of JR. In doing so, one questionable case is anchored onto another, equally questionable case, as if a concatenation of unreliable links could ever produce a strong chain. It is more or less like Thomson and Thomson in Hergé's comic strip Tin Tin who were told to hold on tight but fell because they were holding on to one another (Hergé, 1954, p. 6).

The second problem with case histories is that they do not permit generalisation. Empirical research is designed in such a way that it is clear to which population the results can be generalised. This can go a long way, like in pharmaceutical research on the hormones of mice, or even the genetic systems of algae that have consequences for the medical treatment of human patients. But a case history is sampled on the basis of its outcome, not with the intent of generalisation. Beyond the proof of existence, case histories do not prove anything.

Usually, large numbers of observations are collected in empirical research to increase representativeness and to make generalisation possible. Involving a large number of storytellers in a case-study design does not have the same effect. A study by Williams (1994) may serve as an illustration. She asked 129 women to recall why they were taken to a hospital seventeen years earlier. About 38 percent of these women did not mention the actual reason, that is, suspicion of sexual abuse, and were therefore scored as cases of forgotten sexual abuse. However, there were at least three more reasons why they could have failed to report the abuse, without really having forgotten anything. First, the abuse may not have happened at all; second, at the time of the abuse they may have been too young to remember or realise why they were taken to the hospital; and third, they may have been reluctant to admit the abuse to the interviewers. Together these reasons might explain the number of 38 percent non-reporters, but there is no empirical way to find out. The outcome, therefore, does not inform us about the number of women in the population who really forgot being sexually abused in their youth. Increasing the number of participants in the study would not have increased the representativeness of the outcome. Williams' research is not an empirical study, but a collection of case histories. Of the five criteria for empirical research listed above, it fails on the most important one: public control. There is simply no way in which it can be checked whether or not her subjects were sexually abused, whether they stored such memories, or whether they did not wish to divulge it to the investigators.

Let us compare Williams's study to that of Wagenaar & Groeneweg (1990) on the memory of 78 concentration camp survivors. The subjects in the latter study were witnesses in the trial against the alleged war criminal Marinus de Rijke. Fifteen of these witnesses were interrogated in the years 1943 to 1947 and again between 1984 to 1987. Not a single one of the victims had ever forgotten that they were in the camp. Why is this study more than a collection of case histories? The essential difference with a collection of stories is that the most important facts were corroborated by documentary evidence. There was objective evidence that these people had in fact been inmates of a concentration camp. The accuracy of their descriptions of the camp and its inmates could be verified. On many questions it was possible to compare early and late testimonies. All subjects were under oath when they gave their testimony. Although their participation was voluntary, it was clear that they were very willing to provide answers if they knew them. Under these conditions, where a reasonably objective criterion was available for what was remembered, it could be established which memories were altered and which events were entirely forgotten. As it turned out, most recollections appeared to be well preserved.

Case histories in this book

It may strike the reader as somewhat contradictory that in this book we appear to deal almost exclusively with case histories. Even in the present chapter the argument seems to be based on the analysis of a single case history: the case of JR. The contradiction, however, is only apparent. The case of JR is offered as an illustration of how case studies replace solid empirical proof. The theoretical argument that case studies are not reliable tests of scientific theories is not based on the case of JR or any other case, but on the analysis of the five criteria for empirical research: public control, replicability, generalisability, generally accepted assumptions, and consistency with other data. We argue that case histories do not meet these criteria and therefore can not count as empirical evidence. JR's case merely illustrates that case studies fail these criteria. Likewise, the case histories in the other chapters of this book are only offered as illustrations of general principles, for which empirical support is provided by experimental research.

CHAPTER 6

Not a Good Story or the Disappearance of Maddy and Vicky

The theory of anchored narratives

Every criminal trial begins with an indictment, which is a brief rendition of who did what, when and where, according to the prosecution. At that point, the indictment is only an allegation in need of support by evidence. During the trial, it is the prosecution's task to offer such evidence. It is the defence counsel's task to test critically the evidence offered by the prosecution, if possible, to adduce evidence to the contrary. In an earlier book (Wagenaar, Van Koppen, & Crombag, 1993) we discussed at length the structure of proof in criminal cases. We dubbed it 'the theory of anchored narratives'. Proof in a criminal case consists of an indictment containing a well-shaped narrative of what happened and in which each critical element needs to be supported by evidence in the form of a sub-story. This sub-story, in its turn, may need to be supported by evidence in the form of a sub-sub-story, etc., until each critical piece of evidence can be safely associated to a common-sense presumption (cf. Cohen, 1977), called an anchor, which is an assertion that common sense tells us needs no further exploration or discussion. We demonstrated an example of how one can execute the anchoring process in the previous chapter, where we gradually descended along the hierarchy of the nested (sub)stories that together constituted proof in a criminal case. The present chapter is concerned with the requirement that the indictment must contain a well-shaped narrative. If the indictment contains an a priori impossible or highly improbable narrative, there is no point in taking it to court. The question is, of course, what constitutes a well-shaped narrative or a good story.

Students of various disciplines have designed 'story grammars': sets of rules that a story must obey in order to be a good story. How to choose between those? We picked the one proposed by Bennett and Feldman (1981), because it is empirically based and developed in a legal context. They asked each of 85 students to tell a story. Half of those students were instructed to tell a true story, the other half to invent one. Next, the participants were asked to guess for each story whether it was true or invented. Those guesses turned out to be no better than chance as to the true nature of the stories, but stories that were believed to be true shared a set of properties that the rejected stories lacked. Those shared properties were that (1) they all had a readily identifiable central action and (2) a context or setting that provided an easy and natural explanation of why the actors behaved in the way they did. In a good story, all elements are connected to the central action, and nothing sticks out on its own. The context provides a full and compelling account of why the central action should have developed in this particular manner. If the context does not achieve this effect, then the story is said to contain ambiguities, of which there are two types: missing elements and contradictory elements. Accordingly, a well-shaped indictment tells us that, given the kind of people involved and the circumstances in which they found themselves at the time, it was only to be expected that the defendant did that for which he is indicted. If the prosecuting attorney cannot tell such a well-shaped story, he is, or at least should be, in trouble.

All this may sound rather theoretical. It therefore serves a purpose to illustrate the need for a well-shaped indictment by using a case in which one of us served as an expert witness.

The disappearance of Maddy and Vicky

On 8 June 1997, nineteen-year-old Maddy Becker and her nearly one-year-old daughter Vicky were reported missing. The last person to see them was Maddy's downstairs neighbour Ernie Schwarz, who testified to the police that at 6.45 PM on 8 June he had seen Maddy and Vicky leave their first floor flat in the coastal village of Bergen in the company of Hakan Ciler, Maddy's boyfriend and the (presumed) father of Vicky.

Hakan Ciler was known to the police for all kinds of criminal behaviour, including drug trafficking, prostitution, robbery and assault. He had been sentenced to jail several times. He was also known for regularly and cruelly beating Maddy and other girlfriends that he used to keep on the side. Shortly after being released from jail at the end of May 1997, he beat Maddy so severely that on 1 July she fled with her child to a safe house for battered women in the city of Alkmaar. For these reasons, the police assumed from the very beginning that Hakan was involved in Maddy's and Vicky's disappearance. Perhaps he had abducted them to Turkey, his country of origin, where he still had many relatives.

The police knew one more thing about Hakan, that is, that he was terminally ill with cancer and according to his doctors did not have long to live. Because of his illness, part of one of his feet had been amputated. On 8 June it was Hakan's birthday, and for this reason Maddy decided, against the advice of several of her friends and people of the safe house where she was staying, that she and Vicky should spend some time with him in order to celebrate. In the early afternoon at the railway station of Alkmaar, where Hakan also lived, a friend observed Maddy and Vicky get into Hakan's car and drive off. At 4.15 PM that day, Maddy's downstairs neighbour Ernie Schwarz saw that Hakan, Maddy and Vicky arrived by car at Maddy's flat in Bergen. He saw them enter and subsequently heard them apparently have a terrible row, which was nothing unusual. Schwarz had heard such rows many times before during Hakan's frequent visits to Maddy's flat. Based on all the quarrels he had heard them have, he concluded that they not only quarrelled often, but also that Hakan used to beat Maddy extensively, usually accompanied by loud crying from Vicky. Many times before, Schwarz had filed complaints about this with the owners of the building, the local police and the municipal authorities, but nobody seemed to care or to be able to do anything about the situation. Because of this Schwarz had begun to keep what he called his 'misery diary' shortly after Maddy came to live in the flat above him in November 1996, in which he recorded his observations. On many days he made notes about what was going on: loud noises, shouting and crying, garbage in the entrance hall and occasional threats from Hakan when he dared to complain to him about this. Ernie Schwarz was no friend of Hakan.

On 8 June 1997, Ernie Schwarz wrote in his diary: 'Damn! Between 16.15 and 18.45 yelling and crying. I was real happy to finally see them leave.' From his diary we know that the police, as part of their investigation, had visited him on 12 June and asked him what he had seen on 8 June. On 17 June, the police called him, asking again whether he was sure that Hakan, Maddy and Vicky had left together at 6.45 PM on 8 June. On that day he noted in his diary that he told them that he was indeed sure, but he added: 'Still, some doubt later on.' However, when he was questioned about this by the police on 3 July 1997 he appeared to be sure again: 'At 18.45h I saw the three of them leave,' and he has maintained this ever since. The significance of these details will become clear later on.

However hard the police tried to find Maddy and Vicky in or outside the country, it was to no avail. Hakan repeatedly denied to the police and everybody else, including his mother, that he had in any way been involved in their disappearance. To several people he said that he suspected that Maddy's parents had hidden Maddy and her daughter somewhere, and that he sorely missed them, little Vicky in particular.

Hakan's contacts with the police in the period of June 1997 and May 1998 were not restricted to interrogations about Maddy and Vicky. In September 1997 he was arrested for his involvement, with some friends, in a shooting incident in a café, and in February 1998 for an attempt to rob a bank, in which he or one of his companions also took a shot at a pursuing police car. However ill he may have been at the time, he kept up his criminal career with a vengeance, until he died of his cancer on 18 May 1998, in the jail in Scheveningen, where he was being held in preliminary custody for the attempted bank robbery. He never told anybody (possibly with one notable exception; see further) whether he knew what happened to Maddy and Vicky, but everybody thought that he did, and some may have thought his early death a fine example of divine justice.

Five years later

In the late afternoon of 30 July 2002, one of Hakan's younger brothers, Hasad Ciler, drove by the house in Bergen where Maddy's parents, Carla and Herman Becker, lived. At that moment Herman was busy washing his car in front of his garage. According to Hasad, it was on the spur of the moment that he decided to go talk to Herman. At first, Herman did not recognise him as Hakan's brother. So Hasad reminded him, adding that he was very sorry about the disappearance five years earlier of his daughter and grandchild. During the rather tangled and long-winded conversation that followed, it gradually dawned on Herman Becker that Hasad might have information about the whereabouts of Maddy and Vicky. He invited Hasad into the house and called Carla, who had been having coffee with some of her friends in a local café, to ask her to come home, which she did.

By the time Carla got home, Hasad had already told Herman that both Maddy and Vicky were no longer alive and that their bodies were buried in the dunes nearby. When Carla got home, she was also told that Maddy and Vicky were dead, which she already had come to suspect, but hearing it in so many words shocked her and her husband deeply. Hasad told them that he was very sad about what had happened to Maddy and Vicky, and apologised profusely for not telling them earlier, feeling very guilty about this. At their request, Hasad drove the Beckers to the place were Maddy and Vicky were buried. From the testimony of Carla and Herman it is not clear when precisely Hasad told them how he had come to know where the grave was, before or after they went to look for it.

According to Carla and Herman, at one point Hasad told them the following story. Late in the afternoon of 8 June 1997 Hakan called him and told him to come to Maddy's flat, which he did. Shortly after his arrival there, Hakan left with Maddy, leaving Vicky in Hasad's care. The time must have been about 6.45 PM. At about 8.00 PM Hakan returned to the flat without Maddy, and told Hasad to come along and take Vicky. They drove to a parking lot at the foot of the dunes, got out and walked to a secluded area in the dunes where, according to Hakan, he had once camped (illegally) with Maddy and Vicky. On their way to this spot, Hasad carried Vicky. Upon arrival, Hakan made a slicing movement with his hand across his throat and said: 'You do it.' From this Hasad understood that Hakan wanted him to kill Vicky. Hasad said he could not do that, after which Hakan took Vicky from him, and Hasad walked away. We do not know how far off he walked, but according to him far enough not to see what Hakan did next. After a while – we do not know how long – Hakan rejoined Hasad without Vicky, and they went off, to where we do not know.

After having recounted this, according to the Beckers, Hasad promised that he would go to the police the next day to tell them his story. He asked the Beckers not to inform the police that night, because he wanted first to inform his two other brothers and sister. This the Beckers promised, but they did not keep that promise. Instead, immediately after Hasad had left, they called police officer Esther Baak, who came to the Becker residence. The Beckers repeated to officer Baak what Hasad had told them, which she noted, thus documenting the major points of the story. Officer Baak's handwritten notes are part of the case file. For convenience, we will call this rendition of the events on the evening of 8 June 1997 version A.

The next morning, 31 July, Hasad indeed went to the local police station and told the police that he knew where his brother Hakan had buried Maddy and Vicky five years ago. He said that about a month after the disappearance of Maddy and Vicky, his brother Hakan had taken him to the dunes near Bergen and had pointed out to him where Maddy and Vicky were buried. This is, of course, a very different version of how Hasad had come to know where the burial site was, so we will call this version B.

Earlier, in 1997 (29 October), Hasad had been questioned by the police of whether he had any knowledge of the whereabouts of Maddy and Vicky. At that time he told them that he had not, so even if version B is the truth, he was lying about it then. We think it is important to note that, although the relevant part of version B is quite simple: 'my brother pointed the burial site out to me', when interviewed as a witness by the police on 31 July and 1 August 2002, and as a suspect nine more times between 9 and 16 September, he takes his time to tell this simple story. In the case file the verbatim transcripts of the nine interrogations in September 2002 run close to 300 pages. Although he repeatedly expresses regret about the tragic fate of Maddy and Vicky, and how bad it must have been for Maddy's parents not to know what had happened to them, most of what he says during these interrogations is about his self-pity for how bad he has felt all those years for not being able to tell what he knew and what a burden it had been to 'wear a mask' all that time.

Already on 31 July 2002, the interrogating police officers must have noticed the difference between what Hasad had allegedly told the Beckers and what he told the police right away. One of these officers was Esther Baak, who had heard version A the previous night. But we know from the written report and from the two subsequent interrogations that the police did not confront Hasad with the discrepancy. Obviously, their first priority was to actually find the remains of Maddy and Vicky, so the next day, 1 August, they took Hasad to the dunes and asked him to point out the burial site, which he did, although he did not succeed the first few times. We do not know how many mistakes he made before he got it right, but we think it important to point out that if he got it right after a relatively small number of trials, this performance does not fit well with version A. In version A, Hasad did not stay to see precisely where Hakan dug the grave. In that version he could only know the general area. Even if we assume that this general area was about 30 x 30 metres wide, the chance of accidentally pointing out the right 1 x 2 metre area of the grave in five attempts is still below one percent.

Eventually the police found the remains in a 1.5-metre-deep grave. All that was left of the two victims were their bones. Vicky lay on top of Maddy. Since no remains of clothing were found in the grave, the police investigators concluded that both had been buried without their clothes. They found Vicky's hair, but not Maddy's, which led them to conclude that Maddy's hair must have been removed before she was buried. The police carefully searched the wider area of the burial site, but found no traces of clothing or hair, or anything else that might have been relevant to the case.

The discovery of Maddy's and Vicky's remains attracted widespread attention in the national media, newspapers as well as television. On 2 August, the chief prosecutor, together with the chief of police of Alkmaar, gave a press conference announcing the finding of the remains. Surprisingly, they told the reporters that Hakan had pointed out the burial site to his brother some weeks after he had killed his wife and daughter, i.e., they told the press version B. Also Carla and Herman Becker were interviewed by several reporters, and while doing this they never contradicted version B as given during the press conference. On 3 August, the Netherlands' largest national newspaper, *De Telegraaf*, reported that they had spoken with Carla and Herman. The statement, 'Only this week it became known that Hakan had confided in his brother Hasad by pointing out to him where he had disposed of the bodies on about 8 June 1997,' was attributed to Carla.

The next day, 4 August, Hasad left for a holiday in Turkey, with the consent of the police. On 5 August, the same national newspaper told its readers that there actually were two different stories about the way in which Hasad had come to know where Maddy and Vicky had been buried. In a press release dated 7 August, the chief of police let it be known that during the last few days she had been asked repeatedly about whether Hasad should not be considered an accessory to murder, rather than a witness. To this point she wrote, however, that 'the police as well as the prosecutor's office saw no legal basis for considering this witness (Hasad) as a suspect, but that might change tomorrow, or the day after tomorrow, or next week'.

Well, it did change. After Carla and Herman Becker were interviewed by the police on 15 August, both repeated version A of what they had been told by Hasad on the evening of 30 July. Hasad, upon his return from Turkey on 19 September, was taken into custody and charged with complicity in the murder of Maddy and Vicky.

Corroborating evidence

Confronted with two versions of how Hasad had come to know where Maddy and Vicky were buried, the prosecution was keen to obtain some corroborating evidence for version A, which was known only from the testimony of Carla and Herman Becker. On the evening of 30 July, they had told it to officer Esther Baak in an informal manner. In their official deposition taken on 15 August, they told version A again. But why had they themselves told version B to the press, or at least not protested when the chief of police and the chief prosecutor told version B during the press conference on 2 August? And why did the police and the chief prosecutor, also already aware of version A, tell only version B to the press? And what, knowing both versions, made the police so confidently state to the press that Hasad could not be considered a suspect in the case at the time? Why did they let him leave for a holiday in Turkey? We can think of no good reason for this. Still, only on the basis of version A, which Hasad continued denying ever having told, the prosecution would have had a case against him.

Some corroboration of version A from a different source would therefore be very welcome. To this purpose, the police interviewed many people from Hasad's social circle, hoping to find someone who could testify that Hasad – or perhaps even Hakan – had also told them version A. They thought they had luck with a young woman we will call Liza Blom, the girlfriend of another of the Ciler brothers, Halil. When interviewed by the police on 19 September 2002, she told them that shortly after the remains of Maddy and Vicky had been found, she had overheard a telephone call between Halil and Hasad. At first she called it a 'conversation', but later it appeared to be a telephone call. The difference is of course that in the latter case she heard only half of what was actually said, and the wrong half at that! The conversation was held in Turkish, which she did not know very well but, according to her, well enough to understand words and fragments. Her command of the Turkish language was never tested. According to Liza, Hasad had told his brother Halil version A during this conversation, which was not confirmed by Halil when he was interviewed. However, on the morning of 31 July, when Hasad told the police version B, Liza and Halil had gone first to the police station, where they were told that Hasad had said that Hakan had pointed out to him where he had buried the remains of Maddy and Vicky. From the police station Liza and Halil went to visit Carla and Herman Becker, to tell them how sorry they were that their daughter and grandchild were dead and that Halil's brother had almost certainly killed them. Again according to Liza, the Beckers told them 'in general terms' what they had heard from Hasad the evening before. We do not know what 'in general terms' means, but we think it improbable that they did not include the most remarkable part of the story, that is, that Hasad had been present in the dunes on that fateful evening of 8 June 1997. If we are right in this, it means that on 31 July 2002, Liza already knew version A 'in general terms', and thus also when she overheard the telephone conversation six weeks later.

During her interview with the police, Liza also told them that she had accompanied Hasad on his holiday to Turkey. She said that she had overheard the conversation before they went to Turkey. It is therefore surprising that she also said during that interview that she was in Turkey when she had found out from a Dutch newspaper, on sale in a local newsstand, that there were two different versions of how Hasad had come to know where Maddy and Vicky were buried. She already knew that, possibly from what she had heard from the police and the Beckers on 31 July, and in any case from the overheard conversation. So, whence the surprise?

There appears to be something amiss with Liza's testimony. This became even more apparent when Liza, upon being questioned by the investigating judge on 11 March 2003, told him that she had lied about overhearing a telephone conversation, and when questioned about this by the court of appeal she said so again. Why had she lied to the police about this? According to her, she was pressured to do so by the interrogating police officers, which those officers, of course, denied when they heard about it in court. Now we know that Liza lied at least once, but when? When she told the police that she had overheard a conversation, or when she denied it later on? That was what the court needed to decide if it thought that the testimony by Carla and Herman Becker needed corroboration.

The indictment

When the prosecution brought the case to the District Court of Alkmaar, Hasad was charged with complicity in the murder of both Vicky and Maddy. The latter is surprising, because even if one believes version A, Hasad had nothing to do with the death of Maddy. So what was the prosecuting attorney thinking when he wrote that indictment?

On 20 August 2002, two forensic investigators reenacted digging a grave in the sand dunes near the spot where the remains had been found. That turned out not to be very easy, because part of the walls kept coming down. Eventually the investigator doing the digging reached a depth of 1.5 metres; it took him about an hour. He then found that he could not possibly climb out of it; in the loose sand he could not get a grip to pull himself out. His colleague had to pull him out. On the basis of this experience the two forensic investigators concluded in their written affidavits that 'more than one person must have been involved in digging the grave'. This might explain why the prosecution charged Hasad with being involved with Maddy's death: he might have helped Hakan with digging the grave, or at least with pulling him out of it afterwards. There is no evidence for this and may therefore only have been an assumption on the part of the prosecution to accommodate the findings of the forensic investigators. Actually, we do not know what the prosecuting attorney thought when he wrote the indictment. All through the proceedings the prosecution never offered a well-shaped narrative of the events on the evening of 8 June 1997. In the last chapter of our book *Anchored Narratives* (Wagenaar, Van Koppen, & Crombag, 1993, p. 231ff) we listed ten 'universal rules of evidence', of which the first one reads: 'The prosecution must present at least one well-shaped narrative.' We note that in this case the prosecution did not abide by this rule.

Evidence made into legal facts by the court

On 5 June 2003, the Alkmaar District Court acquitted Hasad of both counts of complicity in the murders of Maddy and Vicky. We do not know why Hasad was acquitted, because in our country courts usually do not explain acquittals in their verdict any further than just remarking that the available evidence did not convince them. But the prosecution decided to appeal the acquittal, and this brought Hasad's case to the Amsterdam Appellate Court. Under Dutch law, the appellate courts are triers of fact, which means that the entire story is reconsidered.

In its decision of 12 July 2004, the Amsterdam Court of Appeals acquitted Hasad of complicity in the murder of Maddy, but convicted him of complicity in the murder of Vicky. In case of a conviction the Dutch law of criminal procedure requires the court in its verdict to list the pieces of evidence on the basis of which it has come to be convinced of the defendant's guilt. By adopting a piece of evidence into its verdict, a court indicates that it considers it to be a fact, and by doing so makes it into a legal fact. Let us see which pieces of evidence the court made into legal facts.[1]

First, the court quoted the part of the testimony by Carla and Herman Becker that contained the whole of version A: on 8 June 1997, Hasad came to Maddy's house at about 6.45 PM, then Hakan left with Maddy, leaving Vicky in Hasad's care. At about 8.00 PM Hakan returned without Maddy and told Hasad to come and take Vicky, upon which they drove to the dunes near Bergen; there Hakan indicated to Hasad that he should kill Vicky, which Hasad refused; Hakan took Vicky from Hasad, who walked away; some time later Hakan rejoined Hasad without Vicky. By quoting this scenario, the court indicates that it takes this sequence of events to be facts.

Secondly, the court quoted from Liza Blom's statement to the police about the

---

1 LJN number: AQ2769; Case number: 23-002377-03.

telephone conversation, during which Hasad had told version A to his brother Halil. Liza's later denials, first to the investigating judge and again in person to the court itself, were not believed by the court. Liza's explanation for her initial testimony, that her interrogators had pressured her into saying so, the court did not believe, since the two interrogators had in person declared to the court that they had not pressured Liza in any way. The court, moreover, wrote that it did not think it likely that Liza, in telling the police about the overheard telephone conversation, had relied on what she had heard before 'in general terms' from Carla and Herman Becker during her visit to them on 8 June 1997, in the company of Halil. To quote the court verbatim on this point: 'The statement was made by Liza Blom in the absence of any indication that she had knowledge about what Carla and Herman Becker had declared.' By writing this in its verdict, the court turned the overheard conversation and its content, 'in so far as she had understood it', into a legal fact.

Also Maddy's downstairs neighbour Ernie Schwarz is quoted by the court in its verdict as having testified that on Sunday, 8 June 1997, he 'had seen that at about 6.45 PM *the three of them* drove off in Hakan's car'. The four words italicised by us in the preceding sentence are astonishing to say the least, as they blatantly contradict the scenario that the court had declared to be a legal fact only one page earlier in its verdict. Schwarz should have seen only Hakan and Maddy leave, not 'the three of them'. Furthermore, he must have missed Hasad's arrival a short while before, and also Hakan's return at about 8.00 PM and the subsequent departure of Hakan, Hasad and Vicky. Apparently, the court assumed that a man who used to hear every move in the apartment above his head, who had made a habit of taking notes on his neighbours in his diary, and who even went as far as recording the licence numbers of the cars used by visitors of Maddy's flat, still could be wrong on so many counts.

All this may serve to demonstrate that the conviction of Hasad for complicity in the murder of Vicky is questionable, and that we therefore find it difficult to understand why the court decided the way it did.

The court's narrative of the events does not make sense

The conclusion of the preceding section is not the real point we intended to make in this chapter. Our real point is that the story does not constitute the well-shaped narrative that we believe is required in order to convict. We need to explain this.

In the first section of this chapter we wrote that a good story has two properties: (1) a readily identifiable central action and (2) a context that provides an easy and natural explanation of why the actors behaved in the way they did. The context should provide a full and compelling account of why the central action should have developed in this particular manner and be free of ambiguities, such as missing or contradictory elements.

In the story that the court chose to believe, the central action is easy to identify: the murder by Hakan of his girlfriend and child. At first that might seem an astonishing, almost unbelievable thing to do. But Hakan was known to be an extremely violent man who, in association with other known criminals, had built an impressive record of violent crime. Maddy appears to have been among his favourite targets for violence. At one time he was heard to say that when he would die, he would 'take Maddy and Vicky with him', because after his death Maddy would probably fool around with all sorts of men, making his daughter 'a whore's child'. The fact that Hakan was diagnosed as terminally ill may well have turned him into a desperado, shrinking from virtually nothing, as indeed his criminal record shows. Perhaps we can understand how a violent and desperate man like Hakan came to murder his girlfriend and child. So far we think we have a reasonably 'good' story. Still, we cannot be absolutely sure that it was Hakan who killed Maddy and Vicky. Everybody assumed it was Hakan, the police, the courts, the press. But perhaps someone else did the killing, on Hakan's request, or maybe not even that. Neither can we be certain that Maddy and Vicky died on 8 June 1997. We only know that nobody has seen them alive since. And maybe they were not killed in the dunes, but only buried there.

Nevertheless, assuming that Hakan at one point in time decided to kill his girlfriend and child, let us next consider the story of how he went about it. He decided to do it on 8 June 1997, at a secluded spot in the dunes near where Maddy lived. Then we may assume that he preferred to do it as fast and efficiently as possible, reducing the risk of being caught at it. A fast and efficient way would have been to go to Maddy's flat and ask her to come for a walk in the dunes and take the child with her. On arrival at the parking lot near the dunes, he might have proposed that they walk to the place were some time earlier they had camped, and Maddy would probably have happily walked with him. Arriving on that particular spot, they may have sit down to enjoy the scenery. Then suddenly.... He would have strangled Maddy first, because killing Vicky first would probably have made Maddy fight like a lion. We do not need to tell the rest of this scenario, because the reader can easily imagine it on his own.

But this was not what happened, according to the court. For reasons that are difficult to fathom, Hakan first called his younger brother to come and babysit Vicky. And Hasad just happened to be available at that very time. Then he somehow persuaded Maddy to come with him without Vicky, and on arriving at the parking lot, got her to walk with him to a spot that she knew. Then he killed her; we do not know how because, when her remains were found five years later, the coroner was not able to establish the cause of death. Next, Hakan needed to go back to the flat to pick up Vicky and Hasad. What did he do with Maddy's body in the interim? Did he hide it in a bush nearby? Or had he already dug the grave, taken off Maddy's clothes, removed her hair and placed her body in the grave – all on his own? If that is what he did, he ran the risk that Maddy's body would be discovered in the open pit by some casual passerby. Did he leave the grave open or did he close it provisionally, to re-open it upon his return? There may not have been many passersby around there at that time, but why would he take the risk at all? Next he went back to pick up Hasad and Vicky. What did he tell Hasad to make him come along and bring the child, in particular since Maddy was no longer with him? Well, in a fatherless Turkish family like his, the oldest son – which was Hakan – is the one whose word is law. Maybe that made Hasad obey. By bringing Hasad along, Hakan needlessly made him a witness to an unspeakable crime, a witness who might eventually decide to talk. Why take such a risk if it would have been more convenient and faster to take both Maddy and Vicky with him at the same time? Surely, he did not expect one-year-old Vicky to interfere while he was killing her mother. Perhaps Hakan needed Hasad's help to dig the grave, to put the bodies in it and pull him out afterwards. But that is not what the court declared to be the facts. The court decided that Hasad only went along to the dunes on the second trip there, handed Vicky over to Hakan and walked away, as in version A. According to the court, Hakan dug the grave by himself, put the two bodies in it, got out of it without help from anybody, and also closed the grave by himself.

This rendition of the events by the court is blatantly at variance with the findings of the forensic investigators who re-enacted the digging of the grave in that particular place. The court chose to ignore this information. It is not even mentioned in the verdict. Reading the court's verdict, you would never guess that the forensic investigators had done anything at all. Their testimony was 'implicitly rejected' as the local law books have it. But more importantly, the story that the court tells in its verdict simply makes no sense whatsoever. Why would Hakan go about his crime in such a circuitous and laborious manner when a simple, straightforward way of committing it was readily available?

Rule 5 of the already mentioned 'universal rules of evidence' in our book *Anchored Narratives* reads: 'The trier of fact should give reasons for the decision by specifying the narrative and the accompanying anchoring.' We already concluded that the anchors that the court gave for its decision were shaky at best. And the court's narrative of the events is not well shaped, meaning that the story of the way in which Hakan is assumed to have committed his crime flies in the face of common sense.

Could there be yet another version?

Does our conclusion that version A of how Hasad came to know where Maddy and Vicky had been buried makes little sense mean that we ourselves opt for version B?

No, we do not, if only because we cannot think of a reasonable answer to the question of why Hakan should have confided in anyone, and in his younger brother Hasad in particular, after having denied having any knowledge of Maddy's and Vicky's fate even to his mother shortly before he died. Our criticism of the court of appeals is not that they did not opt for version B, but that they choose to believe version A. Maybe Hasad did indeed tell Carla and Herman Becker version A, making it more or less up as he went along, but later that night realised, possibly with help from his two other brothers, that version A implicated him in the events, so he decided to dish up a more innocent version to the police the next morning. That would, in any case, absolve Carla and Herman Becker of being confused or lying when they told officer Esther Baak what Hasad had told them.

Interestingly, there was someone who right from the beginning did not believe version A. This was Mary Noom who, at the time of Maddy's and Vicky's disappearance, was the girlfriend of the youngest of the Ciler brothers, Sadi. On being interviewed as a witness by the police, she said that 'if Hakan had needed any help in killing and burying Maddy and Vicky, he would have got it from criminal friends going by the nicknames of Pasja and Chico'. In 1997 the police had already come up with a similar hypothesis when they interviewed Pasja as well as another of Hakan's known criminal friends, going by the name of Boral. To no avail, however, because Boral told them that, even if he knew that Hakan had killed his girlfriend and daughter – the suggestion being that, of course, he did not – he would not tell the police because 'Hakan is my buddy' – Hakan was still among the living at that time. When asked about Pasja, Boral made an interesting comment. According to him, Pasja had already known where Maddy and Vicky had been buried before the media had reported it: 'Maybe he was there when it happened. How else could he have known?' Regrettably, Boral did not explain how he knew that Pasja knew. Pasja himself told the police in 1997 that he had not seen Hakan in a long time, although his telephone record told otherwise. The police simply did not pursue any further the hypothesis that criminal friends of Hakan might have been involved in the death and/or burial of Maddy and Vicky.

Presumably inspired by the media coverage of the case in 2002, a man that we will call Bert Tilman, at the time a prison inmate, wrote to Hasad's defence lawyer that sometime in 1998/1999 a fellow inmate had told him that he had been involved in burying two large plastic bags in the dunes near Bergen and that Hakan as well as two other guys, a certain Benny and a young Moroccan fellow whose name he did not remember, had also been involved. Bert Tilman repeated this information to the investigating judge who, at the request of the defence attorney, interviewed him on 10 April 2003, and that is how this information became part of the case file. Well, one jailbird telling another jailbird a vague tale is not what one would call a strong lead. Moreover, Bert Tilman added that at the time he himself had not really believed his fellow inmate, knowing him as a man who liked to spin stories. Still, the man had known Hakan's as well as Benny's name. The police might therefore have tried to find this other man as well as Benny, but they did not. Evidently, the prosecuting attorney thought version A good enough to present to the court, which he did on 5 June 2003. But that turned out to be a mistake, because the district court acquitted Hasad. Luckily for the prosecution, there was still the Amsterdam Court of Appeals that proved to be more gullible.

Are we suggesting that, on the basis of Tilman's rather vague information, there might be a third version, version C, that describes what really happened to Maddy and Vicky? Indeed we are, but to turn this into a well-shaped narrative of the events, we would need considerably more information. This is lacking because the police apparently did not deem it worthwhile to pursue the lead provided by Bert Tilman. What is most conspicuously lacking from a possible version C is how, if Hakan killed and buried Maddy and Vicky with the help of some of his criminal friends, Hasad came to know where the victims were buried. Was Hasad perhaps one of his partners in crime? Not very likely. For one, Hasad had no criminal record, and nobody who knows him says anything of the sort. Together with another young man, he runs a sort of handyman business, and judging from the way he talks, as we know from his many interviews with the police, he appears to be a fairly naive person of limited intelligence.

Perhaps he became involved in killing Maddy and Vicky as part of some sort of revenge killing to safeguard the Ciler's family honour ('namous') , as is not entirely unknown in some Turkish circles; in these killings, the whole family is expected to take part (cf. Van Eck, 2001). This could be true because some of Maddy's acquaintances told the police, probably not without reason, that she had been unfaithful to Hakan, in particular when he was in jail in the spring of 1997. Indeed, Ernie Schwarz had noted in his diary of this period that Maddy was visited several times by a male visitor other than Hakan. Perhaps Hakan even came to doubt that he was Vicky's father. Perhaps Maddy suggested as much during one of their many quarrels. Taken together these suppositions could make a rather compelling narrative, possibly explaining why Maddy's hair was cut off and Vicky's was not. But unfortunately, there is not a shred of evidence in the case file for such a tale.

Let us, therefore, spin yet another outrageous hypothesis. Let us, if only for a moment, assume that the court of appeals realised that version A was almost certainly not the way in which Hasad had come to know about the burial site, but that his knowledge of the burial site definitely implicated him as part of some narrative about which they could only speculate. Could it be that the court thought: 'OK, version A is almost certainly not what happened, but since he must somehow have been involved, let us convict him on the basis of an indictment for which we can adduce some, if rather shaky evidence. Who cares, so long as we are convinced that

Hasad was involved'? But this way of reasoning would, of course, be a blatant violation of the law. We therefore see no other option than to assume that the court really did believe version A. We find that quite surprising.

CHAPTER 7

Conflicting Scenarios or the Case of the Man Who Needed a Companion

In criminal cases it often happens that the allegation of a victim stands against the denial of the alleged perpetrator and that there is not enough additional information to simply choose between the two versions. However, before bringing a case to court the prosecution must make a choice. This may be done by cherry-picking from among the available, often contradictory pieces of evidence in such a way that the indictment contains a coherent story of the suspect's guilt. All other pieces of evidence are assumed to be irrelevant or untrue, or are simply ignored. This chapter is concerned with the risks of such selective use of evidence in criminal trials as they are conducted in the inquisitorial manner, in use in most countries in continental Europe. Under the inquisitorial system of criminal justice, an extensive case file is compiled by the prosecution prior to the actual trial, containing all evidence collected by the police in the form of written depositions. The defence is not supposed to collect evidence on its own, but can ask the prosecuting attorney and/or investigating judge[1] to investigate certain aspects or to interview particular witnesses and to add such additional findings in written form to the case file. Invariably, the preponderance of documents entered into the case file is supplied by the prosecution. It will be argued that in the adversarial system, used in most Anglo-American countries, many cases reflect the same practice.

The case of Goran Radic: Mileva's story

Goran Radic, a 62-year-old Dutch national of Yugoslav origin, was accused by Mileva Simic, a 27-year-old member of a Roma family living illegally in the country, of

1 In the average criminal case, the district attorney supervises the police investigation. When, however, the police needs investigating methods beyond the authority of the district attorney, e.g., entering a private home, the case must be handed over to the investigating judge.

forcibly detaining her in his house and of beating and raping her repeatedly. According to Mileva, in early September 1999 she received a phone call from Goran Radic, whom she had never met before. He told her that 'someone' had given him her telephone number, telling him that she might be available as a companion. He said he already loved her and wanted her to come live with him. If she would not agree to this, he would kill her.

This is a surprising sequence of events, even more surprising because Mileva decided to accept Radic' invitation. On 11 September she moved to Radic's house, bringing her 3-year-old son with her. We can understand what motivated Radic to invite Mileva Simic to come share his life. More than ten years earlier he had come to the Netherlands from Yugoslavia, leaving behind a wife and two children for, according to him, 'economic reasons'. He got lucky by finding and marrying a woman who had her own business and did not expect him to do anything, which suited him nicely. But after ten years, this marriage failed, and Radic was left to his own resources. This meant that he had to apply for social security; this provided him with a basic income which he came to supplement with the proceeds of petty, though never violent, offences. He often complained to people that no one was 'taking care' of him anymore. So, Mileva might fill this void.

What may have motivated Mileva to accept Radic's sudden offer and to trust herself and her son to a man of more than twice her age, about whom she knew nothing to begin with and who had just called her out of the blue, saying he loved her without ever having met her and threatening to kill her if she did not respond to his invitation? Being an illegal alien in the country, perhaps she hoped that a marriage with a Dutch national like Radic might in time legalise her presence in the country. But until very recently she had been living with another Dutch national, 62-year-old Mr. Peeck, who might have served the same purpose. We do not know whether Mileva ever asked Peeck to marry her and whether he had been inclined to do so. In any case, as long as we restrict ourselves to Mileva's testimony, her motive to accept Radic' invitation is difficult to fathom.

After having moved in with Radic, Mileva stayed there for almost a month, but on 9 October she left with her son, because after the first two weeks Radic had wanted to have sex with her, which she refused. According to her, for this reason Radic began to beat her, and by locking her up, he prevented her from leaving the house. On 11 October she managed to escape and returned to her family.

Radic kept calling her, imploring her to return, which she did a week later, on 16 October. Not for long though, because after a birthday party on the evening of 21 October, attended by most of her family, she left again by climbing from the balcony of the apartment to the balcony of the neighbouring apartment where Mrs. Bergman lived, who admitted she was no friend of Goran Radic. Shortly before Mileva appeared on her balcony, Mrs. Bergman had heard a woman screaming and a man shouting so loudly in Radic's apartment that she decided to call the police. But when Mileva and her son were safely in her apartment, she cancelled this call. The next day Mileva herself went to the police station to file a complaint against Radic for detaining and beating her. Five days later, on 26 October, Mileva visited the local hospital, where a doctor noticed that her body showed signs of physical abuse, but it remained unclear whether she had had those at the time she fled Radic's apartment on 21 October or when she filed her complaint with the police the next day. On 9 November the police took Radic into custody in order to interrogate him. He denied Mileva's accusations. The next day Mileva was interviewed again by the police and then she added rape to her earlier accusations, which Radic also denied and has continued denying ever since.

Goran Radic's story

In early November Goran Radic was interrogated three times by the police. He told them that 'about one and a half months ago' he had met two men in a bar. When he explained to them that he had recently been divorced, they told him that they knew a 'good Roma woman' for him of about 27 or 28 years old. Although he thought that this was rather young for him, he agreed to talk to her, upon which the men gave him a telephone number. 'I understood that this woman needed papers legalising her presence in the country.' The identities of the two men who gave Goran Mileva's telephone number were never established by the police; as far as we know, they never asked.

When Radic called Mileva, she told him that she was willing to accept his offer, but that her family would expect him to pay a dowry of fifty thousand guilders, adding, according to him, that she had already been 'sold' by her family a number of times to a host of other men, but that she had usually returned to her family after about three months. It had been primarily her mother who had organised these transactions. In spite of this rather alarming information, Goran told her that he wanted her to come live with him, which she did, but he refused to pay the required dowry. During her first stay with Goran, Mileva was called almost daily by members of her family, who Goran suspected of encouraging her to press him to deliver on the dowry. But since these phone calls were made in the Roma language he could not be certain of this. After Mileva had left his house the first time, her mother called Goran repeatedly to tell him that if he wanted Mileva back, he needed to pay. This he refused again.

From all this one might surmise that Mileva was some sort of gold-digger, who with some regularity was used by her family to extract money from various men in need of female companionship. Possibly Mileva participated somewhat unwillingly in these confidence games. Perhaps after she had left Goran the first time, she was beaten by members of her family to force her to go back to Radic a second time after the first effort to make him pay had failed, resulting in the injuries that were noticed in the hospital five days after she had left Goran's house the first time. This is what Radic implied when he said to his interrogators that he had noticed Mileva's injuries when she came back to him. During these interrogations he said that in the beginning of Mileva's stay with him things had gone quite well. He still thought of her as 'kind, funny and intelligent'. 'She was good to me and I to her', but things went wrong when her family began to interfere. So Goran believed that, if there had been a confidence game, Mileva had not wholeheartedly cooperated in it, but this belief may be the product of an old man's somewhat pathetic naiveté.

Additional evidence

So far we appear to be stuck with two conflicting scenarios of Mileva's relationship with Goran, and for each of these we have only the word of one of the two protagonists. In order to bring the case against Goran to court, the prosecution decided it needed some corroborating evidence for Mileva's rendition of the facts. For this, the police questioned Mileva's 35-year-old sister Nadja and Nadja's 16-year-old son Milan. They confirmed that, together with other members of the family, they had attended the birthday party in Goran's house on the evening of 21 October. According to them, nothing aggravating had happened. The police also called Mileva's mother. We do not know what they asked her and what, if anything, she told them. In a brief note which they added to the case file, they simply reported that 'no additional information was obtained' from her, which is disappointing because Goran had intimated that the mother might have been the principal instigator of a con game played on him. Perhaps the reason why 'no additional information' was obtained from her was that the police had not been able to talk to her because of a language problem. Language problems may in any case have been the reason why the police had been unable to get more information from and about Mileva's family.

Mileva's 62-year-old former friend Peeck was also interviewed. From this it transpired that Mileva had been living with him for about a year and that she had left his house early in September to go visit a friend, as she told him, which means that Mileva may have gone almost directly from his to Goran Radic's house. After she had left there the first time, she had briefly returned to him, at which time he had noticed that she showed signs of physical abuse, but she never told him who had done this to her. He could not remember the exact day of her return to his house, whether she had come to him directly from Goran's house or had first spent some time at her mother's house. On the latter point, Mileva contradicted herself at different times during the investigation. The matter is important because now it remains unclear at precisely what time and possibly by whom she was physically abused.

Understandably, the investigating police officers thought that there was still insufficient corroborative evidence for Mileva's accusations, and therefore decided that they needed a psychological expert to evaluate 'the degree of reliability, i.e., the veracity and accuracy of Mileva's testimony'. This assignment, given to Professor De Vries, raises two preliminary questions. First, one wonders how, i.e., by using which method or technique, the expert was supposed to do this? Secondly, why was the assignment so one-sided, i.e., why was the expert not also asked to evaluate the 'reliability' of Goran Radic' rendition of the events?

We can be brief about the first of these two questions: at present there is no valid technique by which psychologists can decide whether a witness speaks the truth or not. Often the Criteria Based Content Analysis (CBCA) is used for this purpose. In chapter 11 of this book we explain why this technique cannot serve the purpose for which it is offered, even for children for whom it was designed. We add that, for adult witnesses like Mileva, the diagnostic value of the CBCA hardly surpasses chance level (Landry & Brigham, 1992). Yet, Professor De Vries analysed Mileva's depositions with the help of CBCA. In his report he wrote that he 'did not consider CBCA a hard, scientifically validated method, because there is as yet little[2] research confirming its reliability and validity. The method does not offer proof, only an indication'. Still, the 'indications' were strong enough for him to conclude that Mileva's accusations concerning physical abuse as well as rape or sexual assault were 'very reliable', and he added that according to him there were 'no convincing indications for (...) induction by members of her family', and that 'Mileva also had no obvious motive to make false accusations'.

Still, Professor De Vries also remarked in his report that he found it 'puzzling' why Mileva had decided to go live with a man who had threatened her and, we may add, why she risked the welfare of her 3-year-old son in doing this. And why, De Vries remarks, did she go back to him a second time after what she had experienced during her first stay with him? He writes: 'Pleading and threatening are contradictory, and in going back to him she increased the chance that he would kill her, as he had threatened.' Professor De Vries solved these puzzles by reminding his readers of the *battered woman syndrome*, which is assumed to explain why women who are repeatedly physically abused by their partners often still find themselves unable to leave their abusers (Walker, 1979). Regardless of whether the Battered Woman Syndrome is a real syndrome in the sense of the DSM-IV (American Psychiatric Association, 1994) and is more than a mere description of a surprising phenomenon (Schuller & Vidmar, 1992) remains undecided; in any case, according to the de-

2 This is not a correct qualification: many studies have been done, but the results so far have been disappointing.

scription of its inventor, Lenore Walker, Mileva had not been together with Goran long enough to develop this 'syndrome'.

With the expert opinion of Professor De Vries, the prosecution felt confident enough to bring the case to court. But what about Goran's version of the events? Should that not also have been investigated?

The presumption of innocence

Why should the story of a criminal defendant matter when we have a credible story by his victim? First of all, there is a principled reason for this: the presumption of innocence, which is accepted in every civilised country as a basic principle of criminal procedure. The European Convention for the Protection of Human Rights and Fundamental Freedoms (ECHR) says in its art. 6.2 that 'everybody against whom a criminal investigation is initiated will be considered innocent until his guilt has been established in a court of law'.

To become the subject of a criminal investigation, a 'probable cause' or, as it is called in Dutch criminal law, 'a reasonable suspicion of guilt' is required, which serves to protect people from arbitrary interference by the police and criminal justice authorities. At first, this requirement may appear contradictory to the presumption of innocence, because if there is indeed a reasonable suspicion of guilt, how can we at the same time consider someone innocent as long as a legitimate trier of fact has not established 'beyond a reasonable doubt' that the defendant is guilty? However, the presumption of innocence is not a principle of substantive law, but a matter of criminal procedure, referring to the way in which we are required to treat a suspect. And this implies, among other things, that we take a defendant's rendition of the facts equally seriously as a victim's accusation. And this should be done not only during the trial, but at all stages of the preceding investigation. This is difficult to achieve.

The 'reasonable suspicion of guilt' or 'probable cause' that marks the beginning of a criminal investigation is a hypothesis raised by the police. During the subsequent investigation this hypothesis must be tested by gathering additional evidence, 'additional' to the information that constituted probable cause. Testing a hypothesis is difficult, because in doing so people tend to look primarily, if not exclusively, for information confirming the hypothesis. This general human tendency is called 'confirmation bias' in the psychological literature (Tversky & Kahneman, 1974; Nisbett & Ross, 1980; Evans, 1990; Gilovich, 1993). Ever since Popper, we know that in testing a hypothesis it is equall, if not more important to look for disconfirming or falsifying evidence. We can only really trust a hypothesis if we fail to falsify it, i.e., fail to find any contradictory evidence in spite of vigorous efforts to do so.

Spontaneously, people find it difficult to search for falsifying evidence once they have adopted and perhaps come to cherish a particular hypothesis (Wason & Johnson-Laird, 1972). If you fail to find confirming evidence for an adopted hypothesis, you may console yourself that maybe you have not looked well enough and next time you may still get lucky. There is no logical necessity to drop a 'probable cause', simply because it is not corroborated independently. But now look at the opposite: what do we do when in the investigation disconfirming information is obtained? Do we drop the 'probable cause' without further ado? There is again no logical necessity to do so. Maybe the disconfirming evidence is not what it appears to be; perhaps it can be explained away, although it would have been better if you had never come to know about it. The latter is what people usually prefer, because, in the words of Koehler, 'any task that prompts a person to temporarily accept the truth of a hypothesis will increase his or her confidence in that hypothesis' (Koehler, 1991, p. 502).

The confirmation bias appears to affect every stage of the criminal investigation as often as it occurs in everyday reasoning. The police will only rarely look actively for exculpatory evidence disconfirming the 'probable cause' that led them to the suspect to begin with. If they stumble across it, they may not recognise it as relevant and may therefore not report it. After all, only relevant information, i.e., relevant to the indictment that will eventually be offered to the court, should be in the case file, so as not to confuse the court. But often such disconfirming information does make it into the case file, e.g., when some witness squarely contradicts some quite damning statement by another witness. If the prosecution decides to bring the case to court, the court will be confronted with the contradiction and consequently be forced to make a choice, or dismiss the case altogether. As the latter option is very unattractive, courts may tend to make such choices, even when there are no sufficient logical reasons to do so.

It is not clear whether selection of evidence is legally or ethically wrong. An indictment is not simply a summing up of what the police have come to know during an investigation. It is a coherent story of a series of events, in which each piece of evidence acquires its meaning as a fitting part of that story. 'Nothing is more lost than a loose fact,' George Homans (1951, p. 5) wrote long ago; facts only acquire their meaning from the context of which they are a part. Facts on their own have no meaning. If only for this reason, the prosecution in a criminal case will present its evidence in the form of a coherent story. If there is some contradictory evidence, the formulation of the indictment can only be done by cherry-picking: what fits the indictment is chosen, what does not fit the indictment is ignored and thus left as a collection of loose and therefore meaningless bits and pieces. The court, following the prosecution's lead, may decide to go along. There are many cases with conflicting information, and it is undesirable to dismiss all these cases only for that reason.

But this state of affairs has serious consequences for the defence of a case. The presumption of innocence implies that the burden of proof in criminal cases rests on the prosecution, and that therefore the defence does not have to prove anything. It would, however, be very unwise for the defence to passively wait for the prosecution to meet its burden. Most defence attorneys know this and remain anything but passive during a trial. They offer reasons why the court should not trust the evidence offered by the prosecution, or point out that there is contradictory evidence that is no less trustworthy than the evidence offered by the prosecution. Inconsistency between various pieces of evidence is such a general phenomenon in complex cases that one almost needs an explanation when it does not occur. Did the police never look for it during its investigation, or did they not report it because they deemed it irrelevant? The latter would not be hard to understand if indeed confirmation of the indictment is considered the criterion for relevancy.

In the adversarial system the defence may, more than in an inquisitorial system, conduct its own investigation, especially directed at aspects that may falsify the indictment. Still, it should be realised that in the majority of criminal trials we are faced with an inequality of arms. The government, acting through the prosecution, almost always has immeasurably more resources to investigate at its disposal than the defence. It may well happen that additional inquiries, required by the logic of hypothesis testing, are never made because this would require the type of resources that only the government has at its disposal.

Reconsidering Goran Radic's story

In most complex criminal cases there will be at least some contradictory evidence, often provided by the defendant: he was not present at the scene of the crime at the specified time, or if there is irrefutable evidence of his presence there, he did not take part in the offence, or the sequence of events was different from the one alleged by the prosecution, and so on. The problem with this kind of counter-evidence is that it is the defendant who supplies it. Defendants are expected to lie, and this indeed occurs so often that it may seem safe to routinely ignore the defendant's usually flimsy excuses. This will be particularly easy if the police did not even try to investigate their possible veracity, which may have happened in the case against Goran Radic, although there were good reasons to look somewhat deeper into some of his allegations. During the preliminary investigation he surmised that he had become the victim in a con game played by Mileva's family, as indicated above. We wonder why the police did not think it worthwhile to find out the identity of the two men who gave him Mileva's telephone number in a bar. Who were they? Members of the Simic family? What was their motive? Compassion with Goran's plight, who complained that he had no one to take care of him anymore? We do not need to take

Goran's word for the way in which he came into contact with Mileva. Mileva herself appears to corroborate at least part of this somewhat improbable turn of events: she says that Goran called her out of the blue because 'someone' had given him her telephone number. If this was not what really happened, how else did Goran come into contact with her? There is no indication in the case file, where all investigative actions of the police are supposed to be reported, that the police ever tried to find out who these two men were and what their motive might have been. The court never raised these questions either.

Goran indicated that Mileva's mother might have been the principal instigator of the confidence game and that similar con games had been played before on a number of other men. One of the men with whom Mileva had lived before was Mr. Peeck. The police interviewed Peeck, but failed to ask him whether at any time a dowry was requested. We could understand why Peeck would not report such a thing spontaneously, because he probably would have felt embarrassed if he had actually paid. But that is no reason for not asking him.

The police called Mileva's mother, but only reported that 'no additional information' was obtained from her. What does that mean? What, if anything, did she say? Did she deny having urged Mileva to require a dowry from Goran? Or was the question never put to her? Was she asked whether her daughter had been with other men before Peeck and Goran Radic? Mileva had a three-year-old son by a man living in Germany. Who was this man? Why had Mileva left this man? Did the police try to trace him? Mileva's sister Nadja and cousin Milan were interviewed by the police. They confirmed having attended the birthday party on 21 October. Were they also asked what they knew about Mileva's surprising decision to go live with a man more than twice her age, who had been a complete stranger to her? Had they not been worried about the fate of their three-year-old nephew in the house of a man completely unknown to them and who, according to Mileva, had threatened to kill her if she did not accept his invitation? How many members are there in the Simic family? Why were they not all interviewed and asked these and other questions?

We raise these questions to demonstrate that the police investigated only half of the case against Goran Radic and that the prosecuting attorney did not ask the police to do more. To him, apparently the case looked solid enough, in spite of the earlier mentioned oddities in Mileva's rendition of the events. Moreover, the prosecution had Professor De Vries' expert opinion, in which he explained away at least part of these oddities. Why waste any more of the police's time when the prosecution hopefully had enough to secure a conviction. Why indeed?

Why alternative scenarios are important

We submit that in complex criminal cases, i.e., cases in which there is information contradictory to the indictment, it is of the essence that an alternative scenario be developed and seriously investigated. Perhaps this is too much to expect from the police, as they may be reluctant to do anything that might weaken their case against a suspect. In this they are wrong of course, because a failed attempt to falsify their working hypothesis would only strengthen their case. The prosecuting attorney, however, as 'an officer of the court' should know better. And criminal courts should always insist that reasonable alternative scenarios to the indictment are explored and rejected on the basis of evidence before convicting a suspect. Further on in the text, we will have more to say about what should be considered a reasonable alternative scenario. First we need to explain why a court cannot rationally decide on a criminal case without considering reasonable alternative scenarios.

It was the mathematician the Reverend Thomas Bayes (1763) who already in the eighteenth century explained why a rational decision can only be taken when all possible alternatives are considered. The logic of this can easily be explained with the help of a simple example. The 30 percent chance for a patient to survive an operation may appear regrettably small, but if the alternative to the operation is certain death, the only rational decision under the circumstances is, of course, to have the operation. The rationality of that decision rests on the unacceptability of the alternative. Let us next consider the decision of whether or not to fly with an airline company with a known 30 percent chance that passengers would survive the flight. It would be very irrational to travel with this airline however urgent the voyage might be, knowing that the chance of not surviving the flight with another airline is infinitely smaller. Same chances, opposite decisions. The same logic applies to court decisions: a court can only decide rationally to convict or to acquit the accused if it knows the alternatives. That is why courts must insist upon knowing of all possible reasonable alternative scenarios to the indictment.

Reasonable alternative scenarios

One might think that for any indictment there is always an alternative scenario. Anything is possible if one stretches the imagination far enough; at least that is what many defendants in criminal cases seem to think. How about the suspect who claims that it was not him who killed the victim, but some unknown alter ego residing within him, who suddenly took over his actions? This has actually been tried a few times. Or what about the case of a well-known football player and two of his friends who were accused of gang-raping a girl and claimed that she consented to this?[3] Are such alternatives reasonable and therefore merits serious investigation by the police and consideration by the court? We think not.

We submit that in order to be seriously investigated by the police and considered by the court an alternative scenario must meet the following criteria.

1. A reasonable alternative should not contain elements that are physically impossible. If some alternative scenario requires that a suspect has travelled a distance of 100 miles within a period of twenty minutes, there is no need to investigate such a scenario any further.
2. A reasonable alternative scenario must have some points of contact with the already available evidence in the case file, to which at least part of it can be anchored (see chapter 5 for a definition of 'anchoring'). If there is nothing at all in the available evidence that might serve as anchors for at least some part of the alternative scenario, then it probably does not merit further exploration. The more points of contact there are, the more urgent it becomes to explore it further.
3. A reasonable alternative scenario meriting further investigation must have the potential of being told as a good story, in that it contains a clear central action and a context or setting that easily explains the actions of all the protagonists in the story, as described by Lance Bennett and Martha Feldman (1981). If an alternative scenario can be developed into an equally good or even better story than the indictment, it certainly deserves to be investigated with the utmost care. An alternative scenario that cannot be told as a good story probably merits no further exploration.
4. There must be no virtually irrefutable pieces of evidence in the case file contradicting a critical element in the alternative scenario to make it meritorious of further investigation. One must be careful with this criterion; the discovery of a suspect's DNA on the scene of the crime may be considered irrefutable evidence of his presence there, but not without further ado of his presence there at a particular time.
5. An alternative scenario deserves more careful investigation the more it is recognised as a rather common sequence of events. In other words, common scenarios deserve more initial credit than outlandish ones. Sometimes, however, outlandish events happen. In a high-profile criminal case that was tried in our country in 1995, a young man was convicted by the District Court in The Hague of having killed his mother by shooting a ballpoint pen with a crossbow through her eye into her brain (Rompen, Meek, & Van Nadel, 2000). This is a quite outlandish scenario, but it was adopted by the prosecution because the young man's psychotherapist had told the police that at one time during his therapy he had

---

3 This case occurred in our country some years ago. The police decided not to investigate it, and the district attorney decided not to prosecute it.

told her: 'I have killed my mother. I did it with a crossbow.' The son denied ever having said this, however confused he might have been at the time when he had needed therapy. The alternative scenario offered by the defence, which on appeal led to his acquittal, was that the son had had nothing to do with his mother's death and that she must have fallen accidentally into the ballpoint pen with her eye, which may seem to be an equally outlandish scenario, but in the literature quite a number of similar accidents have been reported.

Not every one of these five criteria is a hard and fast rule. If the criteria 1 and/or 5 are not met, it is probably safe to discard the alternative scenario out of hand, and to convict if no other reasonable scenario can be offered. If, however, there are pieces of evidence in the case file that, if not reasonably explained away, fit an alternative, innocent scenario, and if moreover that alternative scenario has the potential of developing into a reasonably good story which, given the milieu in which it is set, would not be too outlandish, as was the case with the alternative offered by Goran Radic, the court should have insisted that the prosecution investigate it thoroughly and if possible refute it before deciding the case. One could argue that it would have been the task of the defence to investigate the alternative and to offer as much proof for it as possible. In countries with inquisitorial criminal justice systems, however, a defence attorney is not supposed to carry out his own investigation. In our own country this is not explicitly forbidden by any rule of law, but it would be regarded with utter suspicion if he did so. Dutch defence attorneys are dependent on the police do to any additional investigation such as, e.g., interviewing extra witnesses. Under these circumstances the court should have adjourned the trial and have ordered the prosecution to show by additional evidence that the alternative offered by the defence was at least not very plausible. But, as is not unusual in our country, it decided the case on what the prosecution had chosen to offer in evidence. What the defence offered as an alternative could not be anchored onto any evidence other than Radic's allegations, because the police had failed to gather anything else.

It must be stressed that even in an adversarial system, it might have been quite difficult for the defence to gather falsifying evidence. Mileva and the entire Simic family would almost certainly have refused to cooperate with the defence. Probably only the police could have conducted such interviews. Perhaps some information about Mileva's previous relationships could have been obtained from administrative sources, in particular if there had been a marriage, but that would not have been easy. Relationships like the ones she had had with Radic and Peeck would almost certainly be untraceable. A former partner like Peeck, having been the victim of a gold-digger conspiracy, would probably not volunteer to testify against a family clan that he may well have come to fear. However you look at it, the case is an apt example of what goes wrong when the police does only half its job.

How the case ended

Goran Radic was convicted by the Utrecht District Court, but not for illegally detaining Mileva or for rape and aggravated assault. He was acquitted of those serious offences. But he was convicted for simple assault. One wonders why the court decided this. Probably because Mileva did show signs of physical abuse when she visited the hospital on 26 October, i.e., in the interim between her two stays at Radic's house. If Radic had indeed done this to her, she must have had those injuries when she fled his house the first time on 9 October. At some time during that period Mileva returned to the house of her former friend Peeck and he says that he had noticed Mileva's injuries, but he does not remember precisely on which day she came back to his house. It is therefore possible that, upon leaving Radic the first time, she first returned to her mother's house, where she may have been beaten by some family member for returning home without the hoped-for dowry, upon which she decided to flee again, thus turning up at Peeck's doorstep as the only other place where she could go at that time. So there is an alternative scenario that might have been confirmed or refuted by a thorough investigation into the Simic family. Why did the police not do so? The language problem? What about an interpreter? The court, limited by the evidence that was offered, appears to have decided something in between the two scenarios. How this mental feat was performed by the court remains a mystery to us.

Postscript

As stated at the outset of this chapter, we are more concerned with criminal proceedings conducted in the inquisitorial manner, as in use in most countries in continental Europe. In criminal proceedings conducted in the adversarial manner, as in use in Anglo-American countries, the problem discussed in this chapter is less prominent but may occur in a considerable number of cases even though in adversarial proceedings the defence has more freedom to collect and present evidence of its own choice. The wider options of the defence in adversarial systems do not undermine the basic tenet of this chapter, which is that the trier of fact always needs to consider reasonable alternative scenarios to the indictment.

CHAPTER 8

Two Processes Obstructing the Accuracy of Long-Term Memory or the Case of the Stolen Mercedes

It is not uncommon for witnesses to be asked about events that occurred a long time, even years ago. A case in point is the notorious case against John Demjanjuk, who was accused of war crimes in the German extermination camp Treblinka in the years 1942 to 1943. In the period 1979 to 1987, the witnesses were asked to remember what happened and especially to identify Demjanjuk, 37 to 45 years after the event. Understandably, the question was raised as to whether memories may be trusted after such a long period of time (Wagenaar, 1988b). Ever since Herman Ebbinghaus (1885/1966), we know that memory deteriorates with time. We also know that it may become distorted, either by new information or by a sequence of continuous overt or covert rehearsals. In most instances it is unrealistic to assume that memories remain fresh and unchanged across a period of many years. Especially the problem of change over time is highly relevant when the events were personally significant and have therefore continued to play a role in a person's life. In that case it will be difficult to decide what new information was received after the event, which aspects were rehearsed, how often, to what purpose, and how the 'refreshing process' may have changed the details. The case of the stolen Mercedes, discussed in this chapter, is less spectacular than the Demjanjuk case, but the challenges to the witnesses' memories may have been equally formidable. The case is chosen primarily because it offers an apt illustration of the difference between the two major types of forgetting: loss of accessibility, and change through post-event information.

The case of the stolen Mercedes

Mr. Dukes owned a very expensive Mercedes. He always parked it on the premises, never in the street, and it had a sophisticated alarm system. Mr. Dukes was always careful to activate the alarm when he left the car for the night. On the night of 19 December 1995 he came home around 11.30 PM. He parked the Mercedes, activated the alarm (or so he says) and went to bed. The next morning was a Saturday and Mr. Dukes slept late. He got up around 9 AM and discovered to his horror that the Mercedes was no longer where he had parked it. Fortunately, the car was insured with the reliable insurance company Safetycar. The insurance company, however, thought they smelled a rat, since they knew that Mr. Dukes had serious financial problems. Three weeks before, Mrs. Dukes had already reported the theft of *her* car. The alarm on Mr. Dukes's Mercedes was installed on special instructions of Safetycar. It was hard to imagine how the car could have been stolen with the alarm on; with the alarm de-activated, the Mercedes was not insured. Safetycar accused the Dukes of negligence and/or fraud and refused to pay.

Mr. Dukes went to court. The judge appreciated Safetycar's ground for suspicion and ordered Mr. Dukes to prove that his car alarm had been activated on that particular night in December 1995. Now that is a difficult thing to prove. The issue could only be resolved by means of eyewitnesses who might have noticed that Mr. Dukes switched on the alarm in the middle of the night. Still, there were three witnesses, but they were only interrogated for the first time in March 2002, more than six years after the event. All three witnesses swore they remembered definitely that Mr. Dukes had activated the alarm that night. After six years, this is a quite surprising feat of memory. Hence, Safetycar put the question to one of us as an expert witness: how likely is it that witnesses will remember in 2002 whether somebody switched on his car alarm one particular night in 1995?

Forgetting

In the following discussion we will describe two fundamentally different mechanisms of forgetting. The effect of the first mechanism is that the information to-be-remembered is removed from memory, or at least becomes inaccessible. The second mechanism does not really change the accessibility of memories, but alters their contents on the basis of later information. The original information may still be there, but will generally only be accessed under specific conditions. In the present section we will discuss the first of these two mechanisms.

The notion that memory deteriorates with time, although confirmed in many experimental studies, for most people is primarily based on everyday experience: we tend to forget, and more so the longer ago something happened to us. But this is not an absolute law. A closer look tells us that some things may never be forgotten. Some things may even be remembered better after a longer period of latency. This phenomenon is called *reminiscence* (Fitzgerald, 1996). The most extreme form of reminiscence is the much discussed phenomenon of recovered memories. The claim here is that although the memory of a traumatic event has been inaccessible for many years, after recovery it becomes as vivid and detailed as at the time of its acquisition. Whatever the validity of this claim -which we discuss in chapter 5- we must at least conclude that the steady and irrevocable decline of long-term memory over time apparently is not the generally accepted phenomenon that many believe it to be.

It may be helpful to compare autobiographical memory to a library. The library contains an almost infinite number of books, stacked in a systematic manner, although the system may at first not appear to be very conducive to a rapid and successful search process. In our university libraries, books are placed in the order of the date of acquisition and according to size. Those two pieces of information are usually not known to the library users, which prevents them from locating books on the shelves on the basis of such information. Fortunately there is also a catalogue, enabling the reader to use the author's name, the title of the book, the publisher, its subject matter and the year of its publication as retrieval cues. These cues were selected by the catalogue designers because they expected that these types of information would be known by users, and would rapidly limit the search to a single book. If, however, the user only remembers 'a large red book on psychology', the catalogue will obviously be useless. The success of retrieval depends on the fit between the cues foreseen at the time of storage and the cues known to the user at the time of retrieval. If there is no fit between the two, the wanted book is to all practical purposes 'lost' or 'forgotten'. What we know about the process of forgetting in autobiographical memory can be, summarised in a single sentence: damage occurs in the catalogue system, not in the stacks. Most of the memories are probably still there, but can no longer be located among the incalculable number of other, particularly more recently stacked memories.

The use of retrieval cues may go wrong in three different ways. It is possible that the retrieval cues originally used for storage lose their links with the content of a memory. It becomes like an entry in the catalogue that shows no reference to the location in the book stacks, even though the book is still there. This form of forgetting may happen, for instance, when a particular event in which a Mr. Brown played a major role is stored under the cue 'Mr. Brown'. If Mr. Brown is never encountered again, the event itself may still be remembered, but 'Mr. Brown' may no longer function as an effective retrieval cue. When later on Mr. Brown calls and assumes that he will be remembered, an embarrassing situation may develop.

The second possibility is that the retrieval cues are taken mainly from the context in which an event occurred. When next we try to remember the event in a different context, it may happen that the remaining cues prove insufficient. Or worse, it may happen that the new context directs our attention to other cues that lead us to entirely different events. In the library metaphor, this may happen when a book is catalogued only by its title, and we try to retrieve it using the author's name. A somewhat famous example of a similar phenomenon is given by Tversky & Kahneman, when they asked people to estimate either the probability that a word starts with the letter 'R', or the probability that it has an 'R' as its third letter (Tversky & Kahneman, 1973). People solve this type of problem by searching for examples of such words. That is a familiar task for words beginning with an 'R', apparently because the first letter is a search cue already foreseen at the time of storage. The third letter of a word was never foreseen as a search cue, and as a result it is difficult to quickly name even a few such words. The difference in difficulty leads people to believe – quite wrongly – that words have more often an 'R' in the first position than in the third. The incongruence between cues foreseen during storage and cues used for retrieval is at the basis of this often replicated effect. Reinstatement of the original context is a well-known technique for memory retrieval in forensic interviews, of which Geiselman's *cognitive interview* is an example (Geiselman *et al.*, 1984).

A third possibility is that the cues lose their uniqueness, because later on many other events were stored under the same cues. It is like entering Hans Christian Andersen's tales in the catalogue as unspecified 'fairy tales', because it is as yet the only fairy tales collection in the library. Later, the collection of fairy tales may grow to hundreds of titles, thus making 'fairy tales' an almost useless cue for readily finding Andersen's tales. An illustration of the loss of uniqueness of retrieval cues was found in Wagenaar's study of his own autobiographical memory (Wagenaar, 1988d). A real-life example from that corpus was that he once shook hands with Her Majesty the Queen of the Netherlands, which he probably stored under the cue 'the queen', on the assumption that the event would remain a unique experience for him. Little did he realise that much later, as Rector of Leiden University, he would meet the queen on many other occasions, making the cue for the first time he met her in person lose its effectiveness. The other author of this book also shook hands with the Queen once and has never again met her since. For him this was a unique event, which makes it easy to retrieve the verbatim memory of his very brief conversation with her[1].

A much-debated question is whether forgetting is not merely a matter of diminished accessibility, caused by a loss of cue effectiveness, but may also be due to a true loss of stored information. In the library metaphor: not a problem of the catalogue, but a disappearance of books from the stacks. The 'decay theory of forgetting' claims that this may happen, and that the information loss is caused by some sort of automatic decay of memory traces (Baddeley, 1990). Forgetting Mr. Brown's name in the example given above might have been caused by automatic decay, in a manner similar to the fading of graffiti on a wall under the influence of rain. The com-

1 Which consisted of 'Your Majesty, I am Crombag from Leiden University,' to which she replied: 'Ah, from Leiden.'

peting theory of information loss is called 'interference theory'. It claims that new information highly similar to information that was already stored may replace and therefore destroy the original memory trace. The large number of Browns encountered in your life time may have erased all traces of the original Mr. Brown in our example. It will be realised that interference theory is not unlike the loss of cue uniqueness, because it is fed by new and similar contents. The major difference is that in interference theory it is assumed that the memory traces are erased, while according to the theory of cue effectiveness the trace is still preserved but can no longer be found. A vast body of memory research has demonstrated that forgetting is almost always due to interference, and only in pathological conditions to autonomous decay. The decay-theory of forgetting that corresponds with the common-sense notion that forgetting means the automatic erasure or destruction of information in the memory store is incorrect. But, as indicated above, it is very difficult to distinguish memory loss through interference from loss through inaccessibility, because there is no empirical test for the actual disappearance of information. In experiments with human subjects we can only demonstrate that some information cannot be found anymore. There has never been definite proof that information, once stored in memory, can ever be erased.

In order to judge the probability that a witness may correctly remember events from a distant past, we should ask ourselves which cues may best be used in interrogation, and what sort of interference by other but similar information may have taken place. From another study by Wagenaar (1986) it appears that 'what happened at the event' is a much more effective cue than 'where it happened', and 'who was involved'. The worst cue turned out to be 'when it happened'. Still, time is often used as the retrieval cue in forensic interviews, as in the famous question: 'Where were you on the evening of 19 December 1995?'

Retrieving a date

The classic studies on retrieving dates from autobiographical memory were done by Marigold Linton (1975, 1978). She noted in her diary several different events per day, and later used the descriptions of these events to retrieve the date at which they happened. Wagenaar (1986) in a similar study employed a more elaborate setup, in which for each event four pieces of information were recorded: 'what', 'who', 'where', and 'when'. Testing his memory for these events at a later date, these retrieval cues were presented to him separately and in combinations to retrieve the other ones. In this experiment the condition that is identical to Linton's study presented 'what', 'who', and 'where' as retrieval cues, with the task to reproduce 'when'. In the case of the stolen Mercedes, witnesses were asked to confirm that the event of Mr. Dukes activating the alarm happened on a specific date, six years ago. Thus the task was to find a date, given 'what', 'who', and 'where'. Wagenaar's 1986 results show that the chance of remembering an exact date, given the other three aspects as retrieval cues, must be estimated at 5 percent. The score for 'when' was low compared to his ability to remember other aspects: 59 percent for 'what', 76 percent for 'who' and 'where', given the remaining three aspects as retrieval cues. The meagre score for 'when' must mean that dates are rarely encoded exactly. The retrieval of dates is often more a matter of logical inference, or reconstruction with the help of 'landmark' events, like a holiday in India, moving into a new house, the birth of a child, running the New York Marathon, as time anchors, and trying to place the date of the required events relative to such anchors (cf. Loftus & Marburger, 1983; for a general overview, see: Larsen *et al.*, 1996). Whenever witnesses are unable to explain which landmarks they have used to reproduce a date for a trivial event after a time interval of several years, their testimony should be seriously doubted.

Memory changes

The second mechanism that causes loss of information from the memory store is called 'updating'. Older versions are replaced by newer versions, and access is in the first place to these new versions. The major difference with loss of accessibility or interference is that updating is usually not experienced as a form of forgetting. On the contrary, the new versions may be as accessible as the previous ones, and it is rarely realised that a change of content has taken place. We may compare this to taking a book from the library, and replacing it by a newer edition. In that case nothing would go wrong with accessibility, since the catalogue would still give access to the book. But unsuspecting users might not realise that they do not receive the original information. With books one might be alerted by the mention of the date of appearance and the number of the edition. Updating in memory does not leave such traces. The updated version presents itself as an original memory.

Updating is not always bad. It can be very useful to adapt memories to new knowledge and current conditions. One might even argue that a considerable section of our memory is used to keep track of the current status of the world. Our knowledge of the world needs constant updating, and it may be helpful to erase the previous records, or at least to make them less accessible. It serves a purpose to remember where you parked your car today; it may be confusing to remember where you parked it yesterday or the day before. Updated memories may become part of autobiographical memory: the things that eyewitnesses are asked to recall originally belonged to the *status quo* of the world at that time, which was subsequently and routinely updated.

The difference with the type of forgetting discussed in the previous sections lies in the subjective experience: fully accessible but altered memories are not experienced as being forgotten. On the contrary, they may be reproduced with great confidence, even though they are almost entirely inaccurate. The often reported lack of correlation between confidence and accuracy in witness statements is probably due to this effect (Bothwell *et al.*, 1986; Sporer *et al.*, 1995). Confidence is based upon the ease with which these memories are retrieved, their availability, while accuracy depends on the degree to which their content has been altered since they were originally acquired. One might even argue that the updating process may result in a negative correlation between confidence and accuracy: the more often a memory is retrieved for updating, the steadier the retrieval cues will become.

The problems related to witnesses testifying about memories from long ago is apparently twofold: to what extent is access inhibited by the decrease of cue specificity, and to what extent is the content of memories altered through a quite normal process of updating? Let us consider how these problems turn out for the owner of the stolen Mercedes and his witnesses.

Mr. Dukes's testimony

The first and most important witness was Mr. Dukes himself, who testified that activating the alarm in his car for him was a normal and strong habit, because he loved his Mercedes and because this type of car is often stolen by professional car thieves. He also said that the alarm system in his car was of a sophisticated type, especially installed on his request. Why would he forget to activate it? Moreover, he said that he specifically remembered the lights flashing when he switched on the alarm that particular night.

Applying what we know about autobiographical memories and in particular that they are retrieved by means of retrieval cues, we may conclude that Mr. Dukes was faced with no small problem. Why would the rather trivial act of switching on the car alarm on that particular night, an act that was, moreover, part of a routine, be stored in his autobiographical memory with cues that would enable him six years later to retrieve its specific date of 19 December 1995? How could he be so confident? Is it not more likely that his confidence was based on the application of a generic memory (Linton, 1982; Kotre, 1995), i.e., the general script for parking his car, in which activation of the alarm is a fixed step? Could he not have reasoned that he *must* have done it, because it was part of the routine that he always followed? And if indeed it was such a fixed routine, would he be able to remember one particular instance of it?

The rather surprising answer to this question is that an accurate recollection of the critical event was not all that unlikely. His testimony was *not* about a routine event, resembling many other instances. It was, in his version of the story, the *last* time Mr. Dukes followed the routine before the traumatic theft of his cherished

Mercedes. The next morning when he discovered that his car was missing, he must have asked himself: 'How is it possible that I did not hear the alarm? The thieves had no way of bypassing it, did they? Not for all the money that I spent on that system! Am I certain that I activated it last night? Yes, I have a clear memory of doing it!' He will almost certainly have discussed this with Mrs. Dukes and with all the other people to whom he explained in the following days and weeks that his Mercedes had been stolen. The memory task was not to remember the activation of the alarm after six years; the task was only to remember it after no more than nine hours. From then on he will have told -in technical terms 'rehearsed'- the story so often that the cues for the retrieval of the event remained highly effective. He almost certainly will continue to remember it in the coming 40 years, if he lives that long. The controversy with Safetycar will only make long-term recall more likely. The problem of remembering dates after a long time interval, as explained above, simply did not occur for Mr. Dukes.

There is, however, another problem. It begins with the fact that even highly routinised behaviour can go wrong. Although Mr. Dukes had developed a strong habit of activating his car alarm, he may have forgotten it just once. The extensive literature on absentmindedness (Reason, 1984) shows that under some conditions routines may break down. Lapses occur especially when a high degree of automaticity has been achieved, when there is a stressor, like feeling unwell or being in a hurry, or when the deviant behaviour is part of another highly routinised sequence (see also chapter 13). We know too little about the specific situation that night to judge this aspect of Mr. Dukes's behaviour. Although activating the alarm was probably a highly routinised action when parking his car at night, not activating it may have been equally routinised for parking his car during the daytime. Perhaps Mr. Dukes was in a hurry that night, or exceptionally tired. Maybe he was under the influence of alcohol, or was distracted by the sudden appearance of Mrs. Richards walking her dog at the very moment he stepped out of his car (see below). Who knows?

Let us, if only for the sake of argument, assume that indeed Mr. Dukes honestly forgot to switch on the alarm. That must have been an inadvertent act of forgetfulness, because he loved his Mercedes. In that case, he will not have realised his omission and therefore also not have stored it in his memory. When the next morning he tried to remember for the first time whether or not he had activated the alarm, he will not have found a clear recollection of doing it, nor one of not doing it.[2] In that

2 Memories of not doing something do occur: it has happened to many of us that we woke up in the middle of the night with the sudden knowledge of having forgotten to do something important, such as making a phone call or warning a colleague that some meeting has been cancelled.

memory void, his familiar 'locking the car' script may have produced an image of activating the alarm, which next turned into a clear memory of a detail that never happened. A weakness of this scenario is that it supposes the occurrence of two errors: a memory lapse, followed by a memory intrusion. But these errors are not fully independent: one is the ideal precondition for the other.

The situation of making two memory errors in succession has been studied extensively in the context of a frequently occurring real-life problem: taking a medicine at regular intervals, like once or twice a day. Empirical studies show that it is more likely to believe erroneously that one has done so, than to forget that one did (Wilkins & Baddeley, 1978). The result is that skipping a pill is the most likely error, rather than taking one pill too many. The task of remembering whether specific acts were performed or not is called *reality monitoring*. The problem is that the recollection of planning to do something may be mistaken for actually having done it. Reality monitoring is more problematic in young children and the elderly, but it is 'quite common in normal adults, and is an important source of errors in judgments, in action, and in belief' (Cohen, 1989; Schacter, 2001, chapter 2).

The court must estimate the likelihood of a scenario in which Mr. Dukes committed two errors in succession: he forgot to activate his alarm, and then he remembered erroneously that he had done it. In this scenario, the critical retention period is not of the order of six years, but of only nine hours. The alternative is, of course, that he did not in fact make these errors, but did activate the alarm and remembered it correctly.

In the margin of all this, it should be noted that so far in our discussion we have assumed that Mr. Dukes is not the crook that Safetycar suspected him to be. If in fact he sold his Mercedes on the black market and reported it missing to collect the insurance on it, there is, of course, no memory problem. On the other hand, it should also be realised that the logical basis of Safetycar's reasoning is rather weak. If Mr. Dukes is a crook, his alleged recollection of activating the car alarm is false. It is Safetycar's argument that an honest person would not remember whether or not he activated his car alarm on a particular night six years ago. Hence, if Mr. Dukes does remember such an event, his testimony must be false. This is a sort of catch-22. If Mr. Dukes claims that he remembers activating the alarm, he must be a liar; if he does not remember it, he loses his case anyway. Consultation of a memory expert will not resolve this dilemma.

Mrs. Dukes's testimony

Mrs. Dukes stated that she was still awake and up when her husband came home at half an hour before midnight on 19 December 1995. She stated that the Mercedes was always parked in the same spot on the premises, which could clearly be seen from the living room window. The family had the typical Dutch habit of leaving the curtains open at night. She says she actually saw her husband arrive in the Mercedes; she saw how he left the car, locked it and switched on the alarm. She saw the flashing lights of the alarm reflected in the neighbours' windows. She was certain all this happened on the night of 19 December 1995.

For Mrs. Dukes's testimony the same reasoning applies as for her husband's testimony: her problem was not to remember all this after six years. Also, for her the real problem occurred on the morning of 20 December, when the couple discovered that the Mercedes was no longer in its usual place. But there is also a difference between her and her husband: she was not herself responsible for activating the alarm and therefore did not have a memory of doing it, or not doing it. It could therefore not have been very difficult to create a positive memory in Mrs. Dukes's mind through post-event information, for instance by saying: 'You do remember that I switched on the alarm last night, don't you?' Is this what happened? Was she possibly influenced by her husband's suggestive remarks? We do not know the answer, because Mrs. Dukes was never interrogated about this episode.

Mrs. Richards's testimony

Mrs. Richards lived in the neighbouring house, with a clear view of the spot where the Mercedes was usually parked and in fact parked that night. Her neighbour's Mercedes was always something of a nuisance, as it hindered her when she used the side entrance of her house. That was why she had ample opportunity to notice that the alarm indicator on the dashboard was always flashing. Hence she concluded that Mr. Dukes never forgot to activate the alarm. On the night of 19 December 1995 she walked her dog, as she always did, around 11.30 PM. She was outside the house when Mr. Dukes arrived and had a clear view of the taillights of the Mercedes flashing when he activated the alarm. On 20 December she got up at 7.00 AM. The Mercedes was still there, according to her. Around 8.00 AM the car was gone. She thought nothing of it, because Mr. Dukes would usually leave home at about that time. It was only later that she heard that the car had been stolen.

The testimony by Mrs. Richards is surprising, because almost certainly she did not take part in the commotion in the Dukes's residence on the morning of 20 December. Only 'later' did she hear about the theft. Unfortunately, nobody cared to ask what she meant by 'later'; a few hours, a few days, a few weeks? If 'later' means 'a few hours', the same argument applies to her testimony as the one used for the Dukes: she only had to recall the events of the night before, which should not have been too difficult, although she could also have been influenced by suggestions from herself or others. If it meant 'a few weeks', Mrs. Richards would definitively have had a problem attempting to date her memory on the evening of the 19th, instead of on one of the other nights with exactly the same routine. It may therefore be argued that Mrs. Richards is no better a witness than Mr. and Mrs. Dukes, and possibly worse. On the other hand, one might assume that Mrs. Richards is less likely to be party to some sort of conspiracy, since it was not her car. But what do we know of the situation in which a neighbour comes to your door asking: 'You certainly do remember last Friday night, when you saw me come home after you walked your dog, and you saw me switch on the car alarm, don't you?' She might be tempted to be a good neighbour.

Cue specificity and suggestion

Assuming the question was posed to Mrs. Richards as indicated above, it obviously contained quite a number of retrieval cues: 'last Friday night', 'walking the dog', 'saw me come home', 'saw me switch on the alarm'. Such a profusion of cues may be quite helpful for the retrieval of an otherwise trivial event. But the problem is that the cues contained in the question also have the power to direct Mrs. Richards' memory search to the wrong night. Imagine that she saw Mr. Dukes come home on 18, not 19, December. The cues given to her direct her to her memory of what she observed on 18 December, and unless that recollection was explicitly dated, which is by no means likely, she would have no way of noticing that the question put to her led her to the wrong night. On the contrary, when asked after having just been told about the theft, the suggestion may easily have been created that her recollection must be of the night that preceded the theft on Saturday. Once established clearly in her mind in this manner, she would be able to testify about it in total honesty, without realising that she was -perhaps inadvertently- misled by her neighbour's question.

The situation is even worse. In the context of legal proceedings, the question can be phrased in two ways:

– On which day did you see Mr. Dukes switch on the alarm of his car?
– What did you see Mr. Dukes do on the night of 19 December 1995?

Both questions are meaningful, but the first is more difficult to answer than the second. In the first question 'What', 'Who', and 'Where' are the cue, whereas 'When' is to be retrieved. This would be very difficult to do, and without an explanation of the landmark events that Mrs. Richards used to do this, the answer would be rather unconvincing. The second question is in principle not much easier to answer, since the retrieval of an event with a date for a cue will rarely be successful. In this case, however, Mrs. Richards knew full well what the investigation was about, which means that, for all practical purposes, the second question is equivalent to and might have been replaced by:

– Did you see Mr. Dukes activate his car alarm on the night of 19 December 1995?

This, however, is a somewhat suggestive question, with its focus not on the date, but on the alarm. In that case it might easily have escaped Mrs. Richards's attention that the real problem was not *what* she saw, but *when* she saw it.

We do not know precisely which question Mrs. Richards was asked, or in what way she interpreted the question, in whatever form it was posed. Although both wordings of the question are acceptable in principle, in practice only the first question can lead to a useful answer. The second question, combined with what Mrs. Richards already knew about the purpose of her testimony, left nothing to reproduce that was not already present in the retrieval cues offered to her in the question. By using the information to be retrieved as a retrieval cue, the question of whether she saw the lights flashing becomes circular.

Things might have been even worse. Imagine that Mrs. Richards was asked whether she remembered the flashing taillights. If in fact she did not perceive a flashing taillight, the question may have made her add this detail to a memory that did not contain it originally. This effect is known as the post-event information effect and will be explained below. For now, the bottom line is that a question worded in such a way that it contains the answer should be avoided as often as possible.

A type of question often used in police interrogation and court proceedings that suffers from this flaw is the yes-or-no question: 'Did you (or did you not) see the purple pants of the robber?' The question provides the witness with information that he possibly did not yet know, and that may inadvertently be adopted into the original memory. When the next time the correct question 'What colour of pants was the robber wearing?' is asked, the witness may produce the seductive, but misleading information about the purple pants. From this it follows that in the case of Mr. Dukes's the court should be told about the time at which Mr. Dukes approached his neighbour to ask her about the night before the theft, and what question(s) he asked specifically.

The recognition of suspects in lineup tests

A notorious example of including the answer in the question is the recognition of a suspect by means of a lineup test. The procedure is that a set of photographs or of live persons is shown to the witness with the question: do you recognise the person you saw at the scene of the crime? The general rule is that the lineup consists of one suspect and at least five foils, all approximately fitting the description given earlier by the witness. The witness may point out one person only or, if none of the persons shown is clearly recognised, no one at all. The problem with this procedure is that the thing to be remembered, i.e., the appearance of the perpetrator, is possibly contained in the information presented to the witness, namely the suspect's face. When in a recognition test only the suspect is shown to the witness without any foils, the test is reduced to a yes-or-no question. Such single-person identification tests are frequently used by the police in the Netherlands. Being yes-or-no questions, they have been demonstrated to be highly suggestive (Wagenaar & Veefkind, 1992).

The problem is also not entirely avoided in multi-person lineups. Imagine an innocent suspect becoming involved in a criminal investigation because he resembles the real perpetrator. Showing this suspect to a witness in a lineup may lead to a positive identification only because he looks more like the perpetrator than the foils. Such a false identification is not the end of the story. Even if the witness recognises no one, the lineup may still have the effect that in the witness's memory the face of an innocent suspect takes the place of his recollection of the real perpetrator's face. The next time the witness is asked to identify the suspect as the perpetrator, as is not uncommon in courtroom confrontations, the witness may declare himself 100 percent confident that he remembers his face.

Yet another scenario may occur even when the suspect does not particularly resemble the perpetrator, but for some reason the witness' attention is drawn to this particular person in the lineup. This happened in the Demjanjuk case because the foils in that lineup did not fit the general description of the perpetrator given earlier by the witness. This made the lineup a multi-person lineup with only one reasonable candidate, to which therefore all attention of the witnesses was drawn (Wagenaar, 1988b). It may also happen when the photograph of the suspect has a different format than those of the foils; or is in colour while those of the foils are in black and white, or the other way around; or when it has a recent date on it, as is often the case with police photos, while those of the foils have much older dates on them; or when the suspect wears sneakers and the foils have the same black shoes as police officers usually wear. There are hundreds of ways in which the attention of witnesses can be drawn to a suspect by something other than a clear recall of his appearance (for a further discussion, see: Wagenaar, Van Koppen, & Crombag, 1993, chapter 7). The essence of our problem with lineup tests is that, although they are meant to test the first process of losing access to one's memories as outlined above, they may actually introduce a second process, that is, the distortion of memory.

Misleading post-event information

The effect of misleading post-event information was first studied extensively by Elizabeth Loftus (1979). The general procedure of experimental studies of this effect contains three stages. First, some event is presented to subjects by way of a series of slides, a motion picture, or a written account. Then, after a retention interval, a questionnaire is administered with various questions about the story witnessed in the first stage. Some of these questions contain a misleading element, for instance the question 'Did the blue car stop at the traffic light?' whereas in fact it had been a green car. In addition to the group of experimental subjects, there are two control groups. One of these is asked the confirmatory question: 'Did the green car stop at the traffic light?' The second control group is asked the neutral question: 'Did the car stop at the traffic light?' Then, after another retention interval, a forced-choice test is administered to the experimental subjects as well as the subjects in the control groups, in which each question requires the respondents to compare two versions of the story. In the critical question, two versions of the car at the traffic light are shown, one with a green car, the other with a blue car. The question to be answered is which of the two versions the respondents saw originally. Thus, it was established to what extent the memories of respondents in the experimental group were altered by the earlier introduction of the word 'blue'.

In this type of study the outcome is expressed by differences between the groups. Usually the differences between the experimental and control groups amount to tens of percents, meaning that misleading cues may indeed distort memory. Not every subject's memory, though, is altered in this simple manner, and certainly not about everything; altering a motor car into a horse drawn carriage in the memories of experimental subjects is probably not possible.

One clear finding is that small, ostensibly peripheral details are more easily modified than the more central aspects of a memory. The question 'Do you think you were momentarily distracted by the dog that crossed the street the moment you saw the two robbers leave the bank?' may be very effective for introducing a nonexistent dog. A dog is a peripheral detail when one is witnessing a bank robbery. But the ending '... the moment you saw the two robbers leave the circus?' will almost certainly fail to replace 'bank' with 'circus'. For this to happen the connection between 'robbers' and 'bank' is too central to the theme or script of a robbery. A similar reasoning holds for introducing peripheral but implausible aspects into the remembered story. 'Do you think you were momentarily distracted by the elephant that crossed the street?' will fail because it can easily be inferred that an implausible detail like an elephant would have been remembered. The flashing taillights on the night of 19 December 1995 are ideal for the operation of misleading post-event information, because they are peripheral as well as plausible details that do not really affect the general story line of how Mrs. Richards saw her neighbour come home after walking her dog.

It is not really necessary that misleading information is provided by an external source. Common sense inference can have the same effect (Johnson & Raye, 1981). What is true most of the time is probably an integral part of the general 'script' of everyday happenings. In turn, such a script will be used as a framework that directs recall. When no specifics are remembered, they will automatically be 'filled in' on the basis of the script. If Mrs. Richards is convinced that her neighbour always activated the car alarm, the flashing taillights will be part of the script 'Mr. Dukes coming home'. In Mrs. Richards' recollection the script will automatically reproduce the taillights, even if she does not recall the specific instance. Again, the event under consideration appears ideal for such an effect. All witnesses in this case claim that Mr. Dukes always followed a routine for parking his car near his house. On that particular night there was no reason to store more in memory than what was already present in the existing script, because nothing special happened and the theft had not yet occurred. Until the moment of recollection some time 'later', there had also been no reason for rehearsal of aspects that might have differed from the general script.

Misleading information is especially effective when a person's attention is not drawn to the discrepancy. A question such as 'Did the blue car stop at the traffic light?' focuses on the stopping, not on the colour of the car. Likewise, it could be highly effective to ask Mrs. Richards: 'That night when you saw me come home late, that was last Friday, wasn't it?' Now the focus is on Friday. Although the alarm is not even mentioned, it may well be inserted automatically into her memory. Less effective would be: 'When I came home last Friday night, did you see me activate the car alarm?' Now the critical item is part of a question that might be answered with 'no' before the critical item becomes part of the memory. This is the reason why we should know more about the way in which Mrs. Richards was first asked to remember the scene. Her statement, taken six years later, only reflects the end result of a possibly creative memory process. The questioning in court should also be directed at the creation of her memory, not only at the end result.

A highly relevant aspect of the effect of misleading post-event information is the timing of the procedure. Remember the three stages of these experiments: first presentation of a story, next introducing misleading post-event information in a questionnaire, and finally a forced-choice test to establish whether the experimental subjects are indeed misled by adopting the post-event information into their memory. Imagine that the forced-choice test is given a week after the original event. Then we have a choice for the time of presentation of the misleading information: immediately after the original event, or briefly before the forced-choice test. From the results of control groups we know that the critical information, such as the green colour of the car at the traffic light, is almost certainly forgotten after one week. If the misleading information is given immediately after the original story, it may also become forgotten after one week. Hence, with both pieces of information forgotten, subjects cannot do much better than guess. That is exactly what happens: all three groups score about 50 percent correct answers. But when the misleading information is presented briefly before the forced-choice test, many subjects will remember it much better than the almost forgotten original information. They have no reason to question the misleading information, the true version of which they have almost entirely forgotten, and absorb the post-event information easily. In this situation Loftus, Miller & Burns (1978) found that 80 percent of the experimental subjects made the wrong choice. It is not necessary, though, to wait a full week for misleading information to have its effect. After a retention interval of a single day the wrong choice is already made by 70 percent of the subjects, provided that the forced-choice test follows shortly thereafter.

These results of timing can be explained by the quite logical assumption that a weak memory trace is more easily replaced than a stronger one. In the case of Mrs. Richards, the original memory of Mr. Dukes's arrival cannot have been very strong, since for her it was an insignificant event at the time. 'Later', when she was told about the theft, the original trace must already have been quite weak, if there still was a trace at all. If Mr. Dukes had in fact forgotten to switch on the alarm that night, the relevant trace would have been that the taillights did *not* flash. Unless Mrs. Richards realised that she was witnessing the first stage of a drama, which of course she did not, it cannot have left a very strong trace in her memory.

The relevance of our discussion of the possible effects of misleading post-event information is that it may have produced in Mrs. Richards the recollection of something that never happened. If she, in fact, did not see the flashing taillights on the night of 19 December, she may have heard a misleading version from Mr. Dukes at some point in time which she calls 'later'. It may have replaced the original memory in which the taillights did not flash.

Source awareness

Psychologists are not only interested in what people remember, but also in what people know about the operation of their own and other people's memory (see, e.g., Crombag, Merckelbach, & Elffers, 2000). This is called *metamemory.* Quite often witnesses are asked: 'How certain are you about this?' Such a question invites people to reflect upon the quality of their memory, upon reasons why their memories could be wrong and upon other possible sources of information by which they might have become confused. In the green car/blue car paradigm, a reasonable question would be: 'Are you sure that no one else told you about the colour of the car?' This question addresses possible conflicting sources of knowledge in memory. The tacit assumption is that we not only store information, but together with it also the source of that information. We are supposed to remember where our knowledge of the colour of the car came from: from the original observation or from the questionnaire offered afterwards. But a vast body of literature has revealed that this *source awareness* can be rather weak: we know many things without remembering how we obtained the information (the seminal paper is by Johnson *et al.*, 1993). When we briefly return to the metaphor of a library with bookshelves and a catalogue, source amnesia would mean that the catalogue does not say when the entries in the catalogue were made, or by whom. If the position information in the catalogue is mischievously changed so that the entry becomes linked to a new book, a *wrong* book, there is no way to find out that there had been a previous link and to what position the entry used to refer before the change was made. The old book has not been removed from the shelves, but it will be extremely difficult to find.

The effect of misleading post-event information cannot exist without this amnesia for sources. More precisely, it consists of a replacement of sources, not a destructive replacement of information within those sources. The recollection of a blue car does not imply that the green car is forgotten. It only means that the retrieval cue that was linked to the colour green in the original presentation has now become connected to the colour blue introduced by the questionnaire. Extensive research on the precise working of the effect has demonstrated that the original information, like the colour green, is not removed from memory.

An example of how such experiments may be conducted is found in the work of McCloskey & Zaragoza (1985). In the first stage of their experiment, a story was presented in which a toolbox was shown that contained a hammer. In the second stage it was suggested to the subjects in the experimental group that the toolbox contained a screwdriver. Control subjects received no further information about any particular tool. In the traditional setup, during the third stage the subjects were given a choice between 'a hammer' and 'a screwdriver'. As in Loftus' experiments, the misled group displayed a higher preference for 'a screwdriver'. But in a 'modified' condition, subjects were asked to choose between 'a hammer' and 'a wrench'. For the subjects in the control group the substitution of 'a screwdriver' by 'a wrench' should not make any difference, as neither of the two was ever mentioned to them. They would still have a clear preference for 'a hammer'. In the misled group in the modified experiment there should be a tendency to choose 'a screwdriver', but that was not one of the possible choices. For those who replaced 'hammer' in their memories with 'screwdriver', the choice between 'hammer' and 'wrench' would result in a 50-50 guess. Hence the misled group would reveal a lesser preference for 'hammer' than the control group. However, as it turned out, both groups showed an identical 70 percent choice of 'a hammer'. Being misled in a forced-choice test between 'a hammer' and 'a screwdriver' does not imply that the recollection of 'a hammer' is destroyed. It continues to dwell somewhere in memory and can be found if adequate retrieval cues are employed.

Loftus' position was that misleading post-event information destroys the original memory. One argument that seemed to support this notion was that expressed confidence in the choices as equally high for misled and not-misled subjects (Loftus *et al.*, 1989). Another argument came from an extra test, in which subjects were asked to indicate whether pieces of information came from the first or the second stage. Misled subjects had no way of discovering the source of their confusion (Belli *et al.*, 1994). It is obvious from the absence of source awareness in the library metaphor that these two arguments are in line with the notion that misleading post-event information affects the links between cues and stored information, but not the information itself.

In the Dukes's case we may conclude that the three witnesses may all have been influenced by misleading post-event information, either generated by their own logical inference or by the stories they told one another. After such a thing has happened, it will be very difficult to recover the original story, as source awareness will almost certainly be absent. After telling and probably retelling the story during a period of six years, the link between retrieval cues and the revised story has become far too strong to be undone by any type of interrogation.

Our expert testimony

One of us served as an expert on memory problems in this case. The basic arguments presented to the court were:

1. There are two processes that may obstruct memory: a loss of cue effectiveness over time, and distortion caused by post-event information. The problem in the case of the lost Mercedes is not the loss of cue effectiveness in the six years between the theft and the interrogation of the witnesses, but the distortion that may have occurred immediately after the theft was discovered.
2. We know that such distortions may easily occur, especially when the events to be remembered follow routinised scripts and were trivial at the time of their occurrence.
3. Frequent rehearsal of the story as told by Mr. and Mrs. Dukes has made it extremely difficult to find cues that will activate a possibly different original.
4. Distortion of memory through post-event information is especially difficult to discover, both by oneself and by others, because we often do not remember the sources of our recollections.
5. For Mrs. Richards the situation may have been even worse, depending on what she meant by 'later'. If she meant days or even weeks, she will have experienced the difficulty of finding the exact date for the events presented to her as cues. It is even likely that the date to be found in her memory was presented to her as a retrieval cue, which would make her testimony circular.

What the court decided

The court decided that indeed the retention period in this case may have been no longer than a few hours. The supposed effect of post-event information was not more than a speculation because it was not established as a fact that such information had been presented to the witnesses. For these reasons the testimony by Mr. and Mrs. Dukes and by Mrs. Richards was accepted as a sufficient proof of the fact that the Mercedes had indeed been stolen while the alarm was activated. Consequently, Safetycar was ordered to pay.

CHAPTER 9

Confessions after Repeated Interrogation or the Putten Murder Case

Confessions are sometimes called 'The Queen of Proof', apparently on the assumption that no innocent person will confess to a crime he never committed. This assumption, although not unreasonable in many instances, is wrong as an absolute rule, more wrong than many people may realise.

There are a variety of reasons why people may falsely confess. Gudjonsson (1992) distinguishes three major categories: *voluntary*, *coerced-compliant*, and *coerced-internalised* false confessions. In the first category we find people with a morbid desire for notoriety, people with an unconscious need to expiate guilt about previous transgressions, people who make insufficient distinctions between fact and fantasy, and people who for some reason or other try to protect the real culprit. Coerced-compliant false confessions occur when suspects want to escape temporarily from the hardship of the interrogation or the custody. Usually, they harbour the hazardous belief that they can always retract their false confessions later on, and that in any case the truth will come out eventually. Meanwhile, they do not themselves believe in the veracity of their confessions.

In the third category, coerced-internalised false confessions, we find innocent confessors who have come to believe their own confessions, even though they often have no clear memory of committing the offence. This chapter deals especially with a subset of this third category, which we will label 'Coerced-memory-based false confessions'. It concerns suspects who confess based on a false recollection of committing a crime. Our thesis is that some types of interrogations, in particular repeated interrogations, may illicit such false memories.

Autobiographical memory

Sincere false confessions in the category mentioned above are based on what one remembers of episodes in one's life. The question of how a false belief in being guilty of a serious crime may originate comes down to the question of whether a false memory of having performed some action can be implanted in someone's head. Not in just everybody's head; a mere one percent of the population would be enough to create a disturbing number of judicial errors. Empirical research about the malleability of autobiographical memory suggests a considerably higher proportion. In fact, there is no reason to believe that anyone would be exempt from such false beliefs, since the methods for implanting false memories are almost limitless. In chapter 8 we discussed misleading post-event information. There it was demonstrated that the memory of peripheral details of events can be changed easily by providing plausible but incorrect information at a time when the original memory has become sufficiently weak. Still, remembering a criminal offence that was never committed appears of a different order. Murders and the like are neither peripheral nor plausible for the average person. On the other hand, the techniques for introducing misleading post-event information in laboratory experiments are benign when compared to those that are often practised in criminal interrogations. The ethical constraints in laboratory experiments make quite a difference. Where researchers are bound by the rule that no harm must ever be done to human subjects, police investigators often believe that for the protection of society against criminals, harm done to suspects may be justified. This discrepancy between researchers and criminal investigators constitutes a major obstacle to the study of problems of interrogation: we cannot simulate police practices in our experiments. The objection against the outcomes of psychological experiments is often that laboratory studies are not realistic, that they have low 'ecological validity'. And it must be admitted that our admonitions about the effects of suggestive interrogation practices are usually based on extrapolations of the much milder effects in laboratory studies.

Here is an example. Loftus & Pickrell (1995; see also Loftus, Coan, & Pickrell, 1996) suggested to their experimental subjects that in their youth at one time they had been lost in a shopping mall or some other public place. They presented their subjects with descriptions of three autobiographical events provided by their relatives. A fourth, a false description of getting lost in a public place as a child was added to them. This false description was carefully prepared to ensure that it contained a sufficient number of true elements from the subject's life. The false aspect was that the subject had got lost for an extended period of time at the age of five, was found crying in the company of an elderly woman, and subsequently reunited with his family. Subjects were asked to read the four descriptions, to add more details if they could, or to indicate that they did not remember the incident. Thereafter the subjects were interviewed twice, with intervals of about two weeks. Each time the subjects were asked to recall each of the four incidents and to give more details. They were also asked to rate the clarity of their memories. Seven out of 28 subjects said already the first time they were interrogated that they remembered the fictitious event. Six more started to remember the event during later interviews. The clarity ratings tended to increase over time.

With respect to these results, one could argue that most people as children must have been lost at one time or other, in some place or other, and that therefore the induced memories could still be based on some actual experience. But that is not the point: the subjects in this study came to agree that they were lost at the age of five, in a specific place, and that the incident followed a specified scenario. This is not too different from a suspect confessing that he was in a particular place, at a particular time, followed by an elaborate confession containing many details, as we shall see.

Everybody's autobiographical memory is malleable. Some people are more vulnerable to this than others, in particular when carefully designed interrogation methods are used on them.

The Putten murder case[1]

On Sunday, 9 January 1994, the 23-year-old flight attendant Susanne Moebius was murdered in her grandmother's relatively isolated house in a wooded area near the Dutch village of Putten. Some witnesses reported to the police that about the time of the murder they had noticed a blue-green Mercedes in the neighbourhood. Gerald Markhout, who lived in Putten, owned such a Mercedes and was therefore interrogated about his whereabouts on this Sunday afternoon. Interestingly, there was some confusion about the real colour of Gerald's Mercedes. Many shades between light green and marine blue were mentioned by the witnesses, but finally - and conveniently- the witnesses came to agree that the Mercedes they had seen had the colour of Gerald's car. Gerald regularly took rides in his car to walk his dog, often in the company of others, such as his two sons-in-law Harm Francois and Marco Bijk and the somewhat simple-minded Bill Wedman. So, Harm, Marco and Bill were also taken into custody and subjected to lengthy interrogations.

---

1 The names of persons in this case are changed, but the name of the village of Putten and the actual circumstances are kept, because they were already revealed through the massive publicity given to the long sequence of investigations and trials, which lasted from 1994 to 2002. A full description of the case is provided by J.A. Blaauw (2000), *De Puttense Moordzaak*. The various judicial decisions are: Criminal Court Zutphen, LJN-no: AE1685, case 06/030123-94, 19 December 1994; LJN-no: AE1687, case 06/030120-94, 19 December 1994; Court of Appeal Arnhem, LJN-no: AE1889, case 21-000102-95, 3 October 1995; LJN-no: AE1892, case 21-000103-95, 3 October 1995; Supreme Court, LJN-no: AA9800, case 03256/00 H and 03257/00 H, 26 June 2001; and Court of Appeal Leeuwarden, LJN-no: AE1877, case 24-000688-01 and 24-000687-01, 24 April 2002.

In the end, Harm and Marco were accused of the murder, found guilty and convicted, mainly on the basis of their own confessions. Additionally, Gerald and Bill testified that they had actually seen Harm and Marco commit the murder. In court, however, Harm and Marco retracted the confessions they had made to the police. To no avail. Still, their confessions contained many discrepancies, and their stories about what had happened kept changing over time. They did not corroborate each other's testimonies which, moreover, contradicted physical evidence in the house. Also, the testimonies by Gerald Markhout and Bill Wedman were inconsistent, mutually contradicting, and in disagreement with Harm's and Marco's confessions as well as with the physical evidence.

Worst of all, the DNA from traces of sperm found on the victim's body was not from the two suspects nor the two witnesses, but from an unknown fifth person. To explain this, the prosecution argued with the help of an expert witness that the two suspects, after raping Susanne, must have 'dragged' out of the victim's vagina old sperm from an earlier contact she must have had with an unknown person on that same day. The identity of this 'earlier contact' was never established, nor was it in any way excluded that Susanne had simply been raped and murdered by this unknown man. The confessions had brought the police investigations and the judicial reasoning to a definitive halt.

As far as could be established, Harm Francois and Marco Bijk were not put under extreme duress during interrogation, at least not in the physical sense. They were probably not very bright, but they had surely been able to understand that their confessions would lead to long prison sentences. So, why would they confess to the murder of Susanne Moebius in the full realisation that they were innocent? There are a number of passages in the interrogations which indicate that they may belong to Gudjonsson's third category of coerced-internalised false confessors, that is, confessors who have become falsely convinced that they actually committed the crime without really remembering it. Here are some quotes from their confessions[2]:

Harm Francois:

- I must come to the conclusion that I have been in the house. The strange thing is that right now I cannot remember a thing of what happened in or around the house, even though I want to remember it very much (p. 167).
- If I must draw a conclusion, then I am following Marco into the house. It makes me sad and angry that I cannot remember anything... (p. 168).

2 All page numbers in this chapter refer to Blaauw (2000) unless otherwise indicated.

Marco Bijk:

- I experience it as an immense pressure, everything you have explained to me about what has happened, and what I really should have remembered (p. 174).
- The case drives me crazy, as I know for sure that I did not commit the murder (p. 171).

From these quotes one gets the distinct impression that the two suspects have no clear memories about what, according to their interrogators, must have happened, but there are also some indications of their willingness to entertain the idea that they might have been involved. Subsequently, they appear to begin to remember things, albeit hesitantly and fragmentary.

Harm Francois:

- I am following Marco, and we end up behind the house. Now I wonder: Will she invite us to come in? This could be an answer. Why? Because she knew Marco. I will certainly not take the initiative to enter the house. In my head the logical consequence is that she addresses Marco. She asks: Do you want to have a drink? and then it is gone (p. 168).
- The way I experience it, I screwed her first, and then Marco (p. 178).
- I cannot indicate where in the house we have screwed her. I thought it was in the hall. But it is certain that she was also screwed by Marco (p. 179).
- After a right turn I saw a little house on the left-hand side of the [road]. Outside the house I honked, and Marco began to wave his arms enthusiastically. I saw that Susanne was entering the entrance to the house.... Jointly we entered the house through the back door.... Then Marco turned to me and made a sign that she could be screwed.... I also heard Susanne say: 'Man, fuck off.' She was shouting this... Immediately Marco gave her an intentional blow on her head.... immediately I forced her on to the ground. I noticed that she resisted .... Marco kept her at her wrists. I wanted to screw her. When I was ready, Marco came upon her, and started to screw her.... Then there was a struggle and there was some violence. I grabbed a knife.... Then I stabbed her with that knife in her throat.' (Arnhem Verdict, cf. footnote 1 supra)

Marco Bijk:

- I am putting a definitive end to all these proposed flashes, images, fantasies, and dreams. It has just been the reality that on the afternoon of 9 January 1994, I was in that house... [he saw Harm lying on top of the victim] in a door opening at the right-hand side of a hall. [He could not see whether the girl was raped because he was] too close, and looked Harm on his broad back. [The girl did not move]: I could see this, because I was very close. I had the strong impression that the girl

was unconscious. I saw that the girl moved only because Harm moved. Especially her legs and feet. Harm's energy was, so to say, transmitted to this girl (p. 172).
- She was lying with her back on the floor. Her right cheek was touching the floor. Her hair, she had long hair, was on the left side of her face. I told you already that I was the last one to return at the car; Harm, Gerald and Bill were already in it. (Verdict Arnhem, p. 12)

These passages read like true memories, not like something the suspects have come to believe without really remembering it. Still, the overall impression one gets from the large number of subsequent interrogations (see table 1) is that, to begin with, the four men did not remember anything. Then, tricked by their interrogators, they gradually became convinced that they must have had something to do with the murder, even though they could not remember details. Next, they started to remember things, first in the form of flashbacks and disconnected images, that finally evolved into a relatively coherent story. The statements from the final stages of the interrogation were used as evidence and quoted in the various court rulings. That it had taken considerable time for the statements to develop into coherent stories was not really considered by the courts and in any case not mentioned in their verdicts.

There are, of course, two explanations for the slow development of the stories. One is that they were created by the suggestive techniques during the interrogations. The other is that the four men could only gradually be induced to tell the truth. The latter explanation is in accordance with common police experience and simple logic: criminals are not particularly thrilled to confess to rape and murder. So, a little persuasion may help. To the police the first explanation is less likely for two reasons. First, because it assumes the innocence of the suspects. The assumption of innocence may be a basic principle of criminal law, at least in the Western world, but it is certainly not the working hypothesis of police investigators. In their minds a slowly developing confession is no indication for the probable innocence of a suspect. The second reason is that investigators, judges and jury members alike do not really believe that truly innocent people will easily confess to rape and murder. Yet, in this case the final acquittal of Harm and Marco, after having served prison sentences of eight years, indicates that the court of appeals came to believe the first explanation, that is, that the confessions were produced by suggestive interrogation techniques. For this the following arguments – among others – were listed in the final verdict of the appellate court:

a. The suspects were kept in isolation by the police for a period of two months. They suffered from a state of disorientation, also assisted by the inordinate number of interrogations, lasting long and deep into the night.
b. Their disorientation was further promoted by the presentation of pieces of in-

formation as if they were certain, whereas in fact they were uncertain and sometimes blatantly untrue.

c. The suspects were informed about each other's statements, so that a shared story could develop even though they were not in direct contact with each other. The same holds for the key witnesses Gerald Markhout and Bill Wedman. Especially the latter was known to be intellectually backward; he had no resistance against the suggestions of the interrogators, and produced the most damning accusations, which were in turn presented as certain facts to the two suspects.
d. The investigation was exclusively directed at proving the guilt of the two suspects. No attempts were made to falsify the hypothesis of guilt, or to investigate other possibilities.
e. Although there are a few consistent statements in the confessions, there was a remarkable number of inconsistent statements.
f. Many of the elements in the confessions that were interpreted as 'intimate knowledge' were already in the public domain when the two men were arrested.
g. Other details, not in the public domain, were presented to the suspects by the police during interrogation, or at least strongly suggested to them by simply repeating the same questions over and over.
h. Although the examining judge gave the two men the opportunity to recant their confessions, it was obvious to them that by doing so they would worsen the conditions of their detention.
i. The statements can be characterised as speaking in dream images; as speaking in terms of logical conclusions on the basis of facts presented to them; as a continuous change between confessions and denials, even after their confessions had been recorded; as sketching a large variety of ways in which the crime could have been committed. In this sense the pattern of these confessions differs from what the court usually encounters in criminal trials.

From these observations by the appellate judges, it becomes obvious that the court believed that such and similar practices may indeed elicit false confessions, even of murder. Were these practices really employed on such a scale that this unlikely result could have been obtained?

Trickery and deception

The false memories in the 'lost-in-the-shopping mall' study discussed above were brought about by a deceptive trick: information provided by family members was used to produce a compelling but untrue story. The effect of this trick probably worked through the same stages as were found in the Putten interrogations. At first no specific memories corresponding to the description of the event given by the investigators were retrieved. But the subjects did not detect the deception and concluded instead that they must have forgotten it. Then, trying to remember what they assumed they had forgotten, they may have found some vague recollections, possibly of some other, somewhat similar incident or of stories about other children being lost. Their active search for an appropriate memory may create some flash-like images, which gradually and on the basis of logical inference, develop into a more or less coherent story. Losing sight of your parents in a crowded shopping mall must be very scary. Imagining how a child would feel under these circumstance is not difficult, even if you have not experienced it yourself. Asking for help from a trustworthy-looking adult would be the obvious thing to do. Imagining such a scenario, given a sufficient time interval, may well develop into a sufficiently detailed and clear story to be acceptable as a real memory from a confused source (see 'source awareness' in chapter 8).

The starting point of this sequence is the application of a trick. Was such trickery also used in the Putten murder case? Yes, it was! We distinguish six different types of tricks, although they may well have been applied simultaneously. The problem of identifying the occurrence of such tricks, however, is that the interrogations were not recorded verbatim. As is usual in our country, the investigators wrote summary statements at the end of each interrogation, usually no longer than two pages for each hour of interrogation. Our quotations are taken from this indirect source. Here are six different tricks that were applied in this case:

1. *Implanting ideas when the suspect states that his memory is vague and shaky.* An example is the question put to Harm Francois: 'What did you tell Gerald when he asked why you were driving like crazy?' (p. 165). Harm did not remember having been there, let alone having driven very fast, or having talked to Gerald about it. Still, the question may have shaped an image in his mind which, when reproduced later, would fit in nicely with Gerald's statement. Precisely this phenomenon was empirically demonstrated by Crombag, Wagenaar, & Van Koppen (1995). It is also known as the 'When did you stop beating your wife?'-trick.
2. *Inducing the suspect to speak in a hypothetical manner.* The investigators asked Marco to imagine what he could have done after the victim was stabbed to death. He responded: 'I think I would have cleaned up the mess, as I am a caring type… I imagine that I was sitting on my knees, next to the victim, and that I removed some of the traces. It is quite possible, now that I come to think of it, that I put some things away, put a fallen floor lamp upright, and would have covered the girl… I imagine she had no clothes on, and that I covered her with something close by. It was her grandmother's house and there would have been a blanket around, or something' (p. 173). The problem with such an exercise of imagining is that it may leave a more or less clear image in the mind of the suspect that may later be mistaken for a true memory.

3. *Explicit deception* (such as the presentation of fabricated forensic evidence). An example is related to a textile fibre found on the clothes of Harm Francois. From this the forensic laboratory concluded that there was 'a possibility of a contact' between Harm's trousers and the doormat in the home of Susanne's grandmother. But since it was just an ordinary doormat, the fibre could have come from anywhere. Immediately, however, Harm was informed that fibres on his trousers had come from the scene of the crime. Harm's first reaction was still to deny his presence there. But already the next morning he made the statement quoted above: 'I must come to the conclusion that I have been in the house. The strange thing is that right now I cannot remember a thing of what happened in or around the house, even though I want to remember it very much' (p. 167). This is an apt illustration of the crucial step from denial to acceptance, followed by an active search for recollections.
4. *Confronting the suspect with other people's statements.* Harm Francois was told that Marco had said: 'Let us tell nobody that we were in the woods' (p. 165). And also that Marco had declared that Harm had grabbed Susanne and had thrown himself upon her. Harm, instead of simply rejecting these statements, began to worry about his own memory, and tried to remember the things that Marco had said. The second statement also constitutes a clear example of deception, since Marco had said nothing of the kind. On the contrary, the previous day Marco had declared that he had not gone with the others on the usual Sunday afternoon ride.
5. *Informing the suspect about true details of the crime.* Marco Bijk was informed by the investigating judge that the victim was killed by stabs in her neck and throat. When Bijk later on repeated this information to his interrogators, it created the false suggestion that he had intimate knowledge of the events.
6. *Inducing the suspect to make guesses.* Harm was asked to guess where the murder weapon might have come from. His guess was that it came from the boot of Gerald's car, because it was open when they came out of the house afterwards. He further guessed that it might have been dropped in a well, in the Van Eeghenlaan, or in Gerald's barn, or in Marco's house (p. 169). The problem with these guesses is that if one of them would prove to be correct, the conclusion of intimate knowledge would have been drawn. Or, alternatively, the act of guessing might create an image in Harm's mind that might later on be offered as a real memory.

Our colleague Peter van Koppen (Van Koppen, 2000) made an overview of the uses of these deceptive techniques in his written report to the defence. Table 1 presents some of his results.

Table 1 ***The use of deceptive tricks in the Putten murder case (number of interviews)***

Trick	Francois	Bijk	Wedman	Markhout
Memory implantation	17	23	–	10
Hypothetical talk	4	12	2	7
Deception	1	14	1	2
Confrontation with information from others	16	21	4	4
Informing about details of the crime	4	5	2	22
Inducement of guessing	1	6	2	2
Total number of interrogations	67	43	21	61

The overall picture is that Harm Francois and Marco Bijk were exposed to quite a number of interrogation tricks, in particular to memory implantation and the transmission of information from others. Wedman was the least exposed to tricks of all sorts. Markhout was especially fed with factual information about the crime. These differences can probably be explained by the fact that the four men were interrogated by different members of the police team. Also their different roles as suspects and witnesses may have resulted in different repertoires of tricks.

Even though the numbers in table 1 suggest that the situation for the suspects as well as the witnesses has been such that false confessions and false testimony may have been elicited easily, it is still not proven that such techniques actually suffice to create false memories. In the next section we give a brief overview of the research on this problem.

False memories

False memories are most often studied in the context of the so-called 'recovered memory syndrome'. This relates to the phenomenon that some people say they remember psychological trauma which occurred earlier in their lives, and of which they have been oblivious for many years. However, such a sudden return of memory is improbable to say the least. It is more likely that such recovered memories are mistaken, in particular when they have returned under the guidance of therapists using suggestive techniques. Discussions of this can be found in Loftus (1993), Lindsay & Read (1994) and Crombag & Merckelbach (1996). A later discussion of the full breadth of what has since become known as the 'Memory Wars' (cf. Crews, 1995) can be found in the reports of a worldwide experts meeting on the subject held in 1996 (cf. Read & Lindsay, 1997) and more recently in a monograph by McNally (2003).

The debate about the veracity of recovered memories is based on two types of studies: case histories and studies of experimenter-induced deception. Case studies again can be divided in two classes: studies of cases in which the claim of a recovered memory is critically investigated, and studies of the recollections of people who were demonstrably involved in psychologically traumatic events. In the latter category we find victims of accidents, physical violence, war, and violent political action. Examples are studies of children by Malmquist (1986), Pynoos & Nader (1988), Eth & Pynoos (1994), and the study by Wagenaar & Groeneweg (1990) on the memories of concentration camp survivors. The general rule of such 'victim studies' is that the event as such and the rough story line are always well preserved and remembered at any point in their lives. However, the details of the incident may well become changed or forgotten.

In some studies the authors suggest that sexual trauma is a different matter and that, unlike other experiences, sexual trauma may be repressed and thus forgotten to the extent that later on the victim denies having been a victim of it (see for instance: Williams, 1994). However, the problem with such studies is that, unlike with most other traumas, there is no objective, independent evidence for the actual occurrence of the alleged abuse creating an initial memory. The most often-quoted study by Williams involved the recollections of women whose mothers had taken them to a clinic because of a suspicion of sexual abuse. For an unknown number of these women, the suspicion may not have been justified. Some others of these women were younger than three years of age when the abuse was alleged to have occurred, which means that at the time they must still have been in the period of 'childhood amnesia' (Usher & Neisser, 1993) and that the fact that they did not remember it does not necessarily justify the assumption of repression. Whether the totality of these cases accounts for the 38 percent 'repression of sexual abuse' reported by Williams, is unclear.

A solution for these types of problems is to investigate individual cases, for instance on the basis of files of criminal or civil lawsuits. Examples of this approach are found in studies by Schooler, Bendiksen, & Ambadar (1997b), the critical analysis of the case of Jane Doe by Loftus & Guyer (2002), and Wagenaar's analysis of the case of Yolanda (Wagenaar, 1996a). Although at first glance such studies may seem helpful, the truth is that case histories cannot logically prove the veracity of recovered memories for a number of reasons (see also chapter 5 of this book). In the first place, there is no proof of the occurrence of the traumatising event. In the second place, it is logically impossible to prove that an event has been forgotten. In the third place, in such cases almost without exception deceptive information has been supplied, in therapy or otherwise, that could have created the false memory. In the fourth place, it cannot be proven that the final recollection is a reliable copy of the memories that were lost.

Sometimes an attempt is made to bring such discussions to an end by relying on a court verdict: the abuse really happened if a court convicted an alleged perpetrator for it. But here we run into a nasty type of circularity, in that the existence of a particular memory phenomenon is taken to be proven on the basis of a verdict that itself was based on the conviction that such a phenomenon exists, often on the authority of a memory expert who testified to it in court. The 'Memory Wars' have produced two opposing parties called 'believers' and 'non-believers'. If believers are not able to prove their theory by accepted scientific means, it should not happen that the theory is declared proven only because believers testify about it in court.

The other line of reasoning is concerned with the question of whether memories of entire events, such as an extended period of sexual abuse, can be implanted by the use of deceptive techniques. We saw the example of remembering that one was lost in a shopping mall. As a trauma this is benign compared to being abused for many years. The problems faced by experimenters are of two kinds. First, it is unethical to suggest memories of abuse to human subjects. Second, the thesis is not that everybody will be vulnerable to deception of this kind; possibly only a small group of people with a pre-existing psychological problem or disorder could be made to generate a false memory of this kind. Consequently, the empirical studies can always be criticised for not quite proving that false recollections of sexual abuse can be induced by the use of deceptive techniques, like some forms of interrogation or psychotherapy. But here are some examples that come close.

Van Mancius (1994) reported a study in which subjects saw three different crime-related video passages: A, B and C. Immediately after the presentation questions were asked about the subjects' opinions on some of the issues in the videos. Then, two weeks later, subjects in the control group received more questions about the events in videos A, B, and C; subjects in the experimental group received a few questions about A, B, and C, but the majority of questions were about a video D, which they had never seen. Since the subjects were questioned about their opinions, not about the factual contents of the videos, they found it relatively easy to answer the questions. Still, by doing so, some elements of video D were smuggled into their minds from information about it contained in the questions. After another two weeks all subjects were asked to describe the videos they had actually seen. Twenty seven of the 46 experimental subjects described a video with at least some elements from video D. Seventeen of those showed a complete implant, which means that they described only two of the videos A, B, or C, and produced an equally detailed description of video D. The memory of a criminal event was created only by asking questions that provided some verbal knowledge about the events in video D.

It is likely that just imagining an event may lead to the storage of the resulting images in memory. Because of 'source amnesia' there may subsequently be a problem of realising that these events were only imagined. A simple demonstration is found in a study by Garry, Manning, Loftus, & Sherman (1996). To begin with, subjects were asked to fill out the Life Event Inventory, a questionnaire in which subjects estimate the probability that they were ever involved in a number of events like being taken to an emergency room late at night, having found a 10-dollar bill, being saved by a lifeguard, or having broken a window with one's hand. Next, two weeks later the experimenter picked four of these events and asked each subject to visualise them. This is a well-established technique, frequently used in police interrogations. Immediately after the visualisation, subjects were told that the experimenter had misplaced their Life Event Inventory test from the previous week, and they were asked to fill it out once more. The question was if their probability ratings for the four visualised events had gone up.

Table 2 ***Percentages of subjects who changed their probability estimates in the Life Events Inventory in the study by Garry* et al. *(1996)***

	Decreased	Unchanged	Increased
Events not visualised	10%	65%	25%
Events visualised	9%	57%	34%

The results are shown in table 2. The effect is statistically significant in the predicted direction, but not large. It should, however, be realised that the experimental manipulation is not very strong, merely some visualisation. Moreover, the subjects could easily guess what was expected of the manipulation. This effect of visualisation, or imagining, is called *imagination inflation*, and has been found in other studies as well (cf. Paddock *et al.*, 1999).

A subtler design was tested in a study by Mazzoni *et al.* (1999). First-year psychology students were routinely required to take a 'standard' set of psychological tests. One of these tests, administered by the Department of Experimental Psychology, was the Life Events Inventory. In the Department of Clinical Psychology, each student also took part in an individual session of dream interpretation. Here a deceptive design was used in which the dream presented by the student was systematically interpreted as a sign of a forgotten traumatic event dating from before the age of 3. In a number of steps the dream was first related to a particular type of feeling, like fear or loneliness. Then the student was made to agree with this interpretation. Next the feeling was globally related to a class of events that was said to be known to cause such feelings. Finally, a specific event was introduced as the most likely candidate, and it was suggested that this event must have happened to the subject. If there was no recall of this target event, the psychological mechanism of repression was explained to the student. Three to four weeks later the subject again filled out the Life Events Inventory. The results for the suggested events 'got lost in a public space', 'was abandoned by my parents', and 'found myself lonely and lost in an unfamiliar place' are shown in table 3. The conclusion is obvious: suggestive dream interpretation induced a massive shift towards remembering the suggested event.

Table 3 ***Percentages of subjects who changed their probability estimates in the Life Events Inventory in the study by Mazzoni*** et al. ***(1996)***

	Decreased	Unchanged	Increased
Not suggested in dream interpretation	40%	30%	30%
Suggested in dream interpretation	13%	9%	78%

Misleading effects of interrogation techniques

The limits of ethically acceptable experimental manipulation are more or less reached in the design by Mazzoni *et al.* Suggesting a past of repeated sexual abuse would obviously be ethically unacceptable. Equally, the interrogation methods applied to Harm Francois and Marco Bijk would not be acceptable if applied in a psychological laboratory. The question of whether the purpose of criminal investigation is a sufficient excuse is, to our minds, irrelevant; the real worry is not about the ethics of interrogation methods, but the risk of obtaining false evidence. It is obvious that 40 to 60 interrogation sessions with in principle cooperative suspects cannot possibly have been aimed at obtaining more factual information. We do not know how long each of the sessions lasted, because the times of beginning and ending are only reported for 26 of the 244 interrogations. Based on these 26 sessions, we arrive at an estimated average length of two hours per session. After, say, 80 to 120 hours of interrogation there cannot possibly be more to say, even about a murder, in particular when the entire incident cannot have lasted more than at most ten to fifteen minutes. It was also unavoidable that the long sequence of interrogations must have led to visualisations and to some degree of imagination inflation which we now know may well result from this. Did it also cause the two men to remember a murder which they had not committed?

When we closely follow the depositions of the interrogations, even though roughly only 10 percent of what was said is reported, we cannot fail to notice that Francois and Bijk were always in doubt about the reality of their memories. They 'saw' images and flashes, but they never indicated having the concurrent feeling they had actually been at the scene of the crime. They did make positive statements of how they raped and killed the victim, but invariably based on descriptions of their visualisations. They came to what they thought was the logical conclusion, that is, that these visualisations must be of true events, also because of the factual but misleading information given to them by the police. Their confessions were the joint product of images that lacked a concordant 'reality feeling' and logical inference from alleged facts handed to them by their interrogators, which added a context of reality without a clear 'sense of reality'. Hence their confessions fall somewhere halfway between the two categories in Gudjonsson's third category of coerced-internalised false confessions. In the last stage of their trial the fluctuation between believing and not believing their memories ended in total disbelief. But by then the harm had already been done. They argued that their confessions were obtained under strong pressure from the police, endless interrogations at all times of the day and night, and threats. They came to realise that the images in their memories had been implanted by the police. This retraction was not unlike what happens to quite a few people who at one point were made to believe that they had been victims of sexual abuse. Many of those have retracted their stories and sued their therapists for the damages caused by suggestive forms of psychotherapy (Lief & Fetkewicz, 1995). In 2002, eight years after the death of Susanne Moebius, the 'Putten Two' were acquitted by the Appellate Court of Leeuwarden. The verdict argued (see above) that the discrepancies between the two confessions, between the confessions and the testimony of the witnesses Markhout and Wedman, and between the confessions and the physical evidence were simply too large. The course of events as contained in the indictment was considered impossible. This conclusion, combined with the fact that an unknown man had left traces of semen on the victim's body made it less than likely, according to the court, that Susanne had been murdered by Harm Francois and Marco Bijk.

Still, as proof of existence for the implantation of a false memory of having committed a criminal offence, the Putten murder case is not entirely satisfactory. It is no more than a case history and contains all the weaknesses of case histories as scientific proof. We do not know for a fact that Francois and Bijk at any time came to have something like clear, reality-linked memories of the rape and murder. There is ample evidence that they were always aware of the difference between these recollections and normal memories. What is even worse, we still do not really know if and to what extent these memories were created by the interrogation techniques, because we do not know for certain that the two men were not really involved in the crime. The discrepancies in their statements only demonstrate that some parts of their confessions must have been false. This leaves the possibility that some other parts were true. Retraction of the entire set of their statements and the exonerating testimony of their families, stating that the men had been at home on that particular Sunday afternoon, may be construed as a joint effort to help them escape their punishment. The final acquittal by the Leeuwarden Court of Appeals does not constitute scientific evidence of their innocence. Not even the eventual identification of the unknown fifth man, whose semen was found on Susanne's body, or even a complete confession by him would entirely justify the conclusion that false memories were implanted by their interrogators in the minds of Harm Francois and Marco Bijk, since this mysterious fifth person might also falsely confess for some reason or other, including irresponsible interrogation techniques.

What we *do* know, however, is that the interrogation techniques employed in the Putten case, especially the almost endless repetition of the same questions about the same facts, enabling the interrogators to resort to the types of deceptive techniques mentioned above, have been shown to produce false memories in well-controlled experimental conditions. It is not possible to create false memories of sexual abuse or murder in empirical studies. Laboratory studies constitute the best that science can offer. Since the protection of the rights of defendants in criminal trials is a major responsibility of the court, the warning these studies give should suffice. Interrogations should not be prolonged interminably, they must always be documented in their entirety, preferably through audio or video registrations, and trickery as described above should never be employed.

Summary of the experts

Our colleague Van Koppen served as the expert in the Putten case on the effects of misleading interrogation techniques. In his testimony he described and explained the interrogation tricks that were used in the interrogations of the two suspects, indicating all the passages in the depositions where instances of such tricks were to be found. He proceeded by offering an exhaustive list of the thirteen different scenarios described by the witnesses and the suspects. Moreover, he demonstrated that each of the two suspects and the two witnesses switched between different scenarios, and that in the end no stable and consistent choice of a scenario of the events could be obtained. From this the following conclusions may be drawn:

- Given how frequently various forms of deception were used, it is almost certain that at least part of the confessions was not based on any true memory.
- The continuous shifts among different scenarios illustrate the cooperative attitude of the suspects, who were apparently willing to produce hypothetical stories of what might have happened on demand for their interrogators, instead of stubbornly relying on what they remembered for certain.
- The summary depositions of the interrogations make it difficult to reconstruct the way in which the various statements of the suspects were influenced by the information offered to them by their interrogators.

What the courts decided

In 1994, the District Court in Zutphen rejected the complaint that the suspects had confessed under duress. According to the court, the alleged duress was not in evidence from the facts known to the court. On the contrary, the suspects had confirmed with their signature at the end of each deposition that they had made their statements in complete freedom. The fact that the suspects had been interrogated many times, during long sessions, and even during the night, had been approved by the suspects and even requested by them. The court was not aware of any illegal means or methods.

In 1995, the Court of Appeals in Arnhem confirmed the decision of the Zutphen District Court. The interrogators were heard as witnesses and declared unanimously that no illegal or improper methods of interrogation had been used. From the degree of consistency among all the statements, the court also concluded that they could not possibly have been produced without intimate knowledge of the crime.

Yet, in 2001 the Supreme Court of the Netherlands ordered a retrial of the case, though not on the consideration that something was amiss with the confessions of the suspects. The basis for this decision, called a '*novum*', was that the expert witness who had earlier explained the presence of sperm of an unknown person, had retracted his testimony, on the argument that before testifying he had not been given all the relevant information by the prosecution.

In 2002 the Court of Appeals in Leeuwarden in its sentence devoted only one-and-a-half pages out of a total of 32 pages to the problem of the sperm. The rest was devoted to a minute analysis of statements by witnesses and the suspects. It took five-and-a-half pages to discuss the methods of interrogation used and the resulting confessions. The final conclusion was that the confessions were not reliable enough to convict. The prosecution was censured for not addressing the inconsistencies in the confessions and for not responding to Van Koppen's report. It was deemed implausible that the suspects could have committed the crime in any of the ways described in their confessions. It may safely be assumed that the expert opinion of our colleague Van Koppen played a major role in the court's decision.

CHAPTER 10

Collaborative Storytelling or the Artist's Models and an Angry Neighbourhood

The artist and his models

Some years ago the nationally renowned sculptor Edward Green (a pseudonym) got in trouble with the criminal law. The favourite, although not exclusive, subject of his art is the female nude. Characteristic of his work is that it is both sensual and dynamic. The women he portrays are almost always young and beautiful, their postures highly sensual. Moreover, they are not portrayed in some static, more or less elegant posture, but looking at them, they appear to be moving. You can easily imagine what went on before and what is to follow. The combination of sensuality and dynamism gives his work an unmistakably erotic character, but it is by no means pornographic. The women are never portrayed as engaging in sexual behaviour.

Before modelling his subject in wax, Green makes many fast charcoal drawings of his models. Most of the time these models are dancers because, he says, dancers know how to express emotion in their movements. But dancers are not always available as models. Occasionally, he recruits models with the help of advertisements in local newspapers, but models thus recruited have little or no experience with modelling. They must learn how to do the job as they go along. Most of the models thus recruited turned out to be students at the nearby art academy. Sometimes they posed alone, sometimes in pairs.

For the drawings the models are asked to undress, and music is played. They are instructed to move with the music. But the music is not of the rhythmic kind to which you can dance in the way that every young person can. The music serves to create a somewhat ecstatic atmosphere. Its loudness makes communication between the artist and his model(s) impossible. Enveloped in a cloak of noise, the model is expected to surrender to the movement of her body and the emotions this arouses. She is not only expected to reveal her body, but also, and more importantly, her soul.

This is a difficult task. You are asked to put as much feeling and sensuality into your movements as you possibly can, but how do you do that? Perhaps the many drawings of other models on the walls of the artist's studio give some indication of what is expected, but when you ask for more directions, the artist invariably says you need to find out for yourself and follow your intuition. While trying to do what is expected of you on the floor in the middle of the studio, the artist himself is right next to you on the floor, making fast and rough drawings on large sheets of paper, one after another. There is some feedback for the model: so long as the artist is working frantically, you are apparently doing the right thing; when he slows down his drawing or stops altogether, you are apparently not doing the right thing. He may even stop the music and tell the model that she is not giving herself well enough, that she is stiff and inhibited and that she should let herself go. Admonishing his model in this manner makes for awkward moments and builds tension: 'What am I doing wrong? Maybe I cannot do this. What's wrong with me?' She may even start to cry, but when this happens, the artist feels guilty. He will try to reassure her, even embrace and caress her and try to explain his artistic philosophy. Expressed in idiosyncratic language, however, this philosophy constitutes a world of its own, almost impenetrable for outsiders.

The drawings thus made serve as a basis for the artist's sculptures. The final product will be in bronze, so he works in wax, small versions first, and eventually life-sized figures. At this stage the model is not asked to move, but to take a definite position. It may take a while before the right position is found, and finding it may involve touching the model. Touching may also happen during the work, to compare the feel of the developing shape of the work with the feel of the body of the model. What we mean to say is that the way in which the artist works with his model is at times rather physical. It is therefore easy to see how this way of working may lead to misunderstandings with inexperienced models. Which may have happened with some of them.

Trouble

At one point in time, four of Edward Green's models, all women in their early twenties, contacted the police to accuse him of sexually molesting them while they were modelling for him. We shall give them pseudonyms for easy reference: Ann, Babette, Christine and Dora. Ann, Babette and Christine accused Edward of indecently touching them on several occasions. Dora moreover accused him of raping her repeatedly. Confronted with these accusations, Edward did not deny having touched and caressed Ann, Babette and Christine, but according to him they misinterpreted his way of working. As to Dora's accusation of rape, he said that he had had a short-lived affair with her and that the sexual contact between them had been consensual.

The accusations of the four models were not coincidental. Before filing their accusations with the police, the four women had talked extensively and repeatedly about their experiences among themselves and with other people in their environment. Two of them had gotten to know each other because at times they had posed together for Green. The other two had come in contact with the first two because they were all students at the local art academy.

Why did they talk among themselves? Probably because they were uncertain about what exactly had happened in Edward Green's studio and what it meant. Was he just an artist with a somewhat unusual and at times embarrassing way of working and convoluted philosophical ideas to go with it, or was he using his artistic work also as a pretext for his own sexual gratification? And if the latter is the case, why hadn't they noticed this from the beginning and put an early stop to it? Sure, at times they had protested certain aspects of his way of working, but apparently to no avail, because it happened again. Maybe they had not made themselves clear enough about what they considered acceptable and what not. And why had they gone back to his studio again and again after their earlier experiences?

It is easy to see that under the circumstances the four women needed clarification about Green's behaviour and intentions, as well as about their own roles in it, before they could confidently file a complaint with the police. So they talked among themselves and also asked other people for their opinions. At one point in time they contacted the police to ask how they should go about filing a complaint and what would happen next, if they would decide to do so.

It took the women several months to make up their minds. The policeman to whom they had spoken earlier had to call them several times, asking whether they had decided to go through with it or not. In the end they did. Together they told their stories on the police, who next advised each of them separately to put their experiences to paper and to hand in those written reports. Next the police rewrote those in the formal language of criminal complaints and proceeded to take Green into custody for four counts of repeated sexual molestation and one count of repeated rape.

Green was questioned by the police. He denied all the accusations. Several other people were interviewed by the police, among them the sister of one of the alleged victims and the boyfriend of another, as well as a number of other young women who had been or were still modelling for Green. None of the other models voiced any complaint against Edward Green, but the office of the public prosecutor deemed the four incriminating statements enough to bring the case to court.

Evaluating the evidence

On the basis of what we have stated so far, it is not really possible to appreciate the full weight of the evidence against Edward Green. Should statements by four witnesses, all relating similar experiences, not be enough to convict?

Well, there are some problems here. The first is that the four witnesses cannot be considered independent witnesses, and that therefore their statements cannot, without further examination, be taken as corroborating one another. They talked extensively among themselves and with other people. The information exchanged during these talks may have changed or added to their original recollections of what had happened. This is the well-known problem of post hoc information, which is, of course, nothing new (see chapter 8).

But in the case of Edward Green more may have happened than just post hoc information exchange. It took the four women several months to decide to file their complaints. This in itself is not uncommon in cases like these. The accusation of sexual molestation is difficult to bring, because you will be asked embarrassing questions which you would rather not answer. So you hesitate to go forward, and may want to seek reassurance from other people. If there happen to be other probable victims of the same perpetrator, this will be very reassuring: you are not alone. But talking to other people and fellow victims in particular opens your testimony up to the suspicion of post hoc contamination of your testimony.

However, in this and in similar cases there is an extra aggravating problem. To begin with, it was not entirely clear what precisely had gone on in Green's studio. To undress in front of a man you hardly know, is not common behaviour for women. To move to music in this state is even more uncommon. You are instructed to put as much emotion into your movements as you possibly can. Under the circumstances your dominant emotion will probably be embarrassment. Obviously, that is not the emotion that you are expected to express; you are expected to feel sensual. Are you going to fake this feeling or really feel sensual? And if so, what will this do to you? Are you going to be erotically aroused? Are you expected to? And if you do your job well, is the artist not going to become sexually aroused as well? Perhaps that is precisely what the artist hopes for. Maybe his work is only a pretext to become sexually aroused himself and to seduce you. Are the artist's motives purely artistic, or mixed, or perhaps even entirely sexual?

Such questions probably go through your mind. During one session you may convince yourself that everything is alright: this is an honest artist doing serious work. But the next time he says something or touches you in a way that raises your suspicion again. Maybe his intentions are not entirely honourable. And for Dora, with whom Green admits to having been sexually involved for a while, the question may be whether the sex they had was really consensual or whether she was cleverly seduced. None of the models ever mentioned that Green had used force or threatened them in any way, which raises the question of why they did not protest his behaviour more forcefully at the time, if they protested it at all, instead of only feeling embarrassed and maybe even guilty at times.

That the accusing women at the time were not altogether sure about the answers to these and similar questions, is apparent from the fact that they kept coming back to Green's studio after having suffered what they later came to consider unacceptable behaviour on his part. Of course, the alleged victims were asked about this: why did they go back? In her official complaint, Christine answered with this: 'I did not always realise precisely what was happening. Only later on did the full realisation come to me.' Babette said: 'Things became clear to me only after I had stopped working for him.' Ann said: 'I should not have gone back to his studio, but somehow I expected that things would go back to normal.' And Dora, after having had unmistakably sexual encounters with Green, surprisingly said: 'I could not imagine that he wanted something sexual from me. I trusted him and we worked well together.' On the basis of these and similar statements in their testimony we tend to conclude that at the time these models were not altogether sure that something wrong or even felonious was happening to them, but they also were not sure that everything was on the level. They were confused.

After talking among themselves and to other people, things changed. The models came to agree that Green had indeed used his artistic work as a pretext for sexual abuse. Babette says that it was really her sister who convinced her that Green had been abusing her: 'I talked extensively with my sister and the more we talked, the more I became convinced that this had been all wrong.'

The accusing models gave two more reasons for going back to Green's studio. One was that they were paid for their work. Not a very convincing reason, because they were only paid 50 Guilders – about 25 US dollars – per session lasting several hours. Perhaps their anger was motivated by their eventual realisation that they were underpaid. The other reason they gave was that they each felt responsible for the completion of the sculpture for which they were posing. Christine said: 'We talked about this and we all felt that we were responsible for the completion of our sculptures.' That, however, is also not a very convincing reason, because the models knew from experience that it was not unusual for Green to use more than one model to pose for the same sculpture. The completion of any single sculpture was therefore not dependent on the continued availability of a particular model. Perhaps the models realised that their reasons for going back to Green's studio were not altogether convincing, which may have given them an extra motive to compare notes. Their behaviour needed some justification. And so they talked among themselves and to others in order to become clear in their minds about what really had happened and what their own role had been in the events. This, to our mind, was more than mere exchange of post hoc information. It is what we propose to call 'collaborative storytelling'.

Collaborative storytelling

We have taken the phrase 'collaborative storytelling' from the sociologist Jeffrey Victor (1993), but we are not sure that he was the first to use it. In his writings it is the name of the mechanism involved in the development of urban legends, but he does not give a clear definition. So let us try to define it. By collaborative storytelling we mean *a cumulative process of the mutual reinforcement of ideas, which occurs among people during the interpretation of ambivalent information.* Confronted with information that cannot be verified by direct observation, people tend to base their subjective certainty about what was the case on the judgements of others. Confirmation by others who were there or for some other reason may be considered knowledgeable about what happened or must have happened tends to strengthen our conviction that we are recalling and evaluate an experience properly. In particular, moral judgements are often largely dependent on other people's judgements. Whether we or other people present acted properly under the circumstances or whether another course of action would have been possible or preferable depends to a large extent on what other people think or say they think. So we talk about it, and together, bit by bit, we become clear in our minds about what happened and the role that we and others played in the matter.

So far, our account of what may happen when people are confronted with ambivalent recollections is of our own making. Let us see whether there is any support for this 'theory' in the literature. That people become uneasy when confronted with conflicting information and work to diminish the resulting uncertainty by changing their minds about parts of the information available to them is well documented in the literature, in particular the work connected with Leon Festinger's theory of cognitive dissonance (1957). That people are sensitive to other people's opinions and tend to conform their own opinions to what other people think is equally well supported in the literature, in particular in some of the work by Solomon Asch (1956). That people may actively try to pressure members of their group to conform to their own opinions is also well documented in the literature, in particular the work of, again, Leon Festinger and his associates Stanley Schachter and Kurt Back (1950). And finally, that people's recollections may easily become contaminated by their talking to other people is, as already mentioned, well documented by the work of Elizabeth Loftus (1979) and many others.

All this comes close to our 'theory' of collaborative storytelling, but it is not entirely on target. What appears to be on target is Leon Festinger's 'theory of social comparison processes' (Festinger, 1954). This theory is concerned with influence processes in social groups, and in particular with the way in which social processes influence the way in which we evaluate our opinions and our abilities. Now, at first glance, opinions and abilities may seem rather different things, but Festinger claims they are connected because '(a) person's cognition [his opinions and beliefs] (...) and his appraisals of what he is capable of doing [his evaluation of his abilities] will together have bearing on his behaviour' (op. cit., p. 117).

The main hypothesis of Festinger's theory (Hypothesis II) relevant for our purpose here reads as follows: 'To the extent that objective, non-social means are not available, people evaluate their opinions and abilities by comparison respectively with the opinions and abilities of others.' For this sort of comparison we will preferably choose those others whom we perceive as relatively close to ourselves (Corollary IIIA). If the abilities and opinions of those others are initially seen to be somewhat different from our own, we tend to 'change our own position so as to move closer to others' (Derivation Dl), as well as (Derivation D2) to try 'to change others in the group to bring them closer to oneself' (op. cit, p. 122).

In the Green case, the accusing women were uncertain in their opinions about what precisely had happened, as well as about their ability to do something else other than what they had actually done under the circumstances. Festinger addresses uncertainties such as these and, in his theory, postulates a general 'drive' in people 'to determine whether or not one's opinions are correct' (op. cit., p. 118). For the Green case, however, we need not postulate such a general human drive. People probably can and often do live with ambiguities, but if you are considering filing a criminal complaint with the police, you had better first get rid of the ambiguities relevant to your complaint. Moreover, Festinger states that 'with respect to most opinions (...) there is no inherent, intrinsic basis for preferring one opinion over another', as long as you come to agree upon it. This may be true in general, but if you as a group are going to file a complaint with the police, you should be sure that what you are going to report is incriminating enough to justify your complaint, and, moreover, that under the circumstances your own contribution to the events was negligible, i.e., that you were not able to behave in any other way than you did. In general terms, in cases like this all individuals involved in remembering are remembering for a particular purpose.

What we are suggesting is that, in the Green case, the accusing women not only had a strong motive to agree among themselves on what had happened and on their own involvement, but also to move – if they moved at all – in the direction of a more incriminating account of the events. A recent remark by John Kotre may be relevant in this context. He writes: 'When forced to make public statements about what is uncertain, people become very certain, persuading themselves in the course of persuading others' (Kotre, 1995, p. 55). And, we might add, becoming more certain themselves as they succeed in persuading others. Collaborative storytelling works by way of gradual and repeated mutual-reinforcement learning.

We do not mean to suggest that the accusing women in the Green case, during discussions among themselves and with others, decided to lie about Green's behaviour and their own involvement in the events. We believe that witnesses, involved in collaborative storytelling, may unwittingly come to believe the account they build together. While talking repeatedly, they may not realise that they are gradually adding to or slightly changing the events, or that they are gradually diminishing their own responsibility for what happened. This seems particularly likely with respect to their own involvement, because there is a moral issue here. According to their own account, the women kept going back to Green's studio even after they had been repeatedly sexually molested by him. That is of course surprising behaviour, crying out for an explanation. The explanations they came up with after, according to their own statements, having discussed this very issue among themselves were not very convincing, as indicated before. So maybe they changed the events somewhat. Probably not very much, for then they would have noticed the difference themselves, but maybe just enough to carry their account of the events beyond the threshold of a criminal offence.

From collaborative storytelling to co-constructing memories

When people talk about a shared experience, they do not simply exchange information. If that were the case, one might expect that the resulting recollection of their experience would probably be more accurate and complete than their initial recollections. Hyman, testing this very hypothesis, reports that group remembering indeed results in more complete versions of a story that the group members had heard earlier, but that in retelling they also commit more errors and are 'more confident regardless of the accuracy of their responses' (Hyman, 1994, p. 50). Similarly, Roediger *et al.*, wondering 'whether people trying to remember an event in groups can outperform individuals tested alone', conclude that 'in general, the answer seems to be no' (Roediger *et al.*, 2001). What happens when people engage in 'conversational remembering' is that the participants influence each others' accounts of what happened: 'Memories retold in conversation are jointly produced by speakers and listeners' (Pasupathi, 2001, p. 652). Together they 'co-construct' what they remember and 'co-participants, unknowingly, integrate each others' "false" facts into collective memories' (Aronson & Nilholm, 1992, p. 246). 'Both speakers and listeners contribute to the production of a shared recollection' (Pasupathi, 2001, p. 656).

For collaborative story construction during conversation the participants need not all share the experience that is the subject of their conversation, in order to share in the co-construction of a subsequent memory. Through showing belief or disbelief in a speaker's account of an event, through expressing sympathy, indignation or simply recognition, through asking questions, offering suggestions or consolation, a partner in a conversation who has no personal knowledge of an event may change and add to the other person's account of it and its subsequent recollection. The very fact, e.g., that a police officer takes the complaint of an alleged victim of some offence seriously may well strengthen the complainant's belief in his or her own story. When next the police start an official investigation and question possible witnesses, those witnesses may become convinced that their own already existing suspicions and the rumours they may have heard must be true, since the police apparently take the case seriously. When these witnesses next talk with the original complainant, he or she may take the suspicions of these witnesses, now 'confirmed' by the police, as corroboration of their own account and adopt parts of the information of these witnesses into their recollection. 'Experience of reality or meaning is created and maintained for the individual when it is mutually shared with others' (Hardin & Higgins, 1996, p. 30).

When the Green case came to trial, the court of first instance convicted Green of multiple sexual offences against all four women. The court apparently took the statements of the alleged victims as independent and at face value, in spite of all the talking that had preceded them. When next the court of appeals reviewed the case, it did not dispute the facts of the case, i.e., how Green had actually behaved towards these women. There was no need for this, because Green admitted to virtually all of it. However, it also decided that it was not proven to a sufficient degree of certainty that the women themselves had had no option but to tolerate his behaviour. Therefore, the conviction was reversed.

An angry neighbourhood

The Green case is not unique. Some years ago there was the case against a physiotherapist who was accused by a group of his patients of having sexually abused them in the course of their treatment, specifically of having touched them at times in inappropriate places. Also in this case the alleged victims discussed the matter extensively among themselves before filing their complaint with the police, and also in this case outsiders, and even a police officer, took part in those discussions. Also in this case the court of first instance convicted and the court of appeals reversed that decision. The case was a virtual carbon copy of the Green case.

The Green case is a fairly simple sort of case. We think that collaborative storytelling may also have occurred in much more complex cases of alleged multiple child abuse, such as the McMartin Preschool case (see further), the Fells Acre or Amirault case (Rabinowitz, 1995), and the case of Margaret Kelly (Bruck & Ceci, undated), all in the United States. Some time ago, one of us became involved in a Dutch case that was reminiscent of these cases.

The case was located in a medium-sized industrial town in the east of our country, in a low-income, working-class neighbourhood, where unemployment was the rule rather than the exception, and consequently many families were dependent on public assistance. In this neighbourhood there was a problem family, which we will call by the pseudonym of Nab, that consisted of father Harry, mother Irene, and two daughters Maggie (fourteen years old at the time) and Debbie (eleven years old).

There were really two cases. The first of those, case Nab-1, was concerned with the two daughters. They were both troubled children, who made it a habit to terrorise other children in the neighbourhood, bullying and intimidating them, calling them names and often hitting and kicking them. The parents of the victims repeatedly protested about Maggie's and Debbie's aggressive behaviour to their parents, only to find that the father turned against them. At one point father Harry even came to blows with one of his neighbours. The neighbourhood complained to the social services department and the police, who talked extensively to the parents of the two girls, to no avail.

Things changed when the complaints of the neighbours took a sexual turn. Maggie and Debbie were said to have forced other children to lower their pants on occasions, to have pinched the penises of boys and to have penetrated vaginas and anuses with their fingers and objects. If this really happened, it meant that Maggie and Debbie had, probably unwittingly, crossed the border into the more serious territory of sexual child abuse, while for them the sexual violence probably was just one more way to terrorise other children. Now the police really paid attention, for they had had a number of such cases in the city earlier. There was a standing investigative group of policemen, prosecutors and social workers that went by the name of the MOD-team – we never found out what this acronym stood for – that was rumoured to have developed a special method for investigating such cases.

The Nab-1 case received intense media attention from the local newspaper and radio and television stations. The investigative team began to hear many of the alleged child victims, as well as their parents. The result was a host of rather confusing statements. The two girls were finally convicted on the basis of their own confessions that were obtained from them without much pressure from their interrogators; the youngest girl was too young to really be convicted, instead the court ordered her to be placed in some institution. All the offences to which the girls confessed were said to have been committed in school yards, playgrounds and parks. So far on the Nab-1 case.

The Nab-2 case started at the time that the Nab-1 case was about to go to trial. The suspects in the Nab-2 case were the parents of Maggie and Debbie and the brother of the mother, Uncle Charlie, who was a regular visitor to the Nab house. Many people, including the police, had been asking themselves how Maggie and Debbie had become large-scale sex offenders. 'People are not born that way,' one of the interrogating police officers is reported to have said to Maggie, and this was the first indication that the members of the MOD-team entertained the 'transgenerational hypothesis' of sexual abuse, which holds that people who commit sexual abuse often have been sexually abused themselves. In this case the hypothesis would imply that Maggie and Debbie had learned their sexually abusive behaviour from their parents and uncle when they themselves were abused by them. There is some empirical evidence for the transgenerational hypothesis, but the relationship is weak at best (Knudson, 1995). But the hypothesis has many adherents among professionals as well as lay persons. According to Ian Hacking (1995) the transgenerational hypothesis is 'virtually an axiom', and 'it is now a forgone conclusion that an abusive parent will profess having been abused as a child' (p. 60). Even if we take the weak empirical support for the hypothesis seriously, reversing the relationship by concluding from the abusive behaviour of children to abusive behaviour of parents, we make the logical error of confusing a weak implication (If *P*, then *Q*) with a strong implication (If *P*, then and only then *Q*).

At one point in the Nab-1 case the transgenerational hypothesis took hold of the investigating team, and on this basis they started to interrogate Maggie and Debbie, while still suspects in the Nab-1 case, as witnesses against their parents and uncle in the Nab-2 case. Also, many of the child witnesses in the Nab-1 case and their parents became witnesses in the Nab-2 case. Soon virtually everybody in the neighbourhood had heard that the police suspected and probably had definite proof that the parents and uncle had also been involved in massive sexual abuse of their own and other people's children. Reporting on the verdict in the Nab-1 case, the local newspaper wrote – probably incorrectly – that the court had taken into account that the two girls probably had been abused themselves; and sometime later that their parents and uncle had been indicted for sexually abusing children. Rumours about the Nab family became rampant in the neighbourhood as well as in the city at large; for example, it was said that Uncle Charlie had had a sexual relationship with his sister Irene (an unconfirmed rumour of which the source remained unknown), which everybody soon believed to be true.

In the neighbourhood where the Nab family lived, Uncle Charlie soon acquired the reputation of a sex-crazed maniac. But Uncle Charlie himself lived in another part of town, where he had his own circle of friends. When interviewed by the police, many of them described him as a pleasant guy and his behaviour as nothing out of the ordinary. His former wife and three women with whom he subsequently had had relationships described him as a sexually normal person and even a gentle lover. If one compares the testimony of people in the Nab neighbourhood with those of his friends outside that neighbourhood, one gets the distinct impression that the two groups of witnesses are not talking about the same person. Which to our minds demonstrates the power of the collaborative storytelling that went on in the Nab neighbourhood.

Over a period of months, both Maggie and Debbie were questioned more than twenty times by the police concerning the behaviour of their parents and uncle. Although they had readily admitted their own abusive behaviour in the Nab-1 case, for a very long time they kept denying that their parents and uncle had abused them or other children. During these interrogations the police repeatedly made all the mistakes mentioned by Garven and collaborators (1998) in their analysis of the McMartin Preschool case: suggestive questioning, i.e., introducing new information into an interview when the child has not provided that information before; co-witness information, i.e., telling the child that the interviewer has already received information from another person regarding the topic of the interview; differential reinforcement, i.e., giving, promising, or implying praise, approval, agreement, or other rewards for incriminating statements; and repeatedly asking questions to which the child has already given an unambiguous answer (see also our discussion of the Putten murder case in chapter 9). These mistakes, made ad nauseam in the Nab-2 case, were shown by Garven *et al.* (2000) to result in '58 percent false allegations against a classroom visitor, as compared with 17 percent false allegations made by children in a control group'. In the Nab-2 case each new interview of the girls would start with an, often incorrect, summing up of what her sister had said in the preceding interview, and in one interview the interrogating officer even told one of the girls what her sister was definitely going to say in her next interview.

These were not the only mistakes made by the police. On several occasions the interrogating officers told the girls that their mother and uncle were consummate liars, and that their uncle was a sexual pervert, 'doing it' with every woman he could lay his hands on, implying, of course, that it would be quite alright to accuse such despicable and base people. Still, it took the police more than fifteen interviews with Maggie and Debbie before they began accusing their parents and uncle of various kinds of sexual abuse of themselves and other children, of which they next kept changing the details. During her last interview Maggie retracted her accusation entirely, saying that in the end she had simply agreed with what the interrogating officers had told her. This was confirmed by the audiotapes made of most of the interviews: the two girls never accused their parents and uncle on their own initiative, but simply confirmed what the interviewer told them that he or she already knew had happened. Incidentally, all the alleged offences in the Nab-2 case were said to have happened in the Nab family home, as opposed to the offences in the Nab-1 case that were said to have happened in other places outside the family home. The three suspects, during many interrogations, kept denying all accusations.

Other children from the neighbourhood were interviewed in a similar manner, although not nearly as many times as Maggie and Debbie. Also the parents of these children were interviewed, but none of them, of course, had firsthand knowledge of what might have happened to their children. None of them had even had an inkling while all this was going on. Only afterwards were they able to put the horrendous story together, 'like the pieces of a jigsaw puzzle'. With some of these children though, the police got lucky. For instance, nine-year-old Angie told the police that one day Maggie and Debbie had pulled her off her bike and taken her to their parents' house. There, on instruction of father Harry and in the presence of mother Irene, she had been made to undress, had been tied and blindfolded, and sexually abused while being threatened with a handgun held to her head, which, however, was never found in the Nab house, nor was ever seen by anybody. This, according to Angie, was not the only time she was abused in the Nab house; it had happened at least six times. And then there was the even more horrendous story of four-year-old Karl, which included that on one occasion part of his penis was cut off with a knife, which must have been put on again though, because no permanent damage was found afterwards.

Now, one would expect that in particular little Karl's story should have warned the MOD-team that there was something amiss with this case. But it did not. Why? Because the members of the investigating team had themselves become part of the ongoing process of collaborative storytelling. They even became the primary movers of the developing story. They probably did not themselves talk to reporters from the media about the case, but they did talk, as part of their job, to numerous witnesses in the neighbourhood, who in turn had no qualms about talking to other people, including reporters, which through their reporting spread the news to everyone interested in what had been going on. The very fact that everybody gradually came to know what had happened confirmed for everyone that it must be true. What everybody knows to be true cannot be untrue. This is collaborative storytelling.

A caveat

The reader who does not believe that an entirely fictitious case of massive sexual child abuse can develop in this manner is advised to study again the reports in the media and the scientific literature of the McMartin Preschool case. Granted, we do not know for sure that the Nab 2-case was indeed entirely fictitious. Maybe Harry and Irene Nab and Uncle Charlie did somehow abuse their own daughters and even other children. For one thing, Harry Nab was not a nice person, who tended to bully other people. His parental skills and those of his wife were grossly deficient. Their family was a constant pain in the neck of their neighbours. Maybe they did prey sexually on their own and other people's children. We will never know because the investigating team, under the direction of the prosecuting attorney, made a breathtaking mess of the investigation. Of course, they did not do so on purpose. They were not consciously in the business of concocting a false story. From scraps of ambiguous information, provided by confused children and already very angry and anxious parents, they themselves fell victim to a process of collaborative story construction of which they eventually even became the prime movers. They deserve to be criticised for gross incompetence but probably not for bad faith in the matter, if only because all the mistakes noted above were faithfully recorded in the case file of well over 1000 pages. There is a tragic ending to the story: both the district court and the court of appeals convicted the parents and uncle to long prison sentences, which they are still serving as we write. The case was also reviewed by the Supreme Court, which found no legal error and therefore confirmed the earlier findings.

Other types of cases?

Collaborative storytelling is probably not unique to cases of multiple sexual molestation, but cases involving multiple adult victims seem especially vulnerable to it, because in such cases there is almost always the moral issue of the alleged victims own contribution to the events (see also chapter 15). This may give them a strong motive to mitigate or even explain away their own contributions. The need for justification and vindication of their own behaviour seems to us to be a major risk factor for the occurrence of collaborative storytelling. We are, however, aware that stressing the possible contribution of the victim(s) in cases of sexual molestation is a well-known defence strategy. It is called 'blaming the victim'. Advocating this reprehensible defence strategy is, of course, not our purpose in proffering the hypothesis of collaborative storytelling. We think, however, that there are such cases in which the hypothesis of collaborative storytelling must seriously be considered.

Cases of multiple sexual abuse of children, like the Nab 2-case, are also vulnerable to collaborative storytelling. The prime moving factor in such cases is the anxiety and anger of the parents of the alleged child victims. The mere thought that something so terrible may have happened to their child will make them, almost compulsively, seek support from others, not only parents of other possible victims, but from just about everybody else who is willing to share their anxiety. Police officers and prosecutors who show themselves receptive to their worries and willing to investigate are about the best they can hope for.

How strong is the empirical evidence for collaborative storytelling?

Most of what we have offered so far by way of proof for the possible occurrence of collaborative storytelling among witnesses in criminal cases is of an anecdotal nature (Crombag, 1999). How much empirical support is there in the scientific literature? As it turns out, the experimental support for the phenomenon is surprisingly strong, once one knows where to look for it, because it appears in the literature under a variety of different names. Some of this literature we have already mentioned above. Other studies on the subject not yet mentioned are those by Weldon & Bellinger (1997), McGregor & Holmes (1999), Gould & Dixon (1993), Bennett (1992), Kraus (1987), Edwards & Middleton (1986), Novick (1997), Bavelas, Coates & Johnson (2000), and Tversky & Marsh (2000). All these authors have demonstrated in various manners and under different names, like 'collaborative narration', 'social contagion of memory', 'joint remembering', 'co-narration', 'conversational remembering', and 'group remembering', the phenomenon that when people talk about an experience, the resulting memory of it will be the joint product of their individual contributions to the conversation. The resulting memory of the participants will not be a simple accumulation of everybody's contribution, but an unwittingly negotiated compromise of the individual contributions. As Edwards & Middleton (1986) stated some time ago: 'Through dialogue people actually pool their recollections' (p. 426). In doing so, the jointly constructed account of what happened becomes, in the words of McGregor & Holmes (1999), 'a convenient tool for bending the truth to reach certain desired conclusions' (p. 403). In criminal cases, the obvious 'desired conclusion' may well be an acceptable complaint to the police that minimises the alleged victim's own contribution to the events and maximises the alleged perpetrator's guilt. To this purpose the collaborating witnesses need not to be consciously lying, they are merely making up their minds about what 'really' happened.

CHAPTER 11

Allegation of Sexual Child Abuse in a Case of Disputed Visitation or Cindy's Story

It is a well-documented fact that the allegation of sexual abuse is often used as an argument – the 'ultimate weapon' as it was once called in a BBC documentary on the subject – in custody or visitation disputes following divorce (Thoennes & Tjaden, 1990). Typically, the accusation is made by the mother against the father, but it also happens that the father accuses the mother or the new friend or husband of the mother. Statistics show that about 33 to 50 percent of the allegations under these circumstances are false, although not always deliberately so. That number, though, is high enough to scrutinise the evidence critically, even though it must be realised that at least 50 percent of such allegations are probably true.

It follows from the situation of a divorced couple that the accusing party has hardly any possibility to collect other evidence than the story as told by the supposed victim, often a child below the age of six. The legally relevant question is therefore whether the testimony of a child as a witness, largely controlled by one parent for whom the stakes are probably high, can be sufficiently relied upon to convict the other parent who denies the accusation passionately, and in the absence of any other direct evidence.

Cindy's story

Mary and Lawrence were divorced in 1997, when their daughter Cindy was just two years old. Mary took Cindy to her new home in the Dutch village of Loenersloot, before there was a formal agreement about custody or the frequency of visits with Lawrence. In practice, Cindy visited her father about every other weekend. In 1998 Mary remarried with Federico Weinert, of Austrian nationality. In 1999 the couple decided to move to Austria and to take Cindy with them. Lawrence protested this and went to court, because he feared total alienation between him and his daughter. The court decided, against Mary's wish, that Cindy should visit her father for one week in the spring, one week in the autumn, and a full month during the summer holidays. In March 2000 Mary filed a complaint with the Dutch police, in which she accused Lawrence of sexually abusing Cindy during her visits to the Netherlands. The period in which the offence was supposedly committed was set between September 1995 (when Cindy was born) and February 2000 (Cindy's last visit to the Netherlands). Mary requested that Cindy's obligation to visit her father be terminated immediately.

The evidence

The evidence consisted of several items. First, Mary claimed that since the fall of 1998 Cindy had complained about a sore bottom. The father confirmed that Cindy's vagina had been rather red, and that she had needed a special ointment for it, which he had applied regularly after Cindy went to the lavatory, and that he had done so on Mary's explicit instructions. Other witnesses confirmed the infected condition of Cindy's vagina in that period.

Secondly, there was an affidavit of an Austrian paediatrician, specialising in forensic medicine, who stated that Cindy's vagina had a slight scar of a kind more or less typical for a mechanical traumatisation. According to him, it could have been brought about with a finger, but definitely not by penetration with a penis. He thought it unlikely that the child would have caused this herself, as this would have been painful. The time of traumatisation he estimated as from a number of weeks to several months before the examination on 1 July 2000. The paediatrician concluded that Cindy had been sexually abused.

Thirdly, there was a witness, Marijke Heijnis, who stated that in the summer of 1998, when Cindy was just three years old, the girl had said spontaneously that Daddy had touched her bottom. She had told him to stop, but he would not listen. Cindy's mother Mary also said she had heard this.

Fourth, there were two videotaped interviews with Cindy. One was held by a specially trained Dutch police officer in March 2000. In this interview, Cindy did not make any accusation against her father or anyone else, despite quite explicit attempts to let her tell about it. The second interview was done by a psychologist for the Austrian police, in May 2000. This time Cindy said that she herself had stuck her finger in her nose and in her vagina. On further questioning she answered that also her father had stuck his finger in her 'popo', but in a later drawing she indicated that she had meant her anus. The clinical psychologist in Austria, who wrote the report, declared that the statement must be true, as five-year-old children cannot easily be made to lie about such things. She advised that the visits to Lawrence should be stopped.

A fifth source of evidence was an observation made by the mother, but unconfirmed by anyone else. Mary had asked Cindy: 'Did you ever see somebody's willie?' Cindy had answered: 'Yes, Papa's.' Mary: 'And what did you do?' Cindy: 'I lifted it.'

Mary: 'Did it last long?' Cindy: 'Yes, a bit long, Papa sits down till it's ready.' Mary's second husband Federico was not present at this conversation. He also stated that he has a habit of walking in the house without his clothes, so that Cindy would definitively have seen his penis. Lawrence, in turn, confirmed that he regularly bathed with Cindy, just as he had done before the divorce. He said that on one of these occasions Cindy had touched his penis, and he had told her to stop it.

A sixth source of information consisted of statements by Mary's parents. Only repeating what Mary had told them, they moreover declared that they themselves had never noticed any problem in the way in which Lawrence had treated Cindy. Only after they had been informed about Mary's suspicion, they did notice that Cindy had woken up during the night with nightmares related to her sore bottom and her father.

The other scenario

The logical position is that Mary's complaint is pitted against Lawrence's resolute denial. The presumption of innocence requires that as a starting position we take Lawrence's denial as true unless the prosecution succeeds in proving Mary's version, which is that Lawrence sexually abused his daughter. Lawrence's version of the events, however, was never made explicit but may be assumed to be that Mary wants to prevent Cindy from visiting him, and that she therefore has made up a false accusation. She may even have gone so far as to hurt the child herself in order to produce the scar on Cindy's vagina. It is the court's task to assess the likelihood of these two scenarios (see also chapter 7).

The evidence that supports Mary's accusation is presented to the court in an orderly fashion, as the file is organised by the office of the prosecuting attorney. On the other hand, the exculpatory information is scattered throughout the file. First, there was a surprising statement by the assistant of the family's homeopathic doctor, Dr. Alberts. She assisted in the treatment of Lawrence, Mary, and Cindy for several years and thus got to know them well. In December 1998 Mary had asked her to treat Cindy for vaginal spasms. Dr. Alberts had found nothing wrong. She told the police:

> I had the clear impression that these pains did not really exist, but were only suggested by Mary. This idea was strengthened when Cindy asked me whether she would be allowed to live with her father. She said she did not want to go back to her mother.

To this, Dr. Alberts added:

> Some months later Mary called me at home. I was not in and I never returned her call. I was afraid that she wanted to use me again for something. I did not want any

part of that. I am fully convinced that Mary is able to destroy Lawrence completely. She wants the child at any cost. She is using this story to prevent the child from going to her father ever again. I doubt that anything sexual has happened at all. ... I am afraid a game is being played at Cindy's cost.

Secondly, the painful condition of Cindy's vagina was diagnosed as a bacterial infection, which is not uncommon in little girls and usually unrelated to sexual abuse. The treatment, which needed to be continued during the weekends when Cindy visited her father and which is apparently painful, could have resulted in Cindy's remark that Lawrence had touched her, if she ever said this at all.

Thirdly, the expert opinion about a slight scar in Cindy's vagina did not point to any particular perpetrator, meaning that Lawrence is not the only possible suspect. Cindy's statement that at times she herself had touched her vagina needs careful examination. Given that her vagina was itching, it is not unthinkable that she scratched it to such an extent that it left a scar. She would not be the first child to hurt herself by scratching. Sometimes pain is better than an itch. The expert stated that the injury was caused some weeks or months preceding his examination. It should be realised that Cindy saw her father for the last time on 21 February 2000, whereas the examination took place on 1 July. Can a little over four months be considered to be still within the vaguely described period of 'some months'? The expert did not explicitly exclude that the scar was caused by Cindy's earlier infection, or the treatment of that infection.

Fourth, it should be remembered that Cindy did not accuse her father during the first studio interview. In the second interview she said very little. Dutch police experts evaluated the methodology of the Austrian interview and found much wrong with it. To begin with, during that interview Mary had been present behind the one-way screen and Cindy knew this; she approached the screen several times to show things to her mother. The interview was interrupted at least twice to let Cindy talk to her mother. Under such conditions a possible influence of the mother is hard to eliminate (Dekens & Van der Sleen 1997). In the absence of a time indication on the tape, it cannot be established how long these interruptions lasted. Cindy's statements were often rather superficial, but the interviewer did not attempt to obtain more details. Cindy was never asked whether other people like Mary or Federico had also touched her. Obviously, this would have been a difficult thing to ask with Mary behind the screen.

Fifth, even the few statements by Cindy contained a number of contradictions. At one point she said that it had happened in the living room, while later, after declaring that they had no clothes on, she said it had happened in the shower. She said that Lawrence had only touched her behind, not her vagina, and only once. All that conflicts with the evidence about what Cindy had said in the summer of 1998, and with the medical evidence from Austria. She also said that she had never touched Lawrence, which is in conflict with Mary's story.

Sixth, the Austrian psychologist's advice that Cindy must no longer be allowed to visit her father is an indication that she may not have been up to the task, since an expert witness is not supposed to offer therapeutic advice. The role of a therapist is incompatible with the critical attitude required of a forensic interviewer (Greenberg & Shuman, 1997). Maybe this explains why Cindy was not asked for more details and confronted with the contradictions in her statements. The expert's notion that five-year-olds cannot be made to tell a lie is clearly in conflict with the literature about the effects of suggestion on pre-schoolers (Ceci & Bruck, 1993; Jackson *et al.*, 1996).

Seventh, the story about Cindy's experiences when bathing with her father is hearsay in the second or possibly third degree: Cindy told Mary, and Mary told the police, or Mary told her parents who then told the police. No witness other than Mary can vouch for Cindy really saying this. During the studio interview Cindy did not repeat it.

Determining the likelihood: overall statistics

We mention all these details of the evidence that contradict the accusation because it is the very essence of a psychologist's methodology to weigh alternative hypotheses (see also chapter 7). Is it likely that a child's vagina is penetrated and then four months later insists that it was her anus? Or is it more likely that a recollection of her father taking care of her infected bottom, through suggestion by a highly motivated mother, changed into a rather vague story of abuse containing several contradictions? How likely is it that a five-year-old abused child denies this persistently to an experienced interviewer? How likely is it that a child is abused by the father, but nevertheless prefers to live with him rather than with her mother? Might such a preference be better explained as the product of the mother's attempts to create a false memory that is very damaging for her former husband? Is it likely that Mary is the reasonable woman that transpires from her own statements, or is it more likely that she is what Dr. Alberts described her to be, that is, a malicious schemer, hell-bent on hurting her former husband? How likely are experts to be right when they state that children never hurt themselves, or that children do not have enough imagination to lie?

We are also faced with a question that is rarely asked. We tend to think that a mother would not go so far as to suggest sexual abuse to her own child deliberately, thus making it the subject of all sorts of terrifying examinations and interrogations. Compare this to the alternative. How likely is it that a father abuses his baby daughter? We know it happens more often than we care to acknowledge, but fortunately in general it still remains rather unlikely. We know that people are not very good at comparing the likelihood of two unlikely events (Slovic *et al.*, 1982). Obviously, an expert psychologist cannot quantify the likelihood of this sort of event. But asking the questions makes visible the possibilities, and a possibility represents a non-zero probability. The judge or jury should at least try to answer why they are convinced that this non-zero possibility did not materialise in a particular case.

Even though specific likelihoods cannot be established in this case, there are some overall statistics that are relevant as background information. Research has shown that false accusations of sexual abuse in the context of disputed custody are not rare. Thoennes & Pearson (1988) estimate that accusations of sexual abuse are found in 2-10 percent of all contested custody cases. Their estimate of the percentage of false allegations in such cases runs from 30 percent to 80 percent. They also found that in a total of 114 cases of disputed custody, 89 allegations (78 percent) of sexual abuse had been declared by the courts as not involving any abuse. Thoennes & Tjaden (1990) studied the files of 169 cases in which the accusation of abuse was made in the context of custody or visitation disputes. In 129 of those files, the validity of the accusation was reported. In 50 percent the courts declared abuse proven, in 33 percent they decided that the allegation was false, and in 17 percent the ruling was indeterminate. We conclude that the proportion of false accusations of sexual abuse in such cases lies between 33 and 50 percent, which probably is the lower border estimate. Consequently, the likelihood of burdening your child with a false memory of abuse may be equally large as the likelihood of actual sexual abuse.

This does not necessarily mean that parents deliberately burden their children with false memories of sexual abuse. In probably only a minority of cases are false accusations of sexual abuse made with fraudulent intent. The process of unintentionally involving one's own child in a false accusation is described in some detail by Benedek & Schetky (1987):

> Many allegations of sexual abuse stem from borderline situations in which the father may have bathed or slept with the young child during visitation. Anxious mothers may read more into the situation than was intended. What may have been sexually overstimulating to the child but not necessarily intended to sexually gratify the adult becomes abusive in the mother's eyes, and she begins interrogating the child after each visit with the father. The mother's anxiety is soon picked up by the child, who may come to believe that he or she is not safe with the father; behavioural problems around visitation may then ensue. The mother in turn uses this as confirmation that something is terribly amiss, and a vicious cycle is set up.

The essence of this description is that there often is no intention to make a false accusation or unwarranted suggestions to the child. Therefore, the consideration that mothers are not likely to make false accusations deliberately, is not entirely relevant. It does not have to be deliberate.

Jones & McGraw (1987) looked at a more general class of sexual child abuse allegations, not limited to cases of disputed custody or visitation. They found that an estimated 70 percent of the allegations were reliable, and 8 percent definitely fictitious. The difference between the earlier mentioned 30 to 50 percent and 8 percent false accusations makes it tempting to conclude that disputes about custody or visitation increase the risk of false accusations of abuse. Consequently, a court needs to explain in detail how it established that in a particular case involving a custody or visitation dispute, a false accusation did not occur. The case of Cindy is problematic in this respect, because it would be difficult to exclude the possibility of a false accusation. Mary had the motive and the opportunity, and it may not have proved impossible to coach Cindy into saying the few things that transpired in the Austrian interview.

Alan Dershowitz (1994) reports that according to the FBI 8 percent of all rapes reported to the police turn out to be false. The false allegation of rape, therefore, appears to occur about as often as the false allegation of child sexual abuse. The remarkable aspect of this agreement is not so much the numerical correspondence, but the fact that 8 percent false accusations is considerably higher than what is found for any other type of crime. One explanation for this may be that cases involving sex offences can be taken to court with a minimum of supporting evidence, since it is generally known that corroborating evidence is almost always in short supply. But logically, with the prior odds so weakly supporting the allegations, *more* rather than *less* evidence is needed.

In cases of alleged abuse in the context of disputed custody or visitation, the expert psychologist should begin to point out the base rates and their implications for the decision process. Next, he or she should explain how in such cases false allegations may come about more readily than in other types of cases. And finally, reasonable alternative scenarios that could have produced a false allegation should be described and considered. For the case of Cindy the statistics provided by Thoennes & Tjaden (1990) seem quite appropriate, as the resemblance between her case and the scenario described by Benedek & Schetky (1987) is striking.

Motives and opportunities

As in the classic detective literature, it is always useful to consider whether the accusing parent or the alleged child-victim had a motive and the opportunity to concoct a false accusation. This question is especially relevant when there is reason to suspect that the accusation may be deliberately false.

It is obvious that the context of a dispute about custody or visitation rights presents in and of itself a sufficient motive for an accusing parent. It must, however, be realised that often the cooperation of the child is needed, as otherwise it would be difficult if not impossible to coach the child into telling an untrue story. What kind of motive might a child have to cooperate? Is there any conceivable direct or secondary gain from cooperating? Did the accusing parent promise the child some reward for telling the story? Might there be a strong need to please the parent? Could there be a motive to accuse someone of the abuse that was committed by another person? Does the accusing parent or the child have a history of telling lies, or of making false accusations?

The opportunity for the accusing parent to make a false accusation is primarily limited by what sort of credible story the child can be made to present. The child's medical history may cause a heightened preoccupation with things sexual. Genital infection, circumcision, genital surgery, gynaecological examination may offer such an opportunity. Some risky habits of the alleged perpetrators may also promote the opportunity. Examples of these are going about the house without clothes, engaging in sexual activity in view of the child, bathing with the child, sleeping in the same bed with the child, having pornographic magazines about the house or watching pornographic videos in the child's presence. Another type of opportunity for telling a credible but untrue story of abuse is when the child has talked to other children with a history of abuse. This may occur in institutions treating such children, in foster families, or when in the child's own family a case of another child known to the family is discussed.

The opportunity for children to present credible stories about sexual experiences without being abused has been the subject of extensive study. The plausible assumption that abused children have more knowledge than the average child about sexual matters is not generally confirmed (Gordon *et al.*, 1990; Friedrich *et al.*, 1991). The argument that a child with 'inappropriate sexual knowledge' is more likely to be a victim of sexual abuse is not empirically valid. On the contrary, Brilleslijper-Kater (2005) found that abused children show more restraint when discussing sexual matters, so that their experience-based knowledge does not often transpire. The major difference between abused and non-abused children lies not in the amount of their knowledge, but in a more negative attitude with respect to that knowledge.

In the case of Cindy it is clear that the girl has no obvious motive to lie, but her earlier genital infection and her father's risky habits offer excellent opportunities to make her say things that are quite damaging for him in the context of alleged sexual abuse.

The validity of studio interviews: process and product

In cases of alleged sexual abuse of children expert psychologists are often required to evaluate the reliability, i.e., the truthfulness, of the children's testimony, in either qualitative or quantitative terms. Expert witnesses should refuse to do this, as the assessment of truthfulness belongs to the domain of the judge or jury. The expert psychologist can only assist the trier of fact in making that decision through explaining which psychological facts or considerations should be taken into account.

Here two complementary approaches are possible. The expert can analyse either the process or the product. In analysing the process, one pays attention to the manner in which the interview of the victim was held. Below we will list a number of criteria for this. In evaluating the product, we subject the victim's statements to some sort of content analysis.

The distinction between process and product is not an easy one to make. In a simple industrial process there may be a deterministic relationship between the quality of the process and of the product. If the process is correct, the quality of the product is guaranteed; if the process is flawed, it is impossible to obtain a good product. In other instances, however, the relationship may be much looser. It is possible that a witness responds entirely truthfully in a totally misconducted interview, or for a witness to lie unashamedly in a properly conducted interview. In such a case the relationship between process and product is not deterministic but probabilistic. There is a positive correlation between process quality and product quality, but we have no good estimate of its size. Overall, there is no doubt that improper interview methods increase the chances of obtaining false information. It will therefore be helpful to scrutinise the way in which a child was interviewed.

The implications of the process-product distinction are not clear when it comes to criminal court practice. The reason for this is the probabilistic quality of the relationship, which is always difficult to translate into a decision rule. A strict decision rule might be that *only* evidence from a properly conducted interview is declared admissible, because an improperly conducted interview exposes the defendant to an unknown risk. But this is usually not the point of view taken by the prosecution or the court. They are likely to ask the expert whether evidence from an improperly conducted interview is *certain* to be wrong. The answer must of course be negative, which then may lead the courts to decide that the evidence can be used, although with some caution. One reason for such a lenient rule is that suggestive interviews, or interviews that may have influenced the child's memory in any other way, cannot be repeated. Application of a stricter rule would mean the dismissal of many cases, with possibly serious consequences for the children who were actually abused. On the other hand, however, the habitual application of a lenient rule decreases the motivation for the police investigators to follow the best possible practice.

It is odd that while expert opinion must be based on knowledge and methods generally accepted in the scientific community in order to be admissible in court, the same standard of best possible practice is not required of police work. It is even more surprising that the expert who is asked to evaluate the process and product of police work is expected to apply both these standards simultaneously.

In the case at hand, the problem focuses on the acceptability of the Austrian studio interview, which clearly did not conform to the requirements of best possible practice. Should the resulting evidence be left out of consideration, or should the court only be asked to interpret it cautiously? Can the expert in any way quantify the risk of accepting the product of imperfect interviews? Do we know the validity of studio interviews, and do we know to what extent it decreases when children know that their mothers are listening in? Of course, the answers to these questions are negative. Therefore, the expert has little more to offer than a warning.

Let us also consider the opposite problem: can expert psychologists confirm that the evidence resulting from a flawlessly conducted interview can be relied on? They cannot. In such a situation we can only affirm that the defendant is not unnecessarily put at risk. Even if the process was appropriate, the product may still be flawed.

In the case of Cindy, it is obvious that the Austrian studio interview was methodologically flawed, and that for this reason there was a heightened chance that Cindy's statements about her father's behaviour were misleading. The methodological mistakes could have been avoided. The fact that Cindy was only five years old did not preclude a properly conducted interview. Hence the interests of the defendant were unnecessarily put at risk. The question of whether the results from the interview should therefore be disregarded had to be left to the court, because it is not in the domain of a psychologist to assess the amount of risk that can be accepted in the evaluation of the total body of evidence.

Process rules for interviewing children in police studios

There is an extensive literature on how children are best interviewed. Some authorities have issued guidelines for this, like the *Memorandum of Good Practice* (Her Majesty's Stationary Office, 1992) in Great Britain or the brochure *Investigative Interviews of Children* issued by the American Psychological Association (Poole & Lamb, 1998). There is even a fully scripted interview protocol from the National Institute of Child Health and Human Development in Israel (Orbach *et al.*, 2000). Experts may use such guidelines as standards for the evaluation of actual interviews with children.

We offer the following small collection of rules to which studio interviews must conform as a rough indication of what the expert should consider. For a more extensive set of rules we refer to the sources mentioned above.

1. The interviewer is well trained and experienced, and his or her work is subjected to peer review at least once a year.
2. Child and interviewer are the only people present in the interview room. The child is informed that the session is being recorded and that someone else is observing the session from behind the one-way screen. The child is informed that no parent, relative or other custodian is watching or listening in.[1]
3. In the initial stage of the interview, good contact with the child is established. That may take as long as it takes. In that stage the interviewer also establishes that the child can answer simple autobiographical questions in an appropriate fashion, i.e., that he or she understands the concepts of time, place, and number; that she or he understands the difference between truth and falsehood. The interviewer tests whether or not the child yields to suggestion. The interviewer also makes sure that the child understands why the interview is being held, and that anything can be said so long as it is the truth. If the child does not fulfil these necessary conditions, the interview must be discontinued.
4. The interview is held in the child's native language.
5. The child is first invited to tell her own story, uninterrupted by specific questions. In the second stage open questions can be asked. Yes-no questions are always to be avoided. Closed questions are only asked when attempts to elicit information with open questions fail. There is no discussion with the child, but contradictions or unclear points must be elucidated through further questions.
6. The interviewer maintains a neutral, but not uncritical attitude. He or she does not attempt to stigmatise or to implicate the suspected person, nor to offer some sort of therapeutic assistance.
7. The interviewer refrains from drawing conclusions, either during the interview or in a report about the interview.

Whether an interviewer has abided by these rules can be evaluated on the basis of a reliable transcription of the interview, supplemented with some background information about the interviewer. In practice, it may well happen that transcripts differ from what was actually said. We have seen cases in which the differences were large and by no means insignificant. It is therefore always advisable to compare a transcript with the videotaped record. Often objections are raised against making the video or audio recording available to the psychological expert, particularly when the expert is proposed by the defence. In a case in which Wagenaar evaluated

1 However, when the case goes to trial later, at least the accused parent, and probably both parents, will come to know the child's testimony.

an interview exclusively on the basis of a verbatim transcript, the Dutch Psychological Association judged this to amount to professional misconduct, according to the argument that the nonverbal behaviour of the child witness is an important source of information that should also be taken into account by the expert (Nederlands Instituut van Psychologen, 1997). Below we will argue to the contrary.

When we try to evaluate the interview of Cindy by the Austrian expert against the criteria mentioned above, we find that virtually nothing is known about the training experience of the interviewer. Moreover, Cindy's mother Mary should not have been present in the observation room behind the one-way mirror. The interview was conducted in German, whereas Cindy's native language is Dutch. Whether Cindy understood all the relevant notions, including that of the 'truth', was not tested. Although most questions were phrased in open form, no further questions were asked about a number of unclear but highly relevant details, such as where precisely she was touched, how often, and when. In her report, the psychologist concluded that Cindy definitely had been abused and that, for this reason, the visitation rights of the father should be rescinded, thus invading the exclusive province of the court.

Evaluating the product

We can also try to evaluate the reliability of a child's testimony by looking at the product: what did the child say? Such an analysis will not differ much from the way in which every testimony by adult witnesses is scrutinised in a more or less routine fashion. We suggest the following obvious criteria:

- Are some of the reported details perhaps physically impossible?
- Are parts of the statement internally inconsistent?
- Are statements or parts of them inconsistent with previously made statements, or with statements made by other witnesses?
- Are statements inconsistent with other known facts?
- Are there relevant questions that remained unanswered?

The last criterion needs to be supplemented by a list of what the relevant issues are. In a case of alleged sexual abuse, this includes not only the details of the abuse, but also typical details like 'grooming behaviour' and possible rewards and threats. 'Grooming' concerns the manner in which the perpetrator introduced the abuse, usually as something quite innocent; or the way in which it developed from play into abusive acts. Rewards may not only pertain to promising something that the child wants, but also to blackmailing the child into permitting the abuse. Threats are concerned with the manner in which the perpetrator prevented the child from telling others about what had happened. Such details are important, because in case of a mistaken interpretation of the child's story, as described by Benedek & Schetky (1987), they may be expected to be absent. Other relevant questions relate to other possible perpetrators and other instances of abuse, which were withheld by the child or may not have been recognised by the child for what they were.

Apart from these obvious criteria, the expert may want to look at aspects known to correlate with the level of truthfulness, even though such correlations may not be very high. Some are listed in Benedek & Schetky (1987), although we hasten to add that these authors make no reference to supporting literature. Here are some examples of things to look for:

- Is the vocabulary of the child's statements representative for the developmental stage of the child, as opposed to adult vocabulary?
- In subsequent interviews or subsequent repeated passages of the same interview, are the facts consistent, but the wording different, or is there repetition of the same wording and phraseology?
- Is the display of emotion consonant with the content of the testimony, as opposed to emotions incompatible with content?
- Are details freely produced, or are only questions answered?

Answering such questions obviously involves a degree of subjective judgment. Whenever such judgments are made, they should always be accompanied by indications on precisely which part of the material they are based, to enable the court to check on the subjectivity employed.

In the case of Cindy it is not easy to apply these criteria, because she actually said very little. The most striking outcome of applying them is that Cindy occasionally contradicts herself and the accusation made by her mother. The inclusion of the medical evidence in support of the charge can only mean that Cindy's father is suspected of touching or even penetrating Cindy's vagina with his finger, whereas Cindy only mentioned that he touched her anus. Obviously, not all relevant questions were asked.

Criteria-Based Content Analysis

Surprisingly, the mainstream research about product reliability of interviews with children has focused on criteria that are not related to the obvious questions listed above. The technique applied most often is called the Criteria-Based Content Analysis (CBCA; for a description and critique, see: Ruby & Brigham, 1997), and it employs nineteen criteria that are assumed to be indicative of veracity. The more often a child's testimony meets the following criteria, the more it is considered truthful. The most representative criteria in this list are:

- logical structure;
- unstructured production, with less structure indicating more truthfulness;
- quantity of details;
- contextual embedding;
- interactions (with other people);
- reproduction of speech;
- unexpected complications;
- unusual details;
- superfluous details;
- self-deprecation.

The problem with these criteria is that none of them has as yet been demonstrated to relate significantly with truthfulness. By way of example, we consider only one of them: quantity of details. It has never been shown that a detailed testimony is more often true than one with fewer details. As a matter of fact, research with children deliberately telling untrue stories has revealed that fictitious stories on average have as many details as true stories (Jackson *et al.*, 1996). In an analysis of thirteen CBCA evaluation studies, it was established that some factors contributed more often to the discrimination between true and untrue testimonies than others; but even quantity of details, by far the best of all contributing factors, turned out to contribute in only nine out of thirteen studies. Seven factors contributed in five or six of these studies; ten factors contributed 1-4 times; and one factor never contributed (self-deprecation: did the child describe herself as partly guilty?). The criterion 'unstructured production' alone led to a categorisation rate as accurate, as did any combination of any number of criteria. Adding 'quantity of details' did not improve the score (Zaparnik *et al.*, 1995).

The fundamental problem that a method like the CBCA shares with any other method is that the assessment of its validity must be based on an objective and independent categorisation between true and untrue stories. The implication is that the validation must be done either in a laboratory environment in which the veracity of the stories is controlled, or in a field situation with a selection of testimonies that could be evaluated on the basis of other reliable criteria. The disadvantage of a laboratory situation is that, for ethical reasons, story content cannot be comparable to stories of sexual abuse. On the other hand, it has been shown that field studies tend to be limited to a selection of clear-cut cases, which says little about validity in doubtful cases. As a consequence, the validity of criteria validated by such studies will be overestimated.

With these precautions in mind, we can conclude that field studies have not provided a reliable indication of CBCA's validity. Typically, the selection rate is unknown or appears to be very low: in the order of the 5 percent for most clear-cut cases. In laboratory studies the diagnostic value, which is the ratio of hits and false alarms, appears to vary from 3.5 to 0.5. The second value indicates that in some studies there were more false alarms than hits. Elsewhere we have argued that the total diagnostic value of the evidence against a suspect should amount to a ratio of around 200 (Wagenaar, Van Koppen, & Crombag, 2001, p. 101). As diagnostic values of all pieces of evidence are multiplied to obtain the aggregated value of all available evidence in a criminal case, a value of 3.5 or less means that even the best result of CBCA must be supplemented by other evidence worth a diagnostic value of 60 or more. In the worst case the CBCA will even reduce the diagnostic value of the aggregated evidence. Another general finding is that if the CBCA produces the wrong categorisation, it is likely to be a type-II error: untrue stories labelled as true. This renders the method unfit for application in a forensic context.

CBCA also can not distinguish between an untrue story believed by the child and a deliberately false testimony. The diagnostic value of the discrimination between untrue and deliberately false statements, reported by Huffman & Ceci (1997), turned out to be as low as 1.4. This finding is relevant for the case of Cindy, as the defence's alternative explanation was that Cindy was simply presenting elements of her father's uncontested behaviour within a framework that she had learned to interpret as signifying sexual abuse. To put it bluntly: the CBCA cannot assess whether Cindy's story is true, at best it may affirm that Cindy *believes* it to be true. But that was not contested and probably need not be decided anyway. Hence, CBCA can only be used, if at all, when it is suspected that a child is deliberately lying. We suspect that this is only useful in a very small minority of the cases of disputed custody and visitation rights.

Nonverbal communication

The CBCA is an analysis of the verbal content of a child's testimony, made on the basis of a transcript of a studio interview. Nonverbal elements, i.e., facial expressions and gestures, are not the subject of the analysis. As briefly mentioned before, this led the Dutch Psychological Association to reprimand one of us for giving an expert opinion on the basis of a transcript alone. The reason given for this ruling was that the nonverbal communication of the child had been neglected. A strict application of the CBCA would therefore not be allowed in the Netherlands. By way of a solution, proponents submit that the CBCA must be based on both the video recording and the transcript. Although at first this may seem reasonable, it is not clear from the literature (cf. Ruby & Brigham, 1997) that this combination would add anything to the validity of the CBCA.

It appears that analysing nonverbal behaviour contributes little, if anything at all, to the discrimination between true and untrue witness statements.

Although it was found (Ekman, 1988; Vrij, 1995) that in laboratory situations the movements of the extremities and facial expressions are somewhat different in truth-telling and deception, such differences turned out to be very small (Vrij & Semin, 1996) and hardly useful in the context of a police interrogation (Lochun, 1996). Reasons for the differences between the laboratory and the police interview room are:

- Innocent suspects may also be nervous when interrogated by the police, and may therefore display behaviour that suggests guilt (Ekman, 1988). The same may be true for truthful victims who fear that they will not be believed.
- Guilty individuals will probably be highly motivated to deceive the interrogating officer, in particular when their freedom or even their life depends on it (De Paulo, 1994). The same may apply to witnesses falsely claiming to have been victims of abuse.
- Career criminals appear to exhibit less clear nonverbal behaviour when lying (Vrij & Semin, 1996). Also some of the alleged abuse victims have histories of lying and may therefore also be considered experienced liars.
- The interpretation of nonverbal behaviour is usually done without a control group. The interrogator must therefore test the behaviour of a witness or suspect against some fuzzy internal standard. It is possible that distinct expectations of the guilt of the interviewee influence this comparison, yielding a perception of deception where there is none.
- Police officers are not trained to pick up the small predictive nonverbal signals of deception and are likely to employ the unpredictive signals used by lay people, such as the frequency and duration of eye contact. In practice, experienced police officers proved no better than lay persons in distinguishing truth telling from deception (Ekman & O'Sullivan, 1991).

Analysis of nonverbal behaviour in the context of the CBCA will be even less helpful when a distinction must be made between truth-telling and unintentionally telling a lie.

All this leads us to conclude that it is doubtful that inspection of the videotaped interviews with Cindy would reveal whether her story about the sexual abuse is true or false through the interpretation of her nonverbal behaviour.

Summary of the expertise

The expert opinion in Cindy's case consisted of the following elements:

1. In cases of alleged sexual abuse in the context of disputed custody or visitation rights, one must be aware of the prior odds favouring false accusations. Untrue accusations may occur when a parent picks up quite innocent signals from the

child and elaborates them into a suspicion of abuse, which subsequently is confirmed by further information from the child that is either misunderstood or the product of suggestion. Cindy's case could well be an example of such a development. False accusations occur when a parent deliberately makes the child say things that he or she knows to be untrue. Contrary to what many believe that a parent would never be willing to inflict on his or her child, it is by no means rare for a parent to involve a child in a false accusation. Cindy's case file contains several indications that Mary, now living in Austria, would be prepared to take such a drastic step in order to end Cindy's burdensome visits to her father.

2. The studio interview held in Austria did not meet the criteria applied in most countries. The mother should not have been present at the interview, the interview was not conducted in the child's native language, not all relevant questions were asked, and the reporting psychologist invaded the province of the court by drawing conclusions and giving advice that went beyond the limitations of an interview.
3. Cindy's statements were at points contradictory and conflicted with some of the medical evidence.
4. Content analysis of Cindy's statement as well as analysis of her nonverbal behaviour will not help to decide about the veracity of her story. In particular, the distinction between a true story and an untrue story that Cindy may have come to believe cannot be made on the basis of such observable categories.
5. The decision of whether or not to believe Cindy's story and thus assessment of the believability of her story rests with the court. The expert should avoid prejudging this decision and only list which aspects of the evidence, psychological considerations and relevant findings reported in the psychological literature should be taken into consideration by the court.

CHAPTER 12

Psychogenic Amnesia or the Case of the Amnesic Strangler

The case of the amnesic strangler

On 6 June 2002 the District Court in the Dutch city of Assen acquitted Oscar Baarsma (a pseudonym) of murdering his wife Edith, although there was no doubt that Edith had died from strangulation by her husband. They had had a very bad marriage, and Edith had decided that a divorce was inevitable. Oscar disagreed, and he refused to move out of the house or to cooperate in the divorce proceedings. Oscar and Edith quarrelled almost constantly, and sometimes these quarrels became very nasty indeed. On one of these occasions Edith threatened to accuse Oscar of sexually molesting their daughter. At that point, according to Oscar, 'his ears began to ring', he 'began to sweat heavily and became very hot. The light went out of my eyes,' he said, 'and there was total darkness. And then there was nothing at all.' When sometime later he came to his senses, he found himself sitting on the floor next to Edith, his hands loosely around her neck. She was dead, and Oscar had no memory at all of what he had obviously done. He said he felt terribly guilty, but he had no explanation for his behaviour other than that this time Edith had apparently gone too far. But since he had no memory of what had happened, he did not know precisely how and why he had strangled her.

Before the case went to court, three expert witnesses, two psychiatrists and a psychologist, examined Oscar. Each of these experts had two meetings with Oscar, after which they conferred amongst themselves and came to agree that although Oscar had no psychiatric history and also at present appeared to be free of any psychiatric symptom, at the time of the incident he must have suffered from an 'acute dissociative disorder' of brief duration, during which he had had 'no cognitive control' over his actions and could therefore not be held responsible for them. Since in their examination the experts had found no indication for any other psychiatric disorder of a more permanent nature, they judged the chance of recidivism low. And that is how the District Court, adopting the opinions of the experts, came to dismiss the case and sent Oscar home a free man.

Dissociation and dissociative disorders

It was in the third edition of the *Diagnostic and Statistical Manual of Mental Disorders* (DSM-III), published by the American Psychiatric Association in 1980, that the group of dissociative disorders made their first appearance as psychiatric diagnoses. There were, and still are, four of them: the dissociative identity disorder (formerly called multiple personality disorder), dissociative amnesia, the dissociative fugue (formerly called psychogenic fugue), and the depersonalisation disorder. As a psychiatric phenomenon the fugue state – a sudden onset of wandering with clouding of consciousness, followed by amnesia limited to events during the fugue period (Parkin, 1998; chapter 9) – is considerably older than 1980 and was quite regularly reported in the nineteenth century, but nowadays appears to have gone out of fashion, becoming quite rare.

With the publication of the DSM-III, the fugue found a niche among the dissociative disorders, of which the most important is the dissociative identity disorder (DID), which was first adopted in the DSM as the multiple personality disorder (MPD) 'after a lot of jockeying by advocates' of that syndrome, according to Ian Hacking (1998, p. 83). Although since its adoption in the DSM we have seen a real epidemic of cases of the dissociative identity disorder in some countries, in particular in North America[1], it has always been a highly controversial psychiatric diagnosis. Many see it as an iatrogenic syndrome, i.e., a manner in which psychotherapists teach their patients to shape and present their psychological problems. An important aspect of the syndrome is that patients suffering from it have a memory problem: 'Alter personalities (...) are purportedly mutually amnesic.' (Spanos, 1996, p. 217; see also Crombag & Merckelbach 1997, chapter 6). According to Nicholas Spanos this may come about because 'the preoccupations held by therapists concerning the causes of MPD may influence patients to generate memory reports that conform to their therapist's hypothesis concerning the aetiology of their difficulties' (p. 223), which led Ian Hacking to proffer the question: 'Is multiple personality a real disorder as opposed to a product of social circumstances, a culturally permissible way to express distress or unhappiness?' (1995, p. 12). In any case, after a period of great popularity in the 1980s and 1990s, the diagnosis appears on its way out, but is as yet by no means extinct.

The related diagnosis of dissociative amnesia, however, is still very much alive, as illustrated by the case of the amnesic strangler. In the DSM-IV (p. 478), dissociative amnesia is defined as 'an inability to recall important personal information, usual-

---

1 According to Hacking (1998, p. 9): 'In 1972 [...] less than a dozen cases [had] been reported in the last fifty years.'

ly of a traumatic or stressful nature, that is too extensive to be explained by normal forgetfulness'. Furthermore, according to the DSM-IV, it must not be attributable to 'the direct physiological effects of a substance or a neurological or other general medical condition'. This is why dissociative amnesia is often also called 'psychogenic amnesia'. It is also called 'functional amnesia' (Schacter 1986a) or 'hysterical amnesia' (Hodges, 1991). But whatever it is called, it needs to be clearly distinguished from organic amnesia due to substance abuse, closed head injury or some other neurological dysfunction.[2]

Apart from being extremely vague, this definition leaves unexplained what dissociation is. The term is so commonly used among psychiatrists and psychologists that one gets the impression that everyone knows what it is, and therefore it needs no further explanation. The DSM-IV (p. 477) describes 'the essential feature of the dissociative disorders' as 'a disruption in the usually integrated functions of consciousness, memory, identity, or perception of the environment'. To our minds this description is not very informative other than that dissociation may refer to the fact that at times some people may be somewhat confused and less clear-headed about themselves and the world. Dissociation is assumed to be an innate predisposition that comes in degrees and serves to cope with trauma (Hacking, 1995, p. 96). In psychoanalytic parlance it is a 'defence mechanism', another concept that is not clearly defined and the psychological reality of which is assumed rather than empirically demonstrated.

There is a self-report questionnaire called the *Dissociative Experiences Scale* or DES that is purported to measure people's tendency to dissociate (Carlson *et al.*, 1993). It consists of 28 statements of experiences that people may have had and that are assumed to be indicative of people's tendency to dissociate. Respondents are asked to indicate on a one to 100 rating scale how often they have had these experiences. The ratings are then totalled over all 28 items and divided by 28, resulting in a DES score, which is the respondent's average percentage of endorsing the statements. The scale is reported to have adequate reliability because all item-total correlations are positive.

In spite of its internal consistency, factor analysis of the DES revealed that it contains three factors: absorption or imaginative involvement, amnesia, and depersonalisation or derealisation (Ross *et al.*, 1991). Of these three, absorption is taken to be the most common and not inherently pathological. Many people may become absorbed temporarily in a movie or television program, one of the DES

2 Such as temporal lobe epilepsy, encephalitis, anoxia, aneurism in the anterior communicating artery, a tumor in the third ventricle and Korsakoff's syndrome. Summary taken from Schacter, 1986a.

items, and at first sight there seems little wrong with this. Also, amnesia or forgetfulness is not uncommon. On the contrary, most of what happens to us we forget sooner or later. In autobiographical memory forgetting is the rule, remembering the exception. Still, it is surprising that some people endorse DES items like 'being in a familiar place but finding it unfamiliar' or 'not recognising friends or family members'. Endorsing statements belonging to the depersonalisation or derealisation factor, with items like 'feeling as though one's body is not one's own', 'not recognising one's face in a mirror' or 'other people and objects do not seem real', do indeed suggest that something may be wrong with the person endorsing these. Happily, items like these are among the least endorsed in samples of the general population. However, some people at times say weird things. There is nothing new to this, but it raises questions about the psychological make-up of such people.

So there is an operational definition of dissociation, a score on a self-report questionnaire. Which, however, leaves the question, as put by Ian Hacking (1995), 'how creating a system of measurement, such as the *Dissociative Experiences Scale*, can bring a fact – the fact of a dissociation continuum into being' (p. 96). The DES is said to be a measuring instrument, and as such it needs to be calibrated or, as psychologists like to call it, validated. This means that it must be shown to measure what it is meant to measure for example a new type of clock, needs to be calibrated against already existing clocks, showing that the new instrument measures time at least as good and preferably better than the old instruments (Hacking, 1995, p. 98). To what can we calibrate the DES? When the DES was designed by Putnam and Carlson (Bernstein & Putnam, 1986), there were no other instruments for measuring dissociation. Since then other instruments have been developed, that is, a self-report questionnaire called the *Questionnaire for Experiences of Dissociation* (QED; Riley, 1988) and the *Dissociative Questionnaire* (DIS-Q; Vanderlinden, 1991), but these instruments are themselves in need of calibration. All these instruments only reflect a consensus among a network of psychiatrists and psychologists who have come to agree that there is such a thing as dissociation. Calibrating these questionnaires against each other does not constitute an independent validation.

How about calibrating the DES against 'independently' obtained diagnoses of the Dissociative Identity Disorder (DID)? This was done in a study by Carlson and Putnam, the two original designers of the DES (Carlson *et al.*, 1993). The problem with this study, however, is that the MPD (DID) diagnoses were made by a group of psychiatrists who specialised in diagnosing and treating MPD patients. Although these psychiatrists are said not to have depended on the DES score for their diagnoses, they must all have been looking in their patients for self-reported experiences similar to those incorporated in the DES, which leads Hacking (1995) to conclude that this study constitutes 'a calibration of an in-house scale against in-house diagnoses' (p. 101). According to the same author 'the DES is not calibrated against judgments made by a consensus in the psychiatric community, but against the judgments of psychiatrists who are advocates of multiple personality', which makes its calibration or validation virtually circular and 'self-sealing' (p. 108-109).

What about what psychologists call concurrent validity, i.e., the ways in which DES scores correlate with the scores on other measuring instruments that for theoretical reasons are expected to correlate with dissociation? Dissociation is said to be a defence mechanism brought into play against traumatic experiences in the past. If there were correlations between self-reported traumatic experiences and dissociative symptoms as measured by the DES, would that not constitute some sort of independent calibration? In a review study of the literature Merckelbach & Muris (2001) conclude that '1) the correlations between self-reported traumatic experiences and dissociative symptoms reported in the literature are, at best, modest, 2) other factors may act as a third variable in the relationship between trauma and dissociation, and 3) high scores on the Dissociative Experiences Scale are accompanied by fantasy proneness, heightened suggestibility, and susceptibility to pseudo memories'. The last of these points raises the question of whether the self-reported traumatic experiences in these studies can be trusted, as they may be largely spurious in any case.

All this means that it is quite uncertain whether dissociation is anything more than a score on a questionnaire of uncertain meaning, a phenomenon that exists in the world of *some* psychiatrists and psychologists rather than in the world of psychiatry. This, however, is not to say that people scoring high on the DES may not suffer from a variety of troublesome psychiatric symptoms. It only means that as yet there is little reason to assume that such symptoms can fruitfully be brought under the label of a dissociative disorder, and even less be considered as resulting from traumatic experiences.

Types of amnesia

On the basis of the literature three types of amnesia can be distinguished: organic amnesia, psychogenic amnesia (because of the previous discussion we will not use the term 'dissociative amnesia'), and feigned or malingered amnesia. Perhaps there is a fourth type: imagined amnesia, where a person through external influences comes to believe that he/she is amnesic for things that were earlier well remembered. Some authors, such as Christianson & Merckelbach (publication pending), think this is possible. If so, it must be really rare. For this reason we will leave it out of consideration.

Organic amnesia

Organic amnesia is the best-established and least-problematic type of amnesia. It refers to memory impairment due to some neural dysfunction. Such neural dysfunction may result from brain injury due to external influences, blunt head injury or concussion in particular, which is not uncommon among boxers, football and soccer players, and also among victims of traffic accidents. It may also result from a neurological disorder. People suffering from epileptic seizures usually do not remember what happened and what they did during a seizure. People given to somnambulism or sleepwalking may perform quite complicated behaviours during such episodes and be amnesic of them afterwards (Mahowald & Schenk, 1995). Closed head injury may result in what is called 'a post-concussion syndrome', consisting of disorientation, grogginess, concentration problems and anterograde amnesia, i.e., problems with acquiring new memories following the injury. For instance, they may have difficulty recognising words from a list presented to them earlier and in severe cases they may not even remember that such a list of words was ever presented to them. Organic amnesia appears to follow a fixed pattern: often brief loss of consciousness following the trauma, the duration of which correlates with the severity of the trauma, retrograde as well as anterograde amnesia, progressive shrinkage of the retrograde amnesia with old events coming back more readily than more recent ones. In the end the amnesia becomes restricted to the traumatic incident itself (Hodges, 1991; Meeter & Murre, 2004).

Alcohol intoxication may also result in loss of memory for acts performed while intoxicated. This is called an 'alcohol-blackout', but such blackouts are much rarer than popular belief has it. Goodman (1995) found that it takes an excessive amount of alcohol – at least five glasses of whisky or twenty glasses of beer – consumed within the relatively short period of four hours to produce an alcohol-blackout. But if that happens, one may wonder whether the person will be able to do anything else than sleep it off. Common lore, however, has it that also a lower intake of alcohol can lead to memory impairment. In an amusing experiment some subjects were made to believe that they were drinking alcohol, while in fact they were not (and the other way around: subjects who did drink alcoholic beverages while thinking they were drinking non-alcoholic beverages). Subjects who were made to believe that they had drunk alcohol showed symptoms that are commonly taken to be typical of drunkenness, including impaired memory for their actions (Critchlow, 1986). They simply adopted a behaviour pattern that they believed was expected of them under the circumstances. Impaired memory is commonly believed to result from heavy drinking, and pretending not to remember untoward behaviour after drinking may constitute a convenient excuse and is often accepted as such. Criminal offenders may play to this common lore and pretend to be amnesic for their offence. Which is not to deny that many criminal offences are committed by perpetrators who are under the influence of alcohol, making alcohol consumption a prime risk factor for criminal behaviour.

Amnesia resulting from excessive alcohol intake, when it occurs, is a form of organic amnesia, but we add that according to at least some authors, 'amnesia cannot be purely dependent on an intoxicated state' (Parwatikar *et al.*, 1985). This does not exclude that recall may become patchy under the influence of alcohol, and one may wonder what causes this: failing perception and storage during the intoxication or failing retrieval at a later time. Some have proffered the hypothesis that it is due to a failing retrieval process later on, basing this hypothesis on the theory of state-dependent memory (Bower, 1981). This theory states that memories are retrieved more readily when the context in which they were acquired is reinstated. The empirical status of the phenomenon, however, is elusive; according to Daniel Schacter (1996) it has a 'now-you-see-it-now you don't' quality (p. 336, note 14). Moreover, we fail to see why memory impairment due to alcohol intoxication should be attributable to retrieval failure instead of to failing attention and subsequent storage while intoxicated.

Psychogenic amnesia

Psychogenic amnesia is considered to result from a traumatic experience accompanied by extreme emotion, say, from a mental blow. This is called a red-out (Swihart *et al.*, 1991). It is probably the obvious analogy to the possible effects of a physical blow which makes the idea of psychogenic amnesia alluring. But if such a thing as psychogenic amnesia exists, we must assume that a mental blow also can cause some neurological dysfunction in the brain. It is difficult to see how such a thing could come about, and it is, in any case, as yet unclear which of the brain structures concerned with memory would be affected and how (Parkin, 1998, p. 147). If only for this reason, many authors are sceptical about the occurrence of psychogenic amnesia, 'characterized by sudden onset in response to stress, inability to remember precipitating events, loss of personal identity and extensive retrograde amnesia' (McNally, 2003, p. 187). In a brief comment forensic psychologist Arthur Centor (1982) calls psychogenic amnesia 'a myth': 'My own experience, during a period of over eleven years in a forensic unit, failed to confirm even one case of psychological amnesia in the absence of a psychotic episode, brain damage, or acute brain syndrome.' In this he is in the company of Leo Tolstoy who wrote in *Kreutzer Sonata* (1869): 'When people say they don't remember what they do in a fit of fury, it is rubbish, falsehood.' Most contemporary authors take a more careful position to the question of the existence of psychogenic amnesia. If it occurs at all, it is an extremely rare phenomenon, according to Daniel Schacter (1996), short-lived, i.e., temporary, and almost always the result of the combined effects of brain damage and emotional trauma (p. 225). Schacter's Harvard colleague Richard McNally (2003) also considers it a rare phenomenon, but still admits that 'some cases more convincingly suggest that murderers may indeed experience psychogenic amnesia for a crime committed in an extreme state of rage' (p.210). Perhaps we should not entirely exclude the occurrence of psychogenic amnesia in rare cases. However, claims of amnesia among 24 to 47 percent of convicted murderers, as reported by various authors (cf. Taylor & Kopelman, 1984), cannot possibly be called rare.

Feigned amnesia

The problem with psychogenic amnesia is that there is also the possibility of feigning or malingering amnesia and that it is very difficult, if not impossible, to distinguish between real and feigned psychogenic amnesia. According to some authors 'amnesia of 30 minutes' duration or less, circumscribed to the offence, is most likely malingered', while amnesia of longer duration is most likely organic (Bradford & Smith, p. 228).

The case of the amnesic strangler, described in the first section of this chapter, is precisely of this nature in that his amnesia, according to the offender, was restricted to the brief period that it took to strangle his wife. Its onset was sudden, its ending equally sudden. It was, moreover, claimed to be irreversible because also much later during his trial the defendant maintained that he still could not remember his actions during the fatal minutes of committing his offence. How can we or rather how could the court be certain that the defendant did not feign his amnesia? Well, because two psychiatrists and a psychologist said that this was a case of 'acute dissociative amnesia'. Why? We quote from the report of one of the psychiatrists:

> During the offence the defendant acted more or less primitive-emotional, but consistent by strangling his wife, in accordance with his violent (but repressed) anger and in defence against a reality (abandonment) that he considered threatening. In this state became visible primitive and unrestricted infantile attachment reactions in the sense of clinging to and holding on, in a similar way as can be observed, although less aggressively, in young primates during their first post-natal phase under conditions of threat and stress.

That is why! We admit that we chose this quote because we thought it one of the more ludicrous, but by no means atypical, passages in the expert opinions on this case.

Amnesia and cognitive control

All three experts concluded from their diagnoses of dissociative amnesia that the defendant 'at the time of his offence and the minutes preceding it had not been able to determine his will and actions'. Therefore, in the absence of *mens rea* the defendant could not be held responsible for his behaviour at the time. Although this implication of their diagnosis was presented to the court as obvious, it is not so by any means. The amnesia that the defendant claims occurred, *after* the offence was committed if it occurred at all. Remembering something refers to something that occurred in the past: coming to his senses the defendant could not remember what he had done just minutes ago. At the time of the trial, months later, he said he still could not remember it. For the question of whether he was in control of his behaviour *during* the offence, his retrograde amnesia is immaterial. Each of us is amnesic of the vast majority of our actions in the past, and at least some of them we should not have committed because they were less than charitable. Does the fact that we do not remember them now free us from our responsibility for them at the time we committed them? Of course not, so common sense tells us (see also: Wegner, 2002). And we were also told this long ago by an American court in the case of the United States v. Olvera (1954)[3]:

> From amnesia for one's actions during a particular period it does not follow that 'the defendant must necessarily have been unable during the same period either to form a criminal intent, or to distinguish right from wrong. Amnesia is significant only as a symptom confirming other evidence to the effect that the accused did not know the nature and quality of his acts during the period for which he lacked recall.'
>
> The author from whose writing we take this quote concludes: 'Amnesia is – in and of itself – a relatively neutral circumstance in its bearing on criminal responsibility' (Herman, 1986, p. 19).

Also, loss of control does not figure among the diagnostic criteria for dissociative amnesia in the DSM-IV. So what the experts said in their reports on the amnesic strangler amounts to a *non sequitur*. There are cases in which retrograde amnesia occurs together with absence of control while performing an act – as, e.g., often happens with somnambulism – but retrograde amnesia is not a sure or even probable sign of absence of control, and that is what we are saying here.

All this is not to say that people never forget things they did in the past. On the contrary, forgetting the past is the rule rather than the exception. Most of what we

3 United States v. Olvera: 4 USCMA 134, 141, 15 CMR 134, 141 (1954).

did or happened to us in the past we cannot recall at all or only with difficulty and often only partially. And for the things we do remember, we cannot be sure that we recall them accurately. The passage of time plays an important role in this, but it is not the only factor. Another one is that we tend to recall conspicuous events, either positive or negative, more readily than ordinary ones. In the literature, memories of conspicuous events are called 'flashbulb memories' (Brown & Kulik, 1977), a real misnomer. It suggests that we store our memories like pictures in our brain that can be inspected as such when we recall them, while in reality each time we recall something, we need to reassemble the memory anew from components that are distributively stored in the brain. Memory, therefore, is said to be reconstructive, not reproductive. The longer ago something happened to us, the greater the chance that its memory trace has become lost among the myriad of younger memories, or become confused with other, related memories (cf. chapter 8). But really conspicuous events are almost never entirely forgotten. There is no documented case in the literature of someone who has forgotten that he has been an inmate in a Nazi death camp (Wagenaar & Groeneweg, 1990), although many of these victims may well have become confused about the details of their ordeal (Wagenaar, 1988b). The same goes for the many Dutch nationals who were detained in one of the Japanese prison camps in Indonesia during World War II (Merckelbach *et al.*, 2003). Extremely traumatic memories are more readily retrieved and rarely, if ever, fall victim to total amnesia. But this is not to say that those memories are always accurate in every detail. On the contrary, often they are full of mistakes, mostly 'commissions', i.e., false additions and distortions (Loftus, 2003).

Possible motives for feigning amnesia

If we assume that most cases of amnesia without an organic basis claimed by perpetrators of serious crimes are feigned, the next question is why these people pretend to be amnesic of their crimes. The most obvious motive we already mentioned above: a defence based on lack of *mens rea.* We already characterised this argument as a *non sequitur*, but a court, confused by expert witnesses, may fall for it, as happened in the case of the amnesic strangler. There is a German case in which it was used with success (Barbey, 1990), so it may be worthwhile for a defendant to proffer it to a court. A related motive for claiming amnesia for a crime would be the hope that the court will consider amnesia a mitigating circumstance, a hope which rests on the same *non sequitur* that later memory loss is an indication for diminished control while committing a crime.

Another possible motive for feigning amnesia for a crime would be the wish to avoid embarrassing questions about the often ugly details of it. If you do not remember, you cannot answer questions about those details, and maybe, just maybe, the court may not realise how ugly these must have been. But claiming total amnesia for this purpose is a risky strategy. History has it that Rudolf Hess chose it to begin with during the Nuremberg trial, only to realise later that in claiming total amnesia for his misdeeds he also could not contradict anything that was offered in evidence against him. So halfway through the trial he changed his position, telling the court that he had only feigned his amnesia, which a group of prominent psychiatrists had judged genuine earlier (Picknett *et al.*, 2001). A motive related to this would be the wish to frustrate the investigation of the police and the court, hoping that in the end the proof will not be sufficient to convict.

If the latter two motives are envisioned, there is, however, a better and less risky strategy available to defendants: the right to remain silent, which in virtually every jurisdiction is granted to suspects by law, and guaranteed by international treaties.[4] The right not to answer questions and thereby not to be compelled to testify against oneself or to confess guilt can be used selectively by a suspect. It is not an all-or-nothing decision, but can be invoked for every new question and abandoned for the next, whatever suits the defendant. If the motive is to obstruct the criminal investigation, selective use of the right to remain silent is the better strategy, on condition that invoking it cannot be used against the defendant. This is the case in most jurisdictions, with the striking exception in the Netherlands: an obvious attempt to obstruct the court's investigation may lead to a longer sentence (see: Dutch Supreme Court 1964, 1974).[5]

As said before, defendants may feign amnesia in the hope that courts will treat them in a more lenient manner. But how realistic is this hope? To find out, Crombag and Jelicic (unpublished data) designed two versions of a vignette of a criminal case. In both versions the suspect, nineteen-year-old Daniel, was said to have a very troublesome relationship with his parents. After having finished his secondary education he did not go to university as his parents had intended, but instead joined a group of squatters, spending his days in idleness and probably using drugs. Occasionally, he came home, though, to have his dirty clothes washed by his mother. Whenever his father was home on those occasions, they had a row that usually ended with Daniel fleeing the house. But on one of those occasions something else happened: the enraged Daniel brought out a knife and stabbed his father three times in the belly, in the presence of his mother. The father was rushed to a hospital, where he died of his wounds sometime later. Daniel was arrested by the police. At this point in the story, the two versions diverge. In one version Daniel confesses to hav-

4 Art. 14, section 3 sub g, ICCPR (International Covenant on Civil and Political Rights) and art. 6, ECHR (European Convention on Human Rights).

5 HR (Dutch Supreme Court) 3 March 1964, *NJ* 1964, 400; HR 12 Nov. 1974, *NJ* 1975, 41.

ing stabbed his father, but adds that his father had driven him beyond endurance, making him lose his self-control. He had not intended to kill his father and felt very guilty about it. In the other version Daniel did not deny having stabbed his father, since his mother had witnessed it, but said he could not remember a thing about it. His memory for the incident, he said, was a black hole.

Half of a group of 30 District Court judges and 28 prosecutors were offered one version of Daniel's case, and the other half the other version, and were asked to pass judgment on Daniel, choosing from among sixteen alternatives ranging from acquittal to fifteen years of imprisonment, the latter being the maximum sentence under Dutch law for involuntary manslaughter. The average number of years of imprisonment awarded by judges and prosecutors are given in table 1, and were tested for significance. The data in table 1 show that it made no difference to either the judges or the prosecutors whether a defendant claims amnesia or not. So, if defendants hope for leniency from judges and prosecutors by feigning amnesia for their crime, this hope may well be in vain. And this was irrespective of whether the judges and prosecutors in this study thought that Daniel's claim of amnesia was genuine or not.

Table 1 Average number of years of imprisonment awarded in Daniel's case

	No amnesia			Amnesia			F	*p*
	N	Mean	SD	N	Mean	SD		
Judges	15	4.73	1.62	15	4.93	1.67	0.11	.74
Prosecutors	15	5.66	1.95	13	5.54	2.11	0.03	.87
Total group	30	5.20	1.83	28	5.21	1.88	0.01	.98

Detecting malingerers

If the data reported in the preceding paragraph are taken at face value,[6] in criminal cases it may not serve much of a purpose for defendants to feign amnesia. However,

6 Which we hesitate to do as long as they have not been replicated.

we know of a criminal case in which not the defendant, but a victim claimed amnesia and in which the question of whether the court considered the amnesia genuine or feigned was decisive (Nanninga, 2001).

On 15 March 2001, Maya (a pseudonym), a 16-year-and-9-month-old woman of Surinamese-Hindu descent, was on her way home from school. While waiting at a red traffic light before crossing the street, a young Indian man came to stand next to her. Suddenly, Maya felt herself becoming very heavy, and from that moment on she does not remember anything, until several hours later she came to her senses and found herself lying naked on a bed in a strange apartment, while the Indian man was stroking her and penetrating her with his finger. She hastily dressed and ran home. The next day she told the vice-principle of her school about the incident, who informed the police. In spite of her amnesia, Maya was able to lead the police from the traffic light to the apartment where she had been molested, and there they found the almost nineteen-year-old Bandhu (also a pseudonym), who was temporarily living there while visiting the country from India. He did not deny that he had had sexual contact with Maya, but claimed that it had been consensual. Maya denied this, saying that Bandhu had bewitched her with a magic pebble, with the effect that she lost her will and memory.

Maya's purported amnesia posed a logical problem: how could she know that Bandhu had acted against her will if she did not remember anything from the first moment of contact at the traffic light? If the court disbelieved Maya's amnesia, there would be no case to answer.

A reason not to believe it is that Maya had a strong motive to deny her voluntary sexual contact with a stranger, since Hindu women are strictly forbidden to have sex outside marriage. But then she could have kept silent about the whole incident and nobody would probably have known about her transgression. Why did she tell anyone? Because she needed to explain to her parents her lateness in returning home? Had someone seen her in Bandhu's company? We do not know. And lastly, how could Maya have possibly lost command of her will simply by standing next to a man in a very public place? For these reasons one would expect that the court, trying Bandhu, would not have believed Maya's amnesia and loss of will, and would have dismissed the case as another example of how foolish young girls can sometimes be.

Surprisingly, the court decided otherwise: it believed Maya's sudden loss of control and the accompanying amnesia and convicted Bandhu – we quote from the written sentence – for bringing Maya 'in a state of physical helplessness (...) and knowing she could no longer determine her will, had fondled her naked body (...) and had penetrated her sexually', all this leading to a jail sentence of nine months. The court decided this without explaining how Bandhu could have bewitched Maya; quite wisely they did not mention the magic pebble.

We can think of another reason why at times it is relevant to distinguish between feigned and genuine amnesia. For instance, in civil cases in which victims of traffic accidents sue for damages, they may be tempted to maximise the damage they have incurred by exaggerating their symptoms, including memory loss. Also in such cases it may be important to detect malingerers of memory loss.

Distinguishing malingering from genuine amnesiacs

Are we able to somehow distinguish between genuine amnesiacs, be it organic or psychogenic, and malingerers? In 1986 Schacter wrote that at that time there was 'yet no reliable evidence that cases of genuine and simulated amnesia (could) be distinguished'. Still, at about the same time he thought that 'limited amnesia with sudden, sharply defined onset and termination (as was claimed by the amnesic strangler, and Maya as well) should be viewed with caution' (p. 291). In 1998 Parkin reported that 'specific procedures have been devised to 'catch out' people who are faking a memory disorder.' This is because malingerers are often 'not conversant with the true nature of amnesia, and will therefore make mistakes'. The most common mistake often made by malingerers is that they tend to exaggerate their symptoms (see: Schacter, 1986b; Iverson, 1995). According to Parkin, there is a rather straightforward way to distinguish organic amnesia from psychogenic amnesia: anterograde amnesia, i.e., impaired recall for new information acquired after the injury, is typical for organic amnesia, while retrograde amnesia, i.e., impaired recall for events preceding the traumatic event, is typical for psychogenic amnesia (1998, p. 157). He goes on to say that anterograde amnesia in cases with no detectable organic basis is therefore 'in clinical practice (...) regarded as prime evidence for malingered amnesia' (p. 161), apparently assuming that most cases of psychogenic amnesia are malingered. In this he is in the company of many of his colleagues.

The *Structured Inventory of Malingered Symptomatology* (SIMS; Smith, 1997; Smith & Burger, 1997) is a self-report questionnaire consisting of 75 descriptions of highly improbable psychiatric symptoms that individuals suspected of malingering are asked to indicate whether they have them. The test items consist of five subscales concerned various types of psychiatric problems, one of which is concerned with memory impairment and amnesia. The idea is that malingerers will, more than others, confirm that they have such outlandish or at least improbable symptoms, thus revealing their malingering.[7] In a number of studies attempts were

7 One of the items in the memory impairment subscale is: 'At times I've been unable to remember the names or faces of close relatives so that they seem like strangers.' The reader may recall that, surprisingly, the DES contains a nearly identical item.

made to validate the SIMS (Smith & Burger, 1997; Edens *et al.*, 1999). In these studies a group of college students were instructed to malinger psychiatric symptoms, while another group of students were asked to answer honestly. The results were promising in that more than 90 percent of the students instructed to malinger amnesia were identified by the SIMS as malingerers, and also more than 90 percent of the control subjects were classified by the SIMS as honest respondents. The limitation of these studies is, of course, that the experimental subjects were college students, who can hardly be taken as representative of the usual criminal defendant.

Looking for probable signs of malingered amnesia in the ways in which it is presented by the individual claiming amnesia is problematic because one can never be quite sure that in a particular instance one is not dealing with an atypical case. Perhaps it would be safer to treat all cases of claimed psychogenic amnesia, i.e., amnesia in the absence of any organic dysfunction, as cases of feigned amnesia. Still, of all the specialists writing about the subject, no one has categorically stated that psychogenic amnesia can never be genuine, only that, if it occurs, it is very rare indeed.

Recently, another promising method for catching out malingerers was developed. It is called *Symptom Validity Testing* (SVT; Frederick *et al.*, 1995; Denney, 1996). A defendant in a criminal trial suspected of malingering amnesia is presented with a forced-choice recognition test about the particulars of the offence and the circumstances in which it took place. If he indeed suffers from amnesia, he cannot answer these questions, but is instructed to guess whenever he does not know the answer. In such a test, a genuine amnesic will perform at chance level, i.e., 50 percent correct in the case of true/false questions. If the defendant performs significantly below chance level, he is apparently avoiding the correct alternatives, which is an indication that he does have knowledge about what happened and is therefore feigning his memory loss.

Merckelbach, Hauer & Rassin (2002) did a study to find out if feigning subjects could beat this test. Twenty students were instructed to steal an envelope containing some money and subsequently to feign amnesia for this offence while taking a fifteen-question SVT. Of the experimental subjects 53 percent scored well below chance level (fewer than four correct answers) and were thus unmasked as malingerers. This, however, implies that 47 percent of the students instructed to feign amnesia were able to beat the test. But these were relatively smart psychology students, who moreover have come to expect to be deceived in some respect or other in the many experiments in which they are regularly asked to participate. The results might be better if the test was applied to less sophisticated subjects, who moreover could be given more questions to answer. We expect that a real defendant confronting a real police investigator and answering around 40 or more such true/false questions may find it difficult, if not impossible, to keep track of his answers in order to score at chance level, in particular if the interrogator keeps him uncertain during the test as to how many questions there are going to be. In addition the sequence of correct and incorrect answers should be random, which can be checked with a 'runs-test' (see: M.J. Cliffe, 1992).

We think that the SVT is a promising development, but we add that the procedure is laborious, because for every suspect a special test with questions unique for his offence will need to be devised. Moreover, when such a test is devised, the correct and incorrect alternatives first need to be evaluated with a panel of naive subjects, to check whether the incorrect alternative for each question is not more plausible than the correct one, thus avoiding that an genuine amnesic would still be likely to score below chance level. All this probably implies that it only pays to use the SVT in really serious criminal cases.

Concluding remarks

Distinguishing genuine from feigned amnesia in criminal defendants is difficult. Of one thing we are pretty sure: just talking once or twice with such a defendant, as is often done by consulting psychiatrists and psychologists, will almost never suffice. We strongly discourage criminal courts from adopting opinions of expert witnesses based on mere talking to defendants, as was done by the court that tried the case of the amnesic strangler.

If the empirical data that we reported earlier in this chapter are any indication, it often may not matter whether a defendant is feigning amnesia for his offence or not. From not remembering after the fact, it simply does not follow that at the time of the offence the perpetrator did not know what he was doing and had no control over his acts. Judges and prosecutors seem to know this, so long as they are not confused by expert witnesses.

Still, in some cases it is important to distinguish between genuine and feigned amnesia, as in the case of Maya, in which the defendant could only be convicted if the court was willing to believe that Bandhu had magical powers. In this case it might have served a purpose to subject Maya to a well-designed SVT. We suspect she would have failed it. In most of the 26 to 47 percent of the cases in which murderers claim amnesia for their crime, it is probably safe to take their amnesia, when not clearly organic in nature, as almost certainly feigned and in any case irrelevant.

So, what about the amnesic strangler? The court would have been wise not to let him get away with killing his wife.

CHAPTER 13

Obeying Reflexes or Death on the Climbing Wall

The law assumes that people are able to control their behaviour and that therefore they can be held responsible for their actions. There are some exceptions to this general rule, notably cases of self-defence, *force majeur* and insanity. But in general, when none of these exceptions are claimed by the defendant, courts presume responsibility of offenders. For the attribution of legal responsibility, it is not necessary that the perpetrator had a specific intention to cause harm or even was conscious of the possible negative consequences of his (or her) actions. It is sufficient to establish somehow that the perpetrator *should* have thought of the harm that he might inflict on his victim. Drunken driving is a clear example. When a drunken driver causes another person to die in a car accident, there usually has been no criminal intent to kill nor – probably – a clear awareness of the likelihood of a fatal accident. Still, the driver should have realised when he began drinking that later on he would be unable to drive. This should have led him either to refrain from drinking or organise some other way of transportation afterwards. Negligence is the most important case of legal responsibility for harm that was never intended.

People are held particularly responsible for acquitting themselves of their specific duties. A failure in this respect may lead to responsibility for the consequences, even if those consequences were highly unpredictable. Failing to do one's explicit duty is a severe form of negligence. The signal man who fails to throw a switch in time because at that very moment he happened to be engaged in rescuing a child, thereby causing the death of many train passengers, is still considered to have been negligent because he failed to do his promised duty (Sims, 1883).

Psychological theories about the control of one's behaviour are far more complicated than beliefs on the subject commonly held by lawyers. All classical theories assume that there are different levels of behaviour with more or less behavioural control. At the lowest level of this graded set, there is usually something like reflexes, automated behaviour, or preconscious behaviour. 'Consciousness,' Timothy Wilson recently wrote, 'is a limited-capacity system, and to survive in the world people must be able to process a great deal of information outside awareness' (Wilson, 2002, p. 8). Probably the larger part of a person's behaviour occurs on a preconscious level, without conscious deliberation and specific intent (Barg, 1997). Even quite complex behaviour repertoires are often automatically triggered by external stimuli and, once running, cannot easily be stopped. The simplest form of unconscious behaviour is the reflex, such as the corneal reflex, the patellar reflex, and the plantar reflex. Pavlov devised a procedure to build conditioned reflexes on the basis of such innate reflexes, by which almost any type of behaviour can become reflexive through association with an already existing, inborn reflex. To Pavlovian or classical conditioning Thorndike added the mechanism of operant or instrumental conditioning, through which many kinds of behaviour can be 'shaped and maintained' by manipulating their consequences (Skinner, 1972, p. 18). Classical behaviourism aims at describing virtually all human behaviour as resulting from such systematic connections between stimuli and responses. In such a theory awareness, control and responsibility have no place. This is not the proper arena for a principled discussion of the question of whether such a theory is sufficient to accommodate all forms of human behaviour. Instead, we will concentrate on the question of whether it can happen that one person causes the death of another by way of a reflex and can still be held criminally responsible and be tried in a criminal court for the harm he has caused?

The case of John Yonkers

John Yonkers' passion is to climb on climbing walls. He is a highly experienced climber and has won several prizes. Wall climbers always exercise in pairs. The lead climber wears a harness to which a lead rope is attached. This rope runs through a pulley on the ceiling of the hall and from there goes down to the second member of the pair, who remains on the ground and provides 'belay' to the lead climber. This is done by means of a special belay device worn by the belay climber, through which the rope is passed. The device is designed in such a way that the rope can be fed through it smoothly when the lead climber is ascending, but hitches when the lead climber moves down and, in particular, falls. After reaching the top of the wall, the lead climber can be let down through a special device, sometimes called the slot device. The belay climber is attached to an anchor on the floor, so that in case of a fall the lead climber is anchored onto the floor.

The owners of climbing walls usually require that all climbers, lead climbers as well as belay climbers, are well trained and have mastered the specialised skills needed to ensure safety. The rules usually demand that all climbers demonstrate that they know:

– how to put on a climbing harness and buckle it up properly;

- how to feed the rope correctly through a belay device and to attach the rope and belay to the harness in the proper place;
- how to belay properly, i.e., demonstrate the correct hand actions while taking in and feeding the rope, as well as the proper braking action by using the slot device;
- how to use the basic climbing signals; examples of which are the signals for *on belay, climbing, climb, up rope, slack, take, tension and lower*;
- how to climb a route of a certain difficulty level with a good climbing technique and without falling;
- how to belay a lead climber, including how to attach properly to the anchor, how to position oneself in relation to the anchor and the lead climber, how to manage rope, how to feed the lead rope using the correct hand motions, how to brake, how to use prescribed climbing commands, and how to hold a fall by the lead climber.

All these rules imply that wall climbing requires a high level of training, because accidents may happen in a split second.

One day John Yonkers is climbing with his friend Benny Smith. Benny is the lead climber, John provides belay. Five metres away, another pair is climbing: a young boy leads and his girlfriend holds the rope. The young boy reaches the top of the wall and wants to come down, but the girl apparently does not know how to operate the slot device properly. The lead climber has been lowered about one metre and is dangling on the rope. The brake stops the rope and the girl is confused about what to do next. This is what John Yonkers, having observed the event, remembers:

> The girl said: 'Can anybody help me?' And as in a bad dream I saw her hand move to the brake, which would release the rope completely; the lead climber would make a fall of fourteen metres! I rushed to the girl to stop her, and helped her lower her boyfriend in the proper manner. I was shaking all over. The tension did not go away immediately after the boy was safely on the ground.

The real drama, however, had not yet begun. John was still shaking when he made a fatal mistake. After the boy had reached the ground, the slot device needed to be opened to release the lead rope. John meant to open the *girl's slot device*, but in the confusion of the moment he opened *his own slot device*. At the same moment Benny Smith, who had reached a height of twelve metres, made a misstep. He fell the whole distance of twelve metres and was mortally wounded. Three hours later he died in hospital. John was charged with involuntary manslaughter, because he had negligently failed to perform his explicit duty to provide proper belay to Benny. Can it be argued convincingly that Benny's death was an accident, resulting from reflexive behaviour, i.e., behaviour that was not under John's control?

Three levels of control

One of the leading theories on behavioural control, originally proposed by Jens Rasmussen (1983), specifies three levels of control: skill-based behaviour, rule-based behaviour, and knowledge-based behaviour. At the level of skill-based behaviour, everything is fully automated. At the level of rule-based behaviour we apply existing rules in a new situation. At the level of knowledge-based behaviour we generate new solutions for a novel problem, based on existing knowledge in other domains.

Well-known examples of skill-based behaviour are walking, swimming, riding a bicycle, driving a car, speaking. In speaking, for example, each day we pronounce vowels and consonants millions of times, but still we cannot explain how we do it. We learn this through imitation. Even the best teaching method uses nothing but imitation. Appeal to a conscious understanding of the process does not help at all. Native speakers of English will never really be able to pronounce the Dutch diphthongs 'ei', 'eu', and 'ui', whatever their level of education. Not only is the pronunciation automated, but also the finding of words. Words are found in a vast internal 'dictionary', usually without conscious effort and without awareness of how the search is executed. We construct proper sentences with the words in the correct order, again without awareness of the grammatical rules and how the construction process works. While speaking, we may think about the contents of what we are saying, but the speaking itself is completely automated. The automation of speech ensures that this highly complicated skill is performed in real time and almost faultlessly. When an error occurs, there is a speech monitoring system that detects and corrects the error, again without any apparent conscious effort.

Skill-based behaviour often consists of a chain of separate actions. Donald Norman (1981) proffered the hypothesis that such chains are guided by a very simple mechanism: the end of the preceding link constitutes the trigger that starts the next link. For instance, seeing the keyhole in the door of your car is the stimulus for correctly inserting the key. The feeling of the key fully inserted into the keyhole is the stimulus for turning it in the correct direction. While reading this, you may not quite *know* which direction that is, but an adequate stimulus will make you execute the proper movement without thinking. In this manner quite elaborate behavioural repertoires may be executed without any apparent involvement of consciousness: driving home from the office, finding information in the computer, eating a meal, picking up a package from the post office, teaching an introductory class, playing a Beethoven sonata, or skating for the 500 metre championship.

The theory of behavioural control was further extended in the GEMS model of Jim Reason (1990). GEMS stands for General Error Modelling System. The model specifies that skill-based behaviour is the default option. Most of what we do is controlled at the skill-based level. A switch to the higher levels is only executed when there is a clear necessity. For that purpose skill-based operation involves a check at the end of each step. If the result is as expected, go on. If not, a switch is made to *rule-based behaviour*. At this level we engage in some sort of pattern recognition: is the pattern of the observed problem familiar, and do we know a rule that usually solves this problem? If both answers are affirmative, we apply the rule, check whether the problem has gone away and return to skill-based operation. If we do not recognise the pattern, cannot think of an applicable rule, or the rule does not seem to help, we move upwards again to knowledge-based operation. At this level we try to identify the abstract characteristics of the problem, in order to see whether we possess any knowledge that might be relevant for the creation of a novel solution. If no such solution can be found, according to GEMS there is only one step left: panic, usually resulting in repeating a behaviour pattern that has already failed before.

Behavioural errors are made at all three levels, but depending on the level, they differ in appearance. Consequently, there are also three types of errors. At the knowledge-based level we make mistakes. These happen when we execute a consciously chosen plan correctly, but the plan itself is wrong and does not produce the expected outcome. Both Napoleon's and Hitler's invasions of Russia were of that type. At the rule-based level we also make mistakes, but of a different kind: we either misclassify the problem or select a rule that does not apply to the selected type. In the Netherlands we recently had the problem of a leaking dyke. The authorities tried to fortify the dyke with sandbags and a steel wall, in a fashion that was successful during the past 1000 years. But the dyke kept leaking, and the local population was evacuated. After about a week it was discovered that in the body of the dyke there was a leaking water main, explaining why the previous measures had not solved the problem. Although the earlier measures were a logical consequence of the diagnosis, the diagnosis turned out to be wrong. Closing off the water main solved the problem instantly.

At the skill-based level errors take the form of slips and lapses, the kinds of actions to which we react with 'oops'. Examples of these are the verbal slips we regularly make in everyday speech, hitting the wrong keys on our computer, forgetting things we had planned to do, forgetting where we left our car keys, pouring the cat's milk in your coffee cup and coffee in the cat's bowl.

Slips and lapses

In the case of John Yonkers our most important claim is that his error occurred at the skill-based level. He was highly trained in climbing and providing belay. For him the safe arrival of the endangered climber on the ground constituted the trigger for the next link of an automated sequence: opening the slot device. However, he proceeded to the next link of his automated pattern by opening *his own slot device*, not the slot device on the girl's harness, which would have been the appropriate next step. Since at that moment John was no longer engaged in solving a problem, opening the slot device was no longer rule-based behaviour; he was simply following a highly automated routine. It was even less a knowledge-based operation as for him there appeared to be no novel problem that required the conscious search for possibly relevant information in other knowledge domains. The error could only occur at the skill-based level and is typical for this level, as we will see upon further investigating this class of behaviours.

Two aspects of the execution of skill-based action programmes are important for our present discussion: the programmes are highly trained, and their execution is extremely reliable, precisely because of their automaticity. In extreme sports activities, such as motor racing or rock-climbing, almost everything depends on the automaticity of the behaviour. That is why a high degree of training is necessary. This is so because a conscious search of the best solutions would cause unacceptable delays. It is essential that such tasks are executed in real time, often within a split second. In the case of team sports it is also essential that the cooperation between the team members is fully automated. Each participant must follow a fixed pattern and be able to trust that their mates will also not deviate. In doing so, team members make themselves completely dependant on the reflexes of their partners. The safety of motor racing on a racing circuit depends critically on the reflexes of the other participants, and also on the slips and lapses that these participants may occasionally make. Let us consider a short inventory of things that may go wrong in the automatic execution of an action sequence (Reason, 1990).

Errors at the skill-based level will generally occur when the automatic triggering of the next step by the outcome of the previous step goes wrong, *and* at the same time the monitoring and correction mechanism fails. One type of error is called *perceptual confusion*, which occurs when a signal is received that is confused with the trigger for a certain action. As a result, the action starts at the wrong moment. An example is a flashing green light as part of a pharmacy sign near an intersection controlled by traffic lights. The green light in the pharmacy sign may act as a trigger for a driver to move forward.

Another type of error is called *omission following interruption*. The sequence is interrupted and next restarted at the wrong point of the action sequence. An example is a telephone call while cooking. The problem is to go back to the correct next step in the cooking routine after completing the telephone call.

A third category of errors is *reduced intentionality*. The action schema is started, but through interference with external stimuli, the original intention is lost, and some other schema is started. An example of this is when you go to the bookshelves to consult a dictionary, see that a book has fallen on the floor, you pick it up, put it back and forget to consult the dictionary. Intentionality may also be lost spontaneously: you go to the refrigerator to get butter, open the fridge door and cannot remember what you came for.

A fourth category of errors in skill-based actions relates to the execution of two skill-based operations at the same time. These are called *interference errors.* They occur when two actions contain similar links, or links that are triggered by similar signals. Dr. Lovell is applying the stethoscope to Mrs. Bally's chest when the telephone rings. The good doctor says to Mrs. Bally: 'Good morning, Lovell speaking.' This category, together with the earlier mentioned category of *double-capture slips*, are most relevant for the case of John Yonkers.

Double-capture slips involve two distinct, but causally related kinds of capture. In his classical text on this subject, Reason (1990, p. 68-69) describes the double-capture slip as follows:

> First the greater part of the limited attentional resource is claimed either by some internal preoccupation or by some external distractor at a time when a higher-order intervention (bringing the workspace into the control loop momentarily) is needed to set the action along the currently intended pathway. As a result, the control of action is usurped by the strongest schema leading onwards from that particular point in the sequence. Such slips are lawful enough to permit reasonably firm predictions regarding when they will occur and what form they will take. The necessary conditions for their occurrence appear to be:
> a. the performance of some well-practised activity in familiar surroundings,
> b. an intention to depart from custom,
> c. a departure point beyond which the 'strengths' of the associated action schemata are markedly different, and
> d. failure to make an appropriate attentional check.
> The outcome, generally, is a strong habit intrusion, that is, the unintended activation of the strongest (i.e., the most contextually frequent) action schema beyond the choice point.

Examples cited by Reason include:

- 'I brought the milk in to make myself a cup of tea. I had put the cup and saucer out previously. But instead of putting the milk into the cup, I put the bottle straight into the fridge'.
- 'I meant to get my car out, but as I passed through the back porch on the way to the garage, I stopped to put on my Wellington boots and gardening jacket as if to work in the garden'.
- 'I have two mirrors on my dressing table. One I use for making up and brushing my hair, the other for inserting and removing my contact lenses. On this occa-

sion, I intended to brush my hair, but sat down in front of the wrong mirror, and removed my contact lenses instead'.
– 'I went to my bedroom to change into something more comfortable for the evening, and the next thing I knew I was getting into my pyjama trousers, as if to go to bed'.

The readers will not find it difficult to add many more examples of such slips and lapses from their personal life. We perform many of these simple tasks at the skill-based level, which is why we all make these types of errors occasionally.

What must be stressed is the lawful nature of this behaviour. The conditions in which slips and lapses occur are well-known and fully specified. Reason's use of the term 'usurped' is well-chosen: it is an automatic event, controlled by stimulus conditions, and only to be corrected afterwards, after a proper attentional check. Some of the harm may already have been done by that time though.

Application to the case of John Yonkers

It is our contention that John Yonkers was caught in a double-capture slip. When he saw the girl's hand move to release the slot device, he may have made a conscious decision to try to prevent a terrible accident. It is also possible that this decision was made as a reflex, without conscious consideration of the fact that his first duty was to provide belay to Benny. Either way, the next step was the execution of a highly trained, highly automated skill: to safely lower a person hanging on a rope at the height of fourteen metres. He must have executed this skill many times before. The last step in that schema consists of opening the slot device, thus releasing the lead rope. This action is usually performed with the belay device on the climber's harness, not with the equipment on another person. The final step 'safely on the ground, release rope now' is a strong habit, probably strong enough to capture the unusual step of opening another person's slot device. Opening the girl's slot device may therefore be captured by the stronger habit of opening one's own slot device. The condition for this capture to occur is being captured first by an attention-demanding fact or condition, such as a strong emotion. John experienced such a strong emotion when he saw the neighbouring team almost causing a fatal accident.

When John decided to assist the girl and her boyfriend in order to prevent a fatal accident, the risk of double capture was introduced. Whether or not the capture would materialise depended on his level of attention. Given that John's attention for his primary task was interfered with in a virtually unavoidable manner, the necessary separation between the two activities was moved out of John's control. Obviously, an attentional check would have corrected the slip in time, if only Benny had not made a misstep at that very moment. But it is highly representative of dangerous sports that often there is no time or opportunity to correct slips and lapses.

The question remains, of course, whether John should have allowed himself to be distracted by the other couple's problems in the first place. If it was a conscious and reasoned decision that the couple's dangerous behaviour was a sufficient and acceptable reason to leave Benny on his own for a minute, John could be accused of risky behaviour, which in a legal context might be considered negligent. Perhaps he should have warned Benny and asked him to stop climbing. But the whole event happened within a split second: the girl's hand moved towards the slot device. Only by stopping her immediately could John avert a disaster. It is therefore not unlikely that even this part of the process happened automatically, by way of a reflex. In that case it cannot be said that his action was due to a decision under John's full and conscious control.

Who is responsible?

Obviously, the suggestion that John might not be held legally responsible must be very unsatisfactory for the victim's family and friends. It should not be possible that a young man dies after falling from a climbing wall without it being somebody's fault. We need to point out the somewhat surprising judicial habit in cases like these to reconstruct the chain of events that ended in an accident in the reverse order, from the end to the beginning. The first actor we encounter in the backward chain is closest to the actual accident and is for this reason likely to be seen as the cause of the accident. This is sometimes called the *causa proxima* rule (cf. chapter 2 in this book). Since John was the last to do something in the chain of events, he becomes the prime target for attributing blame. But consider our argument that skill-based automated behaviour is shaped by the conditions in which it occurs. John's double capture was possible for two reasons: he experienced a sudden shock, and he became engaged in two highly similar tasks simultaneously. Who was responsible for the first of these two conditions, the sudden shock? The other couple's sudden and unmistakeably very dangerous behaviour. That is where it started. What else than John's assistance could have prevented a fatal accident? One may ask who was responsible for the fact that nobody other than John Yonkers was present who could have prevented the boy from falling to his death.

It must be remembered that the owners of climbing walls are in the habit of requiring climbers to pass a number of proficiency tests. If the other couple had been properly screened in the usual manner, by failing these tests it should have become obvious that they were not yet skilled enough, in particular that the girl had little idea of how the slot device worked. As it turned out, the owner of the climbing wall had not tested the couple at all, nor had he offered any guidance or provided for general supervision and assistance of climbers.

There was no legal obligation for all these things though, because the authorities in the Netherlands have failed to provide the appropriate legislation. Nor do the authorities provide any supervision of facilities for dangerous sports by any health and safety inspectorate. To our minds, it was the sloppy manner of the authorities in dealing with dangerous sports that was the primary cause of the inexperienced couple's trouble, and also brought John in a situation in which his reflexes might take over in a most dangerous manner. The sloppy organisation was obviously not intended to cause accidents but contained all the building blocks for the fatal scenario and can therefore be considered negligent at least. On similar grounds commercial sport schools may be expected to be aware of the risks of such sports and the prevailing professional standards for them. One therefore wonders whether in a case like this the owner of the climbing facility and the municipality that licensed the owner could be held liable under tort law. If that is the case, which we think quite possible, and also wonders whether under criminal law the owner of the climbing wall en the municipal authorities who licensed it should not be held criminally responsible for having acted recklessly, instead of John Yonkers.

Traffic accidents

The case of John Yonkers is just one example of a much larger population of cases. In this type of case, people normally behave in a manner that has not caused problems before, in the sincere belief that this is the proper way of doing things. But one fateful day they are faced with a coincidence of additional factors, by which the situation is dramatically changed, exposing their usual behaviour as remarkably dangerous. Many traffic accidents are of that type, and it is not unusual for people to face criminal charges for causing traffic accidents with behaviour that they used to consider perfectly normal.

Neville Coombs was one of those people. He was driving his truck from Germany to the Netherlands. According to regulations, he could only drive for nine hours on that particular day. So he decided to spend the night in a truckers hotel along the motorway. The parking lot of the hotel was not accessible directly from the motorway. Neville needed to drive his truck over a rather narrow tertiary road, make a sharp left turn, cross the motorway by way of a narrow flyover that could not be seen until the very last moment because improperly trimmed bushes blocked the view. Approaching the spot where the left turn was to be made, Neville reduced his speed to 13 kilometres per hour. Unknown to him, a motorcyclist was approaching from the opposite direction, hidden from view by the bump leading up to the flyover and the untrimmed bushes. Neville looked to the left to see whether the flyover was free and began his left turn. At that moment the motorcyclist hit his truck. Neville had not seen him coming. The motorcyclist died on the spot. The police investigation showed that the motorcyclist had never attempted to break, which means that he also had not seen the truck or had not noticed that the truck was taking a left turn. None of this is surprising, because the truck was hidden from view to the motorcyclist also until the very last moment. The speed of the motorcycle at the moment of impact is not known, but the speed limit was 70 kilometres per hour, which amounts to twenty metres per second. This is dangerously fast in light of the fact that the situation only permitted a view on the intersection during the last 80 metres, i.e., for four seconds.

Still, Neville Coombs was charged with reckless driving and duly convicted. What had he done wrong? His decision to spend the night at the truckers hotel was wise and according to regulations. There was no other way to reach the hotel. He cannot be held responsible for the design of the road or the maintenance of the bushes. Before making the left turn he came almost to a standstill. Waiting longer before making the turn would have served no purpose, since it would not have solved the problem that the opposite road could not be seen from the intersection. At least a hundred trucks pass this dangerous spot on any given day. Neville had passed this spot twenty or thirty times before. Until then, nothing ever had gone wrong. His behaviour and that of others on that spot were almost certainly completely skill-based, as all driving of motor vehicles is.

However, the warning signal that should have interrupted the skill-based action schema was the fact that he could not see the opposite road. For this reason he might have decided not to move forward. And then what? Or perhaps at an earlier time he should have decided never to go to that particular hotel anymore. Perhaps some of his colleagues at some point in time had taken that decision, we do not know, but certainly many of them had not, because the hotel had been in business for at least a number of years and still is. Apparently, few, if any, truck drivers considered the access to the hotel parking lot particularly hazardous. The reason for this is probably that *not seeing something* is not a very efficient warning signal. To be effective, warning signals must be active and conspicuous, thus attracting attention. However, neither Neville nor the motorcyclist saw anything unusual, nothing that would interrupt their normal, completely automated behaviour patterns. It appears that it was just their bad luck that an inherently dangerous situation was not corrected by some authority who could have done so and whose responsibility it is, and that the relative timing of their movements produced the coincidence that caused one of them to die. The fatal outcome of the encounter therefore had nothing to do with any unusual, abnormal, or irresponsible behaviour on Neville's part.

Still, Neville's behaviour was clearly illegal. When making a left turn, the law says that one must give way to traffic coming from the opposite direction. Neville did not do this, thus violating a simple and well-known traffic rule. The problem is, however, that without violating this traffic rule the truckers hotel could not be reached. Moreover, the law appears to deny or ignore the necessity of skill-based operation in complex tasks. One cannot climb rocks or drive cars in a rule-based or knowledge-based mode. Not every slip or lapse in skill-based action can be prevented, since they are an inseparable part of it, precisely because of its automatic character. In this behaviour mode, the control is handed over to a simple mechanism that only once in a while and under the influence of conspicuous danger signals checks the ongoing operation on a higher level, meanwhile running on the basis of simple links between stimuli and responses. The law, however, rather unrealistically appears to assume that all behaviour is rule-based or knowledge-based, i.e., based on at least a certain amount of conscious deliberation. We know that the assumption that all human behaviour is either rule-based or even knowledge-based is not meant to be a strictly empirical psychological assertion; instead, this is a legal fiction meant to encourage people to act as carefully and attentively as they possibly can. However, the knowledge that this convenient fiction is, in many cases, at variance with psychological reality implies that the law and the judiciary should allow for exceptions in cases where the litigious behaviour is obviously of the skill-based kind and the circumstances of the case are such that lapses in routinised behaviour programmes are to be expected for psychological reasons. Both the law and the judiciary often do allow for such exceptions, but sometimes they do not, as demonstrated by the two cases described above.

Accident scenarios

Accidents, especially large-scale accidents in industrial and technical environments, are invariably caused by a multitude of causal factors that combine in a highly unexpected manner (Wagenaar & Groeneweg, 1987; see also chapter 2 in this book). A well-known example is the capsizing of the ferry *Herald of Free Enterprise* just outside the Belgian harbour of Zeebrugge. The proximal cause appeared to be that the boatswain did not wake up in time to close the bow doors through which the cars had entered the ferry. The captain could not see this from the bridge, and the first mate, whose duty is was to inspect the doors before departure, was too busy on the bridge, which the captain must have noticed. Not far outside the harbour the car deck was flooded with water. When the ship made an unusually sharp turn to port, the water began to move across the deck, which caused the already rather unstable ship to capsize. Over 250 people, passengers and crew, died.

The boatswain, the mate and the captain were convicted for having caused this accident. On second thought, however, one could ask whether a ferry company can be excused for arranging its operations in such a way that the safety of a ship with potentially thousands of passengers is critically dependent on the assumption that a boatswain's alarm clock will ring in time to wake him up. How is it possible that such a ship leaves port with its bow doors open? Why does the execution of this quintessential task depend on a single person? Why is there no signal light on the bridge indicating whether the bow doors are open or closed? Why was the first mate too busy to execute a critically important aspect of his task? Why did the captain allow that upon departure the position of the bow doors was not checked? Did he perhaps specifically decide that no inspection of the bow doors was needed? Why did the captain allow or even order the hazardous sharp left turn to be made at full speed? Why was the boatswain asleep at that particular time? Why did the alarm clock not wake him up? Why did none of his superiors check whether everyone, including the boatswain, was at his assigned post at the time of departure? All these questions and many others that could and should have been asked were not answered during the trial, if only to explain why the number of fatalities appeared considerably larger than could be expected even under the given circumstances (Wagenaar 1996b).

It should be obvious by this time that the blame for all the weaknesses in the operation of the ferry cannot possibly be attributed to the boatswain. His error was the failure to wake up. There are many possible reasons for this. His work-sleep rhythm may have been disturbed by the merciless schedule of the Dover-Zeebrugge ferry. His alarm clock may have been broken. He may have made a slip in setting the alarm clock. Maybe the reason for this slip was the one-hour time difference between England and continental Europe. We can think of hundreds of reasons why people do not wake up in time, and occasionally it happens to all of us. Our guess is that most people oversleep at least once a year. Of course, this does not happen intentionally, nor can it seriously be called a matter of gross negligence. Oversleeping for some reason or other, like other slips and lapses, just happens and is characteristic of skill-based, routinised behaviour repertoires. However, if hundreds of people would die each time somebody in the world overslept, we would be in bad shape indeed.

One wonders why we allow specific pockets in our society to be organised in this manner. Why do courts stop at the John Yonkers and the boatswains of this world, instead of holding responsible those who created the conditions under which normal reflexes fail? Legally that would be possible, as was demonstrated in the criminal prosecution of the responsible authorities for the tragedy in Brussels' Heizel soccer stadium, in which 39 visitors died on 29 May 1985. The chaos was started by British hooligans attacking Italian supporters. The opportunity given to these hooligans by the organising authorities was seen by the court as the real cause, more so than the aggressive behaviour of the hooligans. The court convicted the director of the stadium and the responsible police superintendent, not the hooligans ('t Hart & Pijnenburg, 1989).

Free will as a philosophical issue

For more than 2000 years philosophers have argued about the existence or non-existence of free will in human behaviour. A recent overview and critique are provided by Daniel Wegner, in his seminal book *The Illusion of Conscious Will* (Wegner, 2002). These discussions, notwithstanding their intrinsic importance and interest, have little relevance for our current discussion. The real problem is created by the different starting points of two disciplines. The law poses free will as an axiomatic presumption, not because it is philosophically and psychologically sound, but because the presumption is convenient for the entire enterprise of justice. The law cannot afford a discussion about the philosophical basis of the notion of free will. Psychology, in its turn, is governed by Occam's Razor or the principle of parsimony, which dictates that complex explanations be invoked only when simple explanations prove insufficient. In psychology, this logically leads to exclusion of free will as an explanatory concept unless simpler mechanisms cannot possibly explain the behaviour of humans. To many a psychologist, that point may never be reached.

The problem we have discussed in this chapter is not due to a philosophical mix-up but to the adoption by legal doctrine, for reasons of convenience, of a legal fiction as an axiom of human behaviour, as indicated in the introductory section of this chapter, and the exceptions that, again for reasons of convenience, legal theory allows to this axiom. The consideration that this axiom is not always valid undermines the axiomatic character of legal theory, without providing a better axiomatic structure in its place. The court or jury decides whether the exceptions of self-defence, *force majeur* or insanity are available to defendants in particular cases. In this, they are often assisted by experts from non-legal disciplines, which leads to a further weakening of the axiomatic principles of the law. The expert, however, is not supposed to metamorphose into a lawyer. We as psychologists, for instance, are expected to apply psychological principles, even in the courtroom. But without a clear direction about how to translate our psychological principles and findings into legally relevant dicta, we risk a clash between psychology and law.

The law in principle assumes knowledge-based operation as the default option, even in highly automated behaviour patterns. Psychology, however, assumes skill-based operation as the default option, including the unintended slips and lapses that are a part of it, as regrettable but unavoidable side-effects. The real discussion is not about whether there is such a thing as free will but about the desirability of expert testimony on matters that are axiomatic to the law when the default options are so radically different for both disciplines. Still, somewhat surprisingly, we wish to argue that although we think that the psychological account we gave of John Yonker's error is appropriate, we also think that the court should not have relieved him of any responsibility for what happened. The reason for this is not that John needed to be taught a lesson or that Benny Smith's next of kin were entitled to some kind of satisfaction. Our real reason is that in the courtroom a fundamental legal axiom must be given precedence over psychological considerations about the various levels of behavioural control. And indeed, the court duly convicted John for negligently having caused the victim's death (involuntary manslaughter). But the punishment that the court imposed on him was quite moderate, and maybe for that decision the psychological considerations concerning skill-based behaviour were yet deemed relevant by the court.

What keeps bothering us, though, is that this conviction appeared to exculpate the owner of the climbing wall and the municipal authorities supervising such facilities. If after this fatal incident there is any opportunity for knowledge-based action, it is in the boardrooms and at conference tables of those who design, licence, and operate such inherently dangerous facilities. Regrettably, that will not happen. Defining the dramatic event as a direct consequence of criminally negligent behaviour by John appears to effectively prevent the improvement of a dangerously weak organisation.

CHAPTER 14

Visual Acuity or Shooting Mimi the Cat

In most legal systems, eyewitness testimony is limited to what eyewitnesses have perceived directly. Hearsay, guesses, inferences, logical conclusions – no matter how compelling – are excluded as evidence. The rationale seems to be that direct perception and the recollection of it are more reliable than more complex cognitions. Still, there are limits to the precision of human perception and to the recollection of what was perceived. There are good reasons to scrutinise eyewitness testimony even if it is limited to direct perception. The case of Mimi the cat is an apt illustration of how an apparently simple report of what two witnesses saw may contain a wealth of perceptual problems.

The case

On the morning of 1 May 2004, two witnesses reported to the police that a Mr. Church, well known to them, had shot at Mrs. Edgewood's cat Mimi, also well known to them. The witnesses were two Polish seasonal labourers, working on the land of a Mr. Bundy. It was 5.50 AM, twenty minutes before sunrise. They were standing at about 120 metres from the road which runs on top of a small dyke in the polders. They saw a grey Peugeot on that road, being driven by Mr. Church. The Peugeot stopped, the window was rolled down, and the double barrel of a shotgun was pointed out. They saw Mrs. Edgewood's cat Mimi sitting at a distance of about ten metres from the car, on the sloping bank of a ditch. Mr. Church aimed at the cat and fired. The cat ducked and ran away.

This testimony was later corroborated by Mrs. Edgewood, who declared that subsequently Mimi was missing for two entire weeks and then returned home with a scratch on her left paw. Mr. Church denied the accusation, saying that he had been in bed at that particular time, which was confirmed by Mrs. Church. He did not deny, however, that he was an avid hunter, owned a hunting licence and a shotgun, and entertained a habit of hunting in the early morning.

Mr. Church was formally accused of animal abuse, a serious offence carrying a maximum sentence of two years´ imprisonment. For Mr. Church the case was even more serious, because since he had taken early retirement, he had made hunting his major occupation. For him it would be no less than a disaster if the court took away his hunting licence. Moreover, in the small rural community in which he was living a conviction would make life virtually impossible for him. Mr. Church was involved in a severe quarrel with Mr. Bundy, the owner of the land on which the two Polish labourers had been working, and in this quarrel several villagers had taken sides. Mr. Church suspected that the accusation of animal abuse was concocted by Bundy, in an attempt to make him leave the village. The dimensions of the case therefore extended beyond the scratch on Mimi's left paw.

In September 2004 one of the two Polish witnesses told Mr. Church's lawyer that in fact he and his compatriot had seen only a greyish car, heard the shooting and seen a cat run off. It had been too dark to recognise either the gunman or the car. They had mentioned their observation to Mr. Bundy who had said: 'Well that must have been Frank Church, since he is often out hunting in the early morning and owns a grey Peugeot. I think you should report to the police that you saw Frank Church shoot at the cat.' This they did.

When later on the district attorney was told about the subsequent statements of one of the witnesses, he threatened the witness with a charge of perjury, upon which the witness retracted his second statement, saying that the lawyer had put him under severe pressure. By that time, the other Polish witness had already returned to Poland and therefore could not be interviewed about this. The district attorney offered to settle the case with a fine for Mr. Church, but the latter refused to accept this offer; payment of the fine would make him look guilty in the eyes of the people in the village. The defence lawyer decided to seek advice from an expert on the reliability of the observations of the two witnesses.

One of us was asked to provide this advice. There are at least four perceptual problems involved in this seemingly simple case. One is the obvious question of face recognition at a distance of 120 metres, in the twilight before sunrise. The second problem is the recognition of cars under such conditions; not only the make, colour and type of it, but also of identifying a particular car as the one belonging to Mr. Church. The third problem is that of the recognition of a cat. The fourth problem is of perceiving exactly where a gun is aiming from a distance of 120 metres . We will discuss these problems in the four subsequent sections.

Face recognition

Face recognition depends critically on two basic factors: the size of the details in a face that must be recognised and the visual acuity of the observer. Visual acuity is usually measured by way of a simple test, such as the well-known letter chart, the

Landolt C-ring test, or a checkerboard test. In principle, such a test measures the smallest details that can correctly be identified by a person. For instance, the Landolt C-ring test consists of a black circle with a small gap which is in one of four positions: above, below, left or right. The observer indicates where the gap is, which becomes more difficult as the C-ring gets smaller and smaller. The smallest gap that can be seen by a healthy human eye under optimal lighting conditions spans one minute of arc, which is comparable to one centimetre at a distance of 38 metres. The details that must be perceived in order to identify a person's face reliably are in the order of half a centimetre (Wagenaar & Van der Schrier, 1996). Hence, even in clear daylight it is not possible to recognise a person at a distance of more than nineteen metres. This simple calculation was empirically confirmed in a study by De Jong *et al.* on the recognition of the faces of familiar people as a function of distance and illumination (De Jong *et al.*, 2005). At a distance of 120 metres only details of about three centimetres can be perceived, which means that a human face

Table 1 ***The recognition of familiar people (odds) as a function of distance and illumination, after De Jong*** et al. ***(2005).***

	Illumination (lux)			
Distance (m)	**30**	**150**	**300**	**3000**
3	37	>15	>15	>15
5	16	>15	>15	34
7	33	17	36	>15
12	16	30	18	42
20	7	6	<15	7
30	4	3	5	8
40	3	3	2	<15

is reduced to some sort of matrix of 5 x 8 pixels. This is definitely not sufficient to enable reliable face recognition.

In the case under discussion, there are some additional factors that make accurate recognition of Mr. Church even more unlikely. The most obvious factor is the low level of light twenty minutes before sunrise. The effect of illumination on face recognition is presented in table 1. The scores are expressed by the odds of correct versus incorrect recognitions. A score of 3 means three correct recognitions against one false recognition. A value of >15 is entered when the number of false recognitions is very small, which occurs in the favourable conditions of bright light and very short distances. A score of <15 is entered when the observers do not feel they can recognise anyone at all, and consequently the overall number of responses (correct or incorrect) is very low, as is the case with long distances and/or weak illumination. The cut-off score of 15 is used because, as argued elsewhere (Wagenaar, Van Koppen & Crombag, 1994; p. 100-102), recognitions should not be accepted as evidence when the odds are below 15. The rationale is that, at least in our country, recognitions by two witnesses are deemed sufficient to convict. Thus, if each of these has an odds score of at least 15, the total diagnostic value of the evidence becomes 15 x 15 = 225, which leads to an acceptable risk level of judicial error. Table 1 demonstrates that at a twelve-metre distance, all odds scores are above 15, whereas at twenty metres, all scores have dropped below 10. The sudden stepwise decrease as a function of distance is caused by the fact that the critical details of half a centimetre cannot be resolved at distances above nineteen metres. The effect of level of illumination is more gradual. The level of 3000 lux represents daylight on a cloudy day. The levels of 300 to 30 lux represent different stages of twilight. The effect is gradual and in this range not very impressive; the odds diminish by no more than a factor 2 or 3. Hence, the main obstacle to reliable recognition of the huntsman perceived by the two Polish labourers is distance, not twilight.

There are a few other limiting factors. One is that the witnesses declared that they had recognised Mr. Church even before the window of his car had been lowered, which means that they had recognised him through the glass of the window, which may partly have acted as a mirror. Another factor was that during the approach stage, the car had only been visible for a short time, because a farmhouse and some sheds were blocking their vision. A third factor was that before they heard the shooting there had been no particular reason for the two witnesses to pay much attention to a car on the road. Their observation, even if acceptable as a reliable recognition, would have required a purposeful effort. Why would an approaching car on the dyke have deserved their attention at all?

Recognising Mr. Church's car

It is obvious that the problems of face recognition under the given conditions are sufficiently severe to reject the testimony of the two witnesses. But there is more. The two witnesses claimed that they had recognised Mr. Church's small Peugeot. The recognition of cars is fundamentally different from the recognition of persons. Cars are produced in large series of almost identical specimens. Hence, two steps in the recognition process must be distinguished: recognising a type and recognising a particular car of that type. The first is done on the basis of the general shape and a few discriminating details. The second can be done on the basis of licence plates or an individualising mark such as an uncommon colour, lettering or other additions to its appearance, or even the person sitting behind the wheel.

Of these two stages, the first one is already problematic, because at a distance of 120 metres a car is only perceived as a silhouette. The silhouette of Mr. Church's small sedan is not very distinctive, as many other small European and Japanese cars have more or less the same shape. It would probably require some automobile enthusiast to distinguish between all these small cars. Nothing is known about the witnesses in this respect. It is, however, certain that the accurate identification of small details like trademarks, names of makers or type indications require a visual resolution far better than three centimetres.

There is sufficient doubt that even the type of car could be perceived by these witnesses. The identification of specifically Mr. Church's car could only have been done by way of its licence plates, because it had no distinguishing features, and there are more owners of small grey Peugeots in the area. Since the witnesses only saw the car from the side, the licence plates could not have been visible. And even if they were, from a distance of 120 metres each letter and digit would have been reduced to 2 x 3 pixels, which precludes reading.

The perception of the colour of the car is equally problematic. Colour perception diminishes with illumination; in the twilight the perception of red, yellow, and green disappears rapidly, and soon everything takes on shades of blue and grey. It is possible that the 'grey' car perceived by the two witnesses was in fact green or brownish. The only way therefore in which they could have reliably concluded that this was Mr. Church's car was through the recognition of Mr. Church himself. But as argued above, that was highly unlikely.

Cat recognition

The two witnesses declared that they had recognised Mrs. Edgewood's cat Mimi. The first question that springs to mind is whether a cat can be recognised at a distance of 120 metres. Mimi is a black cat with a few white spots. Being black does not really help in the twilight, and spots three centimetres or less in size are not really visible at this distance. Ideally, we would have a table for recognising familiar cats, like the one presented above for recognising familiar human faces. Such a table does not exist, however, and we do not recommend that young investigators take it upon themselves to do research in this direction.

The location of white spots on cats is not entirely random. Usually the spots are on the front and rear paws, the nose, the breast, and around the tail. It requires a high degree of familiarity with cats to distinguish two white-spotted black cats from one another. How well acquainted are two foreign seasonal labourers with the cat of their employer's neighbour? And how is the population of cats in this rural village composed? Are there many black cats with white spots in the village, or is Mimi the only one? In the absence of empirical data it does not seem unreasonable to assume that the recognition of an individual cat depends on visual detail of the same order of magnitude as the recognition of human faces. In that case there is simply no way in which the two witnesses could have reliably identified Mrs. Edgewood's cat Mimi.

Where was the gun aiming?

The witnesses reported that a gun was pointed at the cat, which was sitting on a sloping bank, at about ten metres distance from the car. Since it was a double-barrelled gun, the hunter must have used shot. In that case he must have been a very bad marksman indeed, because missing a cat with a shotgun fired at ten metres is a remarkable accomplishment; remember that the cat had only a scratch on one paw! We know that Mr. Church is not a bad marksman; on the contrary, he is an experienced hunter.

Apart from this, how could the witnesses know where the gun was aiming? There are two aspects to this question: the perception of direction and of height or, as marksmen say, of alignment and elevation. If the cat was located precisely between the gunman and the witnesses, they might have perceived that the gun was pointing in their direction, and therefore also in the direction of the cat. But suppose that the position of the cat was 30 degrees left of this alignment. Could the witnesses have seen in which direction the marksman, with his gun pointed away from them, was aiming? Or, slightly more complicated, suppose the cat was sitting at a distance of ten metres, 30 degrees to the left of the line connecting the marksman and the witnesses, while at the same time a rabbit was sitting at a distance of ten metres, but 40 degrees to the left of that alignment. The cat is visible to the witnesses, but the rabbit is not, because it is too dark. Could the witnesses have seen that the gun was not aimed at the cat, but at a rabbit invisible to them? And even if in principle the distinction could be made, would it not be a matter of simple self-delusion to conclude that the marksman was shooting at the only target visible?

A similar problem occurs with elevation, although elevation is even more difficult to perceive than alignment. Imagine that there are two animals on the line connecting the gunman and the witnesses: a cat at ten metres from the car and a rabbit at 30 metres. Can the witnesses determine which of the two animals the hunter is aiming at? The perception of elevation may be possible when the rifle is seen from the side, but when the gun is pointed in the direction of the observers, it must be nearly impossible to estimate the distance of the target at which the marksman is aiming. And again, if the cat was visible to the witnesses but the rabbit was not, would it not be seductive to conclude that the elevation is just right for shooting at the only visible animal?

One could argue that even if the hunter was aiming at a rabbit and not at the cat, it would have been rather reckless to fire a rifle loaded with shot at a rabbit with Mrs. Edgewood's cat nearby. But that objection assumes that the hunter himself could see the cat, which, however, is not at all certain. The cat was sitting on the sloping bank of a ditch at the foot of the dyke, in the grass. Possibly, the witnesses, looking upward from the land below the dyke, could see a cat at a distance of 110 metres, whereas from above the cat was not even visible at a distance of ten metres. What if the witnesses saw only the cat and not the rabbit, and the hunter saw the rabbit but not the cat? Would that not be the perfect condition for a serious misunderstanding?

To be fair, it is not Mr. Church's defence that he aimed at a rabbit. His defence is that at the relevant time he had been in bed. If anyone shot a gun then and there, it must have been someone else. But that argument does not change the undeniable fact that the two Poles could not have perceived accurately on which target the unknown marksman was aiming.

What the court decided

It is surprising that a case that seems so simple contains so many perceptual problems, problems that have not even been addressed in the field of psychology and law, probably because comparable cases are rare or have been considered trivial. The unexpected complexity of the case may have eluded the prosecuting attorney, which may explain why he did not hesitate the take this apparently trivial case to court. After the presentation of an expert opinion along the lines sketched above, the court realised that it was by no means a simple matter that could be decided on the testimony of two witnesses. Mr. Church was acquitted. It will remain an eternal riddle how Mimi incurred her scratch, but it is very unlikely that it had anything to do with an alleged armed attack on her on 1 May 2004.

CHAPTER 15

Sexual Semiotics or the Case of the Popular Policeman

The human species survives through sexual reproduction. For this reason nature has endowed us with a strong desire to engage in sexual behaviour. Sex is perfectly natural for virtually everyone of us. Generally prohibiting it by law would be hard to imagine, but certain types of sexual behaviour are indeed proscribed, in particular sexual acts against the will of one of the participants. Sexual partners must somehow establish mutual consent, which is however almost never recorded in a written and signed contract. In many cases there is also no explicit verbal agreement, but rather some sort of tacit understanding that may develop almost instantaneously, but also after a considerable period of time. Particularly in the early stages of a sexual relationship, the exchange of nonverbal signals plays a major role. Courtship is a risky process, because the signals are almost often ambiguous, and the penalty for misunderstanding them may be high. Moreover, it may happen that although the signals were clear initially, they may be regretted and denied later on. In a case like that, one of the partners may claim that the other overlooked clear signals meant to discourage sexual behaviour and thus crossed the line dividing courtship from a sexual offence.

Normal courtship and sexual semiotics

The normal processes of courtship may be extensively documented in the world's literature of many ages and cultures, but psychology has only just begun to investigate them systematically, while legal scholarship appears not even to have discovered normal courtship behaviour as a relevant issue. However, the legal perspective on what constitutes normal and abnormal courtship behaviour is critically relevant for cases in which one of the participants believes them to have been abused. It appears that even the normal steps of courtship may be considered punishable whenever one party files a complaint. The law provides no benchmark for distinguishing between legally acceptable and unacceptable courtship behaviour. The demonstration of sexual interest in another person may come close to stalking, and there may be a smooth transition between gentle seduction and sexual assault.

The correct understanding of the function and meaning of signals in the process of normal courtship is important, not only for the success of the process, but also for the safety of the participants. Early on, these signals are almost never explicit and verbal, but as far as we know, predominantly nonverbal (Eibl-Eibesfeldt, 1971; Mehrabian, 1972). It can be a furtive glance or smile, a gesture or touch, the choice of clothing or perfume, but also more elaborate behaviours such as being in a certain place and taking part in certain kinds of activities. Examples of the latter are visiting bars with a certain reputation, hitchhiking alone in the middle of the night, going on holiday with a person and sharing a hotel room or tent, visiting someone late at night without a chaperon. The science devoted to the study of the verbal or nonverbal exchange of signals in courtship behaviour is called *sexual semiotics.* Typical questions are: what are the signals, how effective are they in correctly transmitting the sender's intentions, and what are the differences between men and women with respect to interpretation of these signals. The study of such questions is often inspired by concerns about the use of coercion in situations like first dates, regular dates, steady relationships or marriage. A substantial number of the problems occurring in these situations can be explained as failures of the semiotic system.

In some cases there may be only a few steps between the first meeting and having sex. Often, however, a long sequence of small steps is required, not one of which should be omitted or misunderstood. A single error may well destroy a budding relationship. Empirical studies about the sequences of steps in normal courtship often involve the initial stage of 'flirting behaviour'. The typical environment for conducting such studies is the singles' bar or the dance floor, visited by young people who do not know the other people present but who have come specifically to make contact with persons of the opposite sex. Which signals mean that one is – or is not – interested in a particular person? Moore (1985, 1998) composed two lists of signals that women give to men in this situation, either encouraging or discouraging further contacts.

Here are some of the 52 different *encouraging signals*:

- *facial and head patterns:* room-encompassing glance, gaze fixate, eyebrow flash, neck presentation, hair flip, lip lick, smile, giggle, whisper;
- *gestures:* arm flexion, tap, hand hold, object caress, buttock pat;
- *posture patterns:* lean, breast touch, thigh touch, parade, accept dance, solitary dance, point, aid solicitation.

The catalogue of *rejection signals* contains, among others:

- *facial and head patterns:* yawn, frown, gaze avoidance, upward gaze, stare, negative head shake;

– *gestures:* pocket hands, arm cross, nail clean, teeth pick;
– *posture patterns:* rigid torso, closed legs, body contact avoidance.

The reliability of these and other signals is not a full 100 percent. Not every smile means that a young woman is willing to establish contact with a man. It is the accumulation of encouraging signals that makes it possible to predict reliably that a woman will make contact with a particular man before long (Moore, 1989). Still, the probabilistic nature of such signals implies that men can be severely mistaken about a woman's intentions. Responding to such signals entails the risk of an overt rejection and the accompanying wounded pride or worse, an accusation of sexual harassment.

Advanced courting

Moore's catalogue covers only the beginning of a much more elaborate scenario that in the end may lead to sexual intercourse. The steps to be taken to reach that final stage are called 'advanced courting'. They may be more complicated than the repertoire investigated by Moore and others and will therefore involve more risk. But also advanced courting is often nonverbal and without an explicit and clear expression of mutual intentions. The behaviours displayed in the later stages may encompass inviting a partner into one's home, at night and/or when no one else is present; changing clothes during such a visit, taking a shower; playing romantic music, dimming the lights, lighting candles, etc.

To our knowledge, there exists no orderly catalogue of such behaviours, maybe because the number of possibilities is endless. Empirical research is scarce, probably because experimental manipulation of intimate relationships is hardly feasible. Some indirect approaches have been used, such as *vignette* studies, in which people read a short description of an encounter and are then asked to judge whether the behaviour of both parties is acceptable, or how much responsibility should be attributed to each of the parties. One such example is a study of the impact of condom possession (Hynie *et al.*, 2003). Subjects are presented with a short description of a sexual assault. The independent variable was condom possession by either the male or the female. When the female was carrying a condom, she was generally perceived as more sexually willing, and a claim of sexual assault was perceived as less valid.

A much-quoted study was done by Goodchilds *et al.* (1988). Students were asked under which circumstances it was, according to them, permissible for a male to coerce a female into sex. The results are shown in table 1.

Table 1 Circumstances under which coercion is permitted

Circumstances	Agreeing that coercion is okay	
	Males	**Females**
She is going to have sex with him, then changes her mind	54%	31%
She has led him on	54%	26%
She gets him sexually excited	51%	42%
They have dated for a long time	43%	32%
She lets him touch her above the waist	39%	28%

These results show first that, for this group of respondents, the overall answer is definitely not 'under no circumstance', which would be the correct answer according to the law. And the second conspicuous outcome is a consistent tendency for men to interpret the rules more liberally. Clearly, initially agreeing to sex is a very strong signal for a majority of the male and a substantial number of the female respondents, which cannot always be nullified by a subsequent refusal. For only about half of the men and 70 percent of the women, the general rule 'no means no' applies unconditionally. We are not sure what surprises us more: the other half of the male respondents or the substantial minority of women who appear to think that coercion may be justified in certain circumstances.

Still another study, illustrating the gender difference in the interpretation of dress signals, was conducted by Haworth-Hoeppner (1998). Among other things, she submitted agree/disagree statements to her subjects like, 'If a woman wears a low-cut blouse, she should expect men to make sexual comments'. The results of this study show that wearing a short, tight-fitting skirt or a low-cut blouse is more likely to be perceived by men than by women as displaying sexual interest or communicating sexual intent. Men more often than women perceive such signals as requesting a sexual response.

Individual differences

Typically, such studies focus on signals given by women and received by men. Little is known about the reverse situation, possibly because there are hardly any legal cases in which women are accused of sexually assaulting men.[1] If it is true that misinterpretation of nonverbal signals is a major cause of harassment or plain sexual assault, then individual differences with respect to the system of sexual semiotics must be taken into consideration. Uncertainty about the meaning of signals is proportional to their variety. Gender may be a major if not the most important source of such differences, as demonstrated above, but other candidates can easily be imagined: social background, ethnicity, geographical origin and age. The specific circumstances of an encounter may also shape the semiotics. There may well be a difference between meeting someone in church or in a singles' bar. It may matter whether the encounter happens in the context of a business contact or in a holiday resort. In some instances the legislator is aware of such differences: we hold the relationship between two students to a more liberal standard than the relationship between a student and a professor. From a professor we expect considerably more reticence in the interpretation of sexual signals, even up to the point where almost no signal will provide him with a valid excuse when a complaint for sexual assault is brought against him by a student.[2] The complexity and situational variability of semiotic rules constitute a considerable risk factor for those who engage in courtship, especially when there is a lack of experience with the semiotic culture of the other party.

The fact that during the past 30 years the rules for sexual behaviour have been subject to rapid change in Western culture complicates the problem of how to court someone even further.

- There was a time in which generally accepted societal rules prescribed that sexual relationships were limited to married couples. In a system where marriage precedes sex, there is little risk of misinterpreting the signals. A formal proposal, a sincere talk with the girl's parents, an extended engagement period, and the festive closing of the marriage contract were sufficiently clear steps to exclude any misunderstanding about the final objective of the arrangement. These days the order seems to be reversed in that marriage is often the end of a process of which progressive intimacy and sex are major parts, with the accompanying uncertainty about mutual consent during the early stages.
- Nowadays, most adolescents engage in multiple sexual relationships, with no further purpose in mind than finding out about it. This is called sexual experimentation. Each of these relationships involves the risk of getting it wrong, with

1 There is, of course, the fictional case of Tom Sanders in Michael Crichton's novel *Disclosure*, also made into a motion picture with Michael Douglas and Demi Moore as the leading characters.

2 This issue is impressively staged in the play *Oleanna* by David Mamet (1992).

victimisation of one party and the risk of becoming accused of sexual abuse for the other. Movies, television programmes, the mass culture of going out in town to large music events or dance parties provide models for changing and transient sexual contacts between young people. Also for steady couples there is an increasing tendency towards partner-swapping or joining partner clubs.
- People marry later, thus extending the period of risky courtships. In our country the average age of marriage has increased by about ten years within one generation.
- In most countries, including our own, the cultural diversity of the population has increased considerably, due to both migration and a very effective worldwide system of mass transportation. This diversification confronts people with new, unfamiliar and sometimes conflicting sexual semiotic systems.

The issue here is not a moral judgement on these developments but the simple observation that an increasing number of sexual relationships and a widening horizon for the search of prospective partners makes normal courtship behaviour more hazardous than it used to be not too long ago. If only for these reasons, the number of accusations of sexual misconduct may be expected to increase, as well as the demands on the understanding of judges and juries. The latter point is critically important. If judges and juries are only familiar with a single sexual semiotic code, which may be outdated or limited to the societal niche in which they themselves were educated, their legal judgement of a complaint or accusation may well put people in jeopardy who were only following their own courtship rules in which they saw no harm, and in any case without any intention to cause harm.

Male and female roles

It is obvious that the roles of men and women in the context of courtship differ substantially. The vast majority of accusations of unwanted intimacy and sexual assault are made by women against men. Why is this? Are men less sensitive to the sexual signals than women? Or are men more primitive creatures than women, with an insatiable hunger for sex, which for them extends the limits of acceptable behaviour beyond norms set by most women? This is a common belief.

The literature suggests a third possibility though, which is that in the exchange of signals women are more often the senders, and men the receivers. In a study of behaviour in singles' bars, Perper (1985) demonstrated that 70 percent of the contacts came about on the initiative of the women. The reason for this may be that women have different, more stringent selection criteria, which encourages them not to wait passively for someone to make a pass at them. Remoff (1984) found that women are primarily interested in partners who can offer emotional and financial stability. On the basis of interviews with 10,047 people from 37 different cultures, Buss (1989) found that men prefer young and attractive women, while women look for men with a satisfactory economic status or at least potential. As an underlying rationale for this difference, it is submitted that having children has more lasting and far-reaching consequences for women than for men. Because women's investment in a sexual relation and its probable results is greater than it is for men, women must be more selective right from the beginning of the courtship process. This selectivity is achieved through active control over the exchange of encouraging and discouraging sexual signals, which tends to make women the senders and men the receivers. As a result men and women are prone to making different kinds of errors. Women are more likely than men to send the wrong signals; men are more likely to produce the wrong interpretations. Both types of errors may lead to a situation in which the woman experiences an unwanted invasion of her privacy or, in extreme cases, falls victim to sexual assault. Most accusations are therefore made by women and directed against men.[3]

Hindsight context changes

Another aspect of this complex problem is hindsight bias, which is the tendency to judge and re-evaluate the past on the basis of our current knowledge (Fischhoff, 1975). When a relationship ends in an unpleasant manner, there often is a tendency to place the behaviour of the former partner in the context of the outcome, and to judge it more negatively than at the time of its occurrence. The same holds for one's own feelings and behaviour. It is possible that already during the relationship there was some unspoken uncertainty about mutual feelings, intentions and expectations. After the failure of the relationship, this uncertainty becomes a certainty, and outspoken negative feelings substitute earlier hesitations. One can easily forget which signals were exchanged in the initial stages, especially when they were not sent in full awareness, as is often the case. A similar change of context may occur during the courting process, well before the final stage is reached. When one suddenly realises that the relationship is not really wanted, one wonders how it got that far, and in order to answer this question there may be a tendency to conclude that the partner must have missed or misinterpreted the otherwise clearly discouraging signals. An evening visit that was originally agreed to in retrospect becomes a violation of the privacy of one's home. Sexual innuendo in a series of SMS messages becomes stalking by telephone. Sexual intercourse in which the woman undressed

3 Might this be related to the fact women take the initiative in divorce cases more often than men?

voluntarily and participated without protest may in hindsight become rape. The problem with the reconstruction in hindsight is that, when it occurs, it is almost always done unintentionally and without awareness. It is also irreversible, since the original context, no longer part of one's world, can no longer be reinstated. Testimony about intentions, feelings that were present, and events that happened before the change of context can be absolutely honest and at the same time absolutely false. Often the context change makes the behaviour of the alleged victim largely incomprehensible to herself and others. If she felt bad about what had happened, why did she not protest? Why did she not defend herself, or scream, or tell others afterwards? Why did she not leave? Why did she come back to the perpetrator several times? If a woman was indeed stalked for months in succession, why would she have agreed to have sex with the stalker? If she had been raped by an acquaintance, once or even several times, why would she agree to accompany the perpetrator on a holiday trip? We have seen many criminal cases in which these or similar questions were raised. We have also seen cases in which the courts failed to raise such questions or accepted obviously unsatisfactory answers out of a misplaced consideration with the alleged victim's plight. We want to stress that accusations after a change of context are not necessarily perjurious, but may yet be false in the sense that they reflect a reality that never existed.

Political background

In her somewhat rallying but insightful collection of essays under the title *The Morning After: Sex, Fear, and Feminism,* Katie Roiphe (1993) explained that discussions concerning the problems outlined above often have a distinct political overtone. In the 1980s, the issue of rape, especially date-rape, was taken up by the feminist movement and put high on the feminist agenda, in particular in the United States. Suddenly, date-rape seemed to be everywhere, especially on university campuses. A survey study by *Ms.* magazine 'revealed' that at least 25 percent of college women at one time or another fell victim of rape or attempted rape by their male colleagues, but according to Roiphe the number of 50 percent also circulated.

What does rape mean in this context? Gilbert (1992) argued that the definition used by *Ms.* must have been rather broad, as about three-quarters of the women classified as rape victims did not themselves think they were raped; only *Ms.* thought so. Roiphe argues that there is a political reason for this: 'Rape is a natural trump card for feminism' (p. 56) and 'By blocking analysis with its claims to unique pandemic suffering, the rape crisis becomes a powerful source of authority' (p. 57). Roiphe further quotes a former director of Columbia University's date-rape education program as saying: 'Every time you have intercourse there must be explicit consent, and if there's no explicit consent then it's rape.' This definition not only illustrates where the date-rape statistic comes from, but also why we see increasing numbers of prosecutions and convictions for sexual assault. When two people engage in sexual intercourse without an explicit, consciously articulated consent, one of the two partners, in retrospect regretting what he or she agreed to do in moments of diminished alertness, may change her or his mind afterwards. Then the intercourse becomes rape and one of the partners a victim of a 'retrospective trauma'. Roiphe quotes this reasoning in a critical manner:

> Regret can signify rape. A night that was a blur, a night you wish hadn't happened, can be rape. Since verbal coercion and manipulation are ambiguous, it's easy to decide afterward that he manipulated you. You can realise it weeks or even years later (p. 80).

Being, or rather becoming, a rape victim in retrospect is no doubt emotionally painful. The victim may also decide to take the case to court, since consent is a mutual thing. But consent may be withdrawn after the fact. It is apparently difficult to admit that the complaining party may have contributed decisively to energise the semiotic system up to the point where intercourse followed almost naturally. Why is this difficult? Roiphe seems to suggest that it is a matter of political correctness: one is simply not allowed to say that a self-proclaimed victim co-operated in what she subsequently experiences as a criminal offence. Are courts also subject to the politically correct idea that regret always means rape?

The case of police officer Rhine

Barney Rhine, a police officer, was accused of sexual harassment and rape of thirteen women, all of them colleagues. It came as a big surprise to him. He had just celebrated his 12½-year anniversary on the police force, his colleagues had thrown him a big party, and he was awarded an official commendation. Barney Rhine just seemed about the most popular policeman in the district, and then this happened. It had begun with a single accusation, but soon a couple more followed, and then management decided to interview all female employees in the precinct, and this produced quite a number of new accusations. The problem was, however, that virtually all these women had been friendly with Barney, many of them had dated him and had even had a prolonged sexual relationship with him, and some of them had lived with him for extensive periods of time. Had he forced all of these women into these relationships? Perhaps some of the relationships with Rhine had originally been voluntary, but were regretted later on, resulting in a reconstruction of the memories of these women of what was once a non-controversial part of their lives? This question can only be answered by taking a closer look at the police culture in this precinct.

Police work requires close working relations between colleagues, at all hours of the day and night, often under difficult or stressful circumstances. Police officers depend on their colleagues' alertness and professionalism. As a result, they develop strong bonds of mutual appreciation and trust. However, in this particular precinct social relationships went further than usual. Groups of police officers adopted a habit of going out on the town together on Friday and Saturday nights. They frequented various bars in their own district, drank a lot, often to excess, and sometimes even used drugs. This was not unknown to the management; on the contrary, many high-ranking officers participated in these parties. From these activities, inevitably, many short-lived or some longer relationships developed within this group of merry friends. Barney Rhine may have been the champion among them, but for12½ years, no one saw anything exceptional or objectionable in his behaviour. Then, suddenly all this changed.

We will not discuss all thirteen complaints, because that would make for tedious reading. We restrict ourselves to two of the more serious accusations.

Ricky Venables The case against Rhine started with Ricky Venables filing a complaint against him for stalking, harassment and sexual assault. At one time she did a nightly round with Barney Rhine in a police car. He touched her legs and said that she was a very attractive woman. A couple weeks earlier Ricky had given him her mobile phone number, when members of the squad were planning a tour of the bars in the Belgian city of Antwerp. At the end of their round, Barney promised Ricky that he would send her an SMS message and also asked her to join him and some other colleagues next Friday night on one of the regular drinking tours in town. They returned the police car to the precinct, and Barney offered to drive Ricky home in his private car. She accepted the ride. She did not invite him in, but reminded him that he had promised to send her an SMS. Barney did so within the hour and, according to Ricky, he asked her whether she was in bed, what she was wearing, and adding what a shame it was that she was alone while they could have been good to one another. Her reply came a few minutes later and was recorded in Rhine's cell phone. It said: *Hi handsome! I am in bed and very horny, big surprise after being with you a whole night! I am naked, maybe that will give you beautiful dreams!* The technical department verified that this message had really come from Ricky's phone. In the next two months there were fourteen more phone calls from Ricky to Barney.

Yet another two months later, Ricky filed her complaint for stalking, unwanted visits, and sexual assault. She said that she had never given Barney any reason for believing that she wanted a relationship with him. He had sent her many e-mails, SMSes and phone calls. She had answered only 10 percent of these and, according to her, never in an encouraging manner. The SMS quoted above she did not remember. Perhaps she did send it, but that would have been atypical for her. During the outing on Friday night, he had touched her in a crowded bar and pressed his genitals against her body, which she now considered sexual assault. Three weeks later, Barney had come to her apartment at a moment when she was only dressed in a T-shirt and underpants. Someone rang the downstairs doorbell, the intercom was noisy, so she could not hear who it was. She pressed the button to open the downstairs door anyway. When the visitor rang the bell at her own front door, she looked through the spyhole but saw nobody. She opened the door and to her surprise, Barney stepped inside. He looked at her 'in a certain manner' and commented on her scarce clothing. She asked him to leave, which he did after a while.

Again two months later, someone rang the downstairs doorbell while Ricky was taking a shower. Since she had a date with her colleague Martin, she asked through the intercom: 'Martin, is that you?' The answer was 'Yes'. She opened the doors, both the one downstairs and the one of her own flat, and went back into the shower. When she stepped out of the shower, to her dismay she saw Barney Rhine. She told him to leave immediately, which he did. However, her neighbours told her that Rhine had been near her flat at least four times later that day. Ricky got scared and for a while slept in the homes of various friends.

Barney Rhine has a different perspective on these facts. In his experience Ricky was a nice and spontaneous colleague. They had lots of fun together during the regular police outings. During the tour of duty on that particular night, he had indeed touched her knees. She had not reproached him but, on the contrary, had invited him to send her an SMS when he got home. Her instantaneous response to his SMS had been sex-loaded, which he took as an encouragement. During the outing on the next Friday night, they had again great fun. Some weeks later he visited her in her flat. She opened the door for him with almost no clothes on, which he again took as an encouragement. When she said she needed to sleep because she was on the night shift, he had left almost immediately. On his next visit, she opened the door for him while she was taking a shower. This aroused him, but again she asked him to leave, which again he did. He went to visit another colleague, Kitty, who lived in the same building. Kitty was nice to him. The neighbours' reports on his presence in the building were probably related to that visit.

On being interrogated by the examining judge, it came out that Ricky sometimes performed pole dancing in public bars, pictures of which could be found on the internet. At a police party she had at one time demonstrated various sexual positions. Her comment on this was that sometimes she did not know what she was doing when drunk, and furthermore that police management had never reprimanded her for it.

Should Barney Rhine's behaviour be considered criminal? He had not attacked

Ricky, nor ever raped her, and he had never refused to leave when she asked him to. It is true that he had touched her, that he had asked her to go out with him, that he had called her and sent her messages with a distinct sexual content, and that he visited her twice at her flat, uninvited. Do such actions constitute criminal offences? Ricky and Barney were both single adults, and Ricky had shown her interest in sex publicly. Why would it have been wrong if Barney tried to hit it off with her? Isn't that what adults often do? Are such actions significantly different from what is expected in a normal courtship? Did Ricky make it clear to Barney that she did not wish to get intimately involved with him? Or did she string him along for kicks, to a limit that she did not wish to cross? We know that Ricky unmistakably encouraged Barney at least once. That either was a mistake from the very beginning, or she changed her mind at a later time. Either way, how was Barney Rhine to know? And more importantly, how can a criminal court confidently judge what really went on between these two? Is this problem still within the domain of the finder of fact?

Maria Lopes Graus Maria also filed a complaint against Rhine for stalking and sexual assault. She had had a sexual relationship with Rhine for a period of six months. Next they decided to share an apartment together, but at that time, according to Maria, 'they were just friends, sharing the apartment only for financial reasons.' Still, she admitted that even then they had occasionally slept together. At one time, Maria had given up her job in a local gym to go work with the police. She had specifically asked to be assigned to Barney's precinct. Maria was introduced to Barney's parents, who soon came to consider her as their daughter-in-law.

In that period, however, Rhine had two other relationships. One with Trudy, with whom he had once lived together for four years, and with yet another woman called Ruby. When Maria found out about Trudy and Ruby, she strongly objected, accusing Barney of not being faithful to her, which is remarkable given that according to her they were just friends. Then Maria discovered that Barney called sex lines on her telephone. She confronted Barney, and then they decided to split up. Maria moved to a new place and did not want Barney to know her new address. She had become afraid of him, although Barney had never been violent with her. She describes her feelings toward him as 'double'.

Maria's father accidentally gave her new address to Barney, and soon thereafter she began to notice Barney's car in the vicinity of her new apartment, several times a week at first, and then almost every day. She also began to receive anonymous telephone calls and was convinced that they came from Barney. She became totally paranoid, keeping her curtains closed during the day and not turning on the lights in her apartment at night, so that Barney would not know if she was home.

The affair came to a climax when, one night in October, Barney climbed up to her balcony. The door from the balcony to the apartment was locked, but Maria, dressed in her nightwear, unlocked it and let him in. When asked, she could not explain why she had done this. She does not remember it distinctly, but says she assumes that she told Barney to leave, but he embraced her, and she felt his erection. She grabbed his scrotum and twisted it forcefully. He let go of her and left. According to Maria this was sexual assault. About half a year later Maria ran into Barney on the street, and she told him that he had ruined her life that evening. After that, all contact between Barney and Maria was broken.

Barney's version of these events is quite different. He knew Maria from various bars in town, but he did not really fancy her. He had not had sex with her until she moved in with him in his apartment. Sharing the apartment for Barney was a purely financial arrangement; he was still not sexually interested in Maria. But Maria fell in love with him and wanted to sleep with him almost every night. She changed jobs in order to be with him almost constantly. They had sex occasionally, but not nearly as often as Maria wanted. This situation lasted for about a year and a half. He admits that he had called sex lines, but not often. His explanation for the high telephone bill is that Maria used to receive many other boyfriends in the apartment when he was not present, mostly doorkeepers and bouncers of local bars. Barney told Maria that contacts between a police officer, which Maria had become, and people from the local scene were clearly undesirable. According to him, those visitors had used the telephone in the apartment and apparently had called sex lines.

Still within Rhine's perspective, Maria's decision to move out of the apartment came as a surprise. She gave him her new address, and they kept in occasional contact. A few times Maria invited Barney to her new flat, often with the request to bring some food. On several of those occasions Maria touched his genitals, but since by then he had a new partner, he did not want to have sex with her. Maria kept calling him, took to waiting for him at the exit of the gym he frequented, sent him SMS messages in which she invited him to have sex with her, etc. He regularly drove by her house on his way to his mother's house where he now lived, and because the way to his best friend was through Maria's street.

With respect to the balcony scene, Barney says that he had called Maria half an hour earlier, asking her whether he could drop by. She agreed. Climbing up to her balcony had just been a joke. She let him in, and nothing really happened. As usual, they talked, maybe took a drink, and then he went home. He had not assaulted her and she had not twisted his scrotum. The meeting in the street, in which she asked him to stop harassing her, never happened. There was a witness who testified that Maria had been sad when Barney had left her. 'This town will be never be the same again,' she was heard saying.

Maria's case is quite different from Ricky's. In Ricky's case, both parties agreed about all the facts; even the sexually loaded SMS sent by Ricky was not really contested. The difference between them is a matter of interpretation of the uncontested facts. In Maria's case, there is a considerable disagreement between the parties about the facts. According to Barney, it was Maria who consistently took the initiative in establishing and maintaining their sexual relationship, even after she had moved out of his apartment. Maria denies that she invited Barney to her new apartment, or that they still had a friendly relationship when Rhine climbed up to her balcony. The discrepancy was not further investigated, and there were no witnesses to confirm or contradict either version. Still, these aspects are critical for the appreciation of Maria's case against Barney. If, at the time of the balcony incident, Maria and Barney were still friends, and Maria was indeed expecting him on that particular night, entering via the balcony could well have been some sort of joke. Maybe not a good joke, but why would it be a criminal offence? If in fact Maria had invited Barney to her place, if they had in fact had meals together, if in fact she had called him and sent him SMS messages, if in fact she had touched his genitals in a soliciting manner, can we still expect Barney to have understood that Maria felt threatened and harassed? To that purpose, we should know more about precisely which signals Maria did or did not give. And whether she in fact kept her curtains closed and the lights off in her apartment.

There is one weak point in Barney Rhine's story. Why did Maria suddenly decide to move out of his apartment? Her explanation is that they had a row over telephone bills. Barney's story about visiting doormen and bar bouncers calling sex lines is not very credible. But then, Barney was not indicted for calling sex lines. His explanation is that Maria left because she felt deserted by him when he had temporarily moved out of the apartment to go live with his mother after his biological father had unexpectedly died. It transpired that his father had three daughters and a son, about whose existence Barney had never been informed. This was quite a shock to him, and he got depressed. To restore his balance, he went to live with his mother, where he said he would have a better chance to think matters over. According to Barney, Maria concluded that he no longer wanted to share the apartment with her, after which she moved out. Readers of chapter 6 may recognise the elements of a bad story here, but no attempt was made by the police investigating his case to find out about the circumstances of Barney's moving to his mother's house.

In a friendly relationship involving occasional sex, it is not unusual to call one's partner regularly, to send messages, to pay visits, to touch, to hold, to kiss and to have an occasional erection. Such things are only reprehensible, and perhaps punishable, in the absence of a consensual intimate relationship. But how can we judge the intimacy of a relationship that has existed several years ago, if the two partners now disagree about its existence? Could this be one of those cases of retrospective sexual assault as described by Roiphe (1993), resulting from a redefinition of past events? Is it possible that Maria changed her perspective on the very nature of her former relationship with Barney when he entered a relationship with some other woman? Did jealousy or wounded pride reshape her memories? Or did that perhaps happen because of the rumour spread in the police force that Barney Rhine was a kind of Don Juan, who had used and betrayed virtually every one of her female colleagues? In the absence of any further evidence, the final judgement of whether Barney's behaviour towards Maria must be considered a criminal offence depends entirely on the acceptance of Maria's present perspective. If her negative feelings towards him had already been present at the time, his behaviour toward her may indeed have been entirely inappropriate. However, if Maria's negative feelings toward Barney are only a recent creation, his behaviour toward her appears not to have been outside the realm of normal courtship.

As mentioned before, after Ricky had filed her complaint against Barney Rhine and several other cases had emerged, the chief of police called a meeting of all female employees in the precinct, explained what he had come to know and urged them to support Ricky and the other women who had already come forward. Although, of course, he did not instruct them to lie about anything, some of these women reported that they had felt considerable pressure to show their solidarity. Maria was one of the women who in response to this appeal filed a complaint against Barney.

Final analysis

The process leading from getting acquainted for the first time to regular sex consists of a number of steps. At a certain point these steps involve sexually loaded allusions, gestures, intimate touching and the like. In principle, such actions may be punishable, even though they occur all the time without causing problems. It is not the behaviour itself that makes such acts punishable, nor even the intention with which they are done, but the reception by the other party. However, it is in the very nature of courtship that this reception is not entirely predictable. On the contrary, such actions are explorative, used to find out about the other's intentions and feelings. Logically, if such explorations turn out not to be welcome, an awkward episode develops in which the behaviour of the one is rejected by the other. The attempt at rapprochement will probably be repeated once or twice before the party who took the initiative finally gets the message, and the courtship process ends. Those repeated attempts are particularly hazardous, because they may be framed as sexualised behaviour by one party against the will of the other. Sending an SMS or climbing up to one's balcony may be part of such repeated, but unwelcome attempts which afterward are labelled as stalking, or breaking and entering.

If it is indeed the reception by the other party that defines criminal behaviour in normal courtship, to decide whether an offence has really been committed we must be able to establish:

- What was the reception at the time when it occurred?
- How was that reception made clear to the accused?
- Was the reception masked by other behaviours of any kind that could have been interpreted as signs of encouragement?

In the case of Barney Rhine these questions were not answered for any of the thirteen complaints brought against him. Despite this, Rhine was convicted by the district court. His case will come up for appeal.

Postscript: Psychological Expertise and the Law

The basic problem of introducing psychological expertise in the framework of a legal trial, civil or criminal, is that it almost inevitably causes a clash of disciplines. Legal decisions are made on the basis of the law, either statutory or common, and interpretations of the law according to legal scholarship. Psychological interpretations of the law are irrelevant in a context in which primacy rests with another discipline. Because of the large and fundamental differences between psychological science and legal scholarship, it is often questionable whether it serves any purpose for courts, judges, and juries to take notice of psychological expertise. Clearly, a set of rules is needed for the way in which only selected elements of psychological reasoning can find a place within the often doctrinaire structure of the law. What then is the difference between the approaches of the two disciplines?

Legal scholarship is axiomatic

Among the scientific disciplines, legal scholarship resembles mathematics more than any other discipline does. Legal reasoning is based on a particular ordering of reality that makes it possible to place concrete events, situations or actions in fixed categories for which legal rules have been developed. As an example, take the problem of *force majeur*, discussed in chapter 13. It is concerned with situations in which people, through conditions beyond their control, can react in only one possible manner. If that reaction constitutes a violation of the law, should it be punished? Traditionally, a distinction is made between *vis absoluta* and *vis compulsiva* (cf. Cleiren & Nijboer, 2000, Art. 40). The first is a strong form in which there simply was no deliberate choice. An example is being pushed in a dense crowd and thereby injuring another person. The second is a weaker form, in which there was a choice in principle, but the situation was such that all options except one were virtually impossible. A well-known example is self-defence when one's life is threatened. In the class of *vis compulsiva*, again two subclasses can be distinguished: situations in which a severe pressure made it impossible to weigh the alternatives, versus situations in which there is a dilemma, characterised by the fact that all available choices involve behaviour proscribed by the law. An example of such a dilemma is the signalman's choice between saving a child playing on the railway tracks and staying on duty in order to throw the switches for an oncoming train (Sims, 1883). John Yonker's dilemma in the climbing wall tragedy, as described in chapter 13, may have been of this type. Hence, we must distinguish three classes of *force majeur.*

Another distinction that is usually made refers to *justification* versus *exculpation. Force majeur* may provide justification for one's actions, which logically excludes prosecution and punishment. It may also happen that, notwithstanding the condition of *force majeur,* the chosen behaviour was still unjustified. Then it may be possible that the exceptional situation provides an excuse, leading to exculpation. The classical example of this case is the resistance fighter who betrays the names of fellow fighters under extreme duress.

It should be obvious that these distinctions, *vis absoluta* versus *vis compulsiva,* severe pressure versus choice dilemmas, and justification versus exculpation, are artificial and do not necessarily correspond with clear distinctions in the reality of everyday life. On the contrary, reality is characterised by gradual transitions from one class to another, with continuity rather than discreteness, and boundary cases that will always create problems for the legal authority deciding on the class to which a particular case belongs. In this sense, the law enforces an orderly structure on a reality that of itself does not reflect this structure, or any structure.

This characterisation of legal scholarship suggests that the discipline is axiomatic. Its ordering of real life is not based on extensive empirical observation and research, but on the application of a limited number of logical principles and distinctions. It cannot be challenged in any particular trial; the discussion there must be restricted to questions of how the ordering applies to a specific case. Such discussions may well lead to the definition of ever more subclasses, and finally to a vastly complicated and refined structure with dozens of sub-sub-categories, criteria to distinguish them, and lists of authoritative precedents.

But still, such structures reflect the original and often age-old principles which themselves are not under discussion. It is understandable why this is done: without maintaining the preconceived order, it is impossible to adjudicate in a systematic, reliable and predictable manner. Without an a priori ordering of reality, the law becomes a tombola, not serving the societal stability for which it was designed.

It is also clear, however, that such an inflexible a priori ordering has a disadvantage. Around the boundaries of the categories, cases will be classified as belonging to one category, although it could easily be argued that they belong to another adjacent category. The development of legal categorisations through legislation or precedent does not make decisions about such individual cases predictable and thereby superfluous. Even if a majority of situations clearly fall in one or the other category, there will always be a significant minority of cases that need to be decided through the decisions of a court of law.

In situations like these, psychological expertise may be brought in to tip the scale one way or another. The *Battered Woman Syndrome* (Walker, 1979) may serve as an example. The argument here is that women who are systematically abused by their husbands cannot be expected to escape from that situation, because the repeated physical abuse brings them in a condition of learned helplessness, a feeling of being powerless. Through the (arbitrary) alternation of love and violence, they have come to believe that their husbands are basically good men, and that they themselves are the cause of their husbands' aggression. At the same time, they may well come to believe that their husbands might eventually kill them. Thus, a dilemma is created: they cannot escape although they fear to be killed. As a result, they may come to believe that their only option is to kill their husband. The initial legal discussion on this issue is found in the case of Ibn Tamas v. United States (Monahan & Walker, 2002, p. 410-418). Psychological expertise about the Battered Woman Syndrome may result in placing the murder of one's spouse in the category of *vis compulsiva*, subclass severe pressure, suggesting that justification may not be in order, but exculpation is. Without the psychological expertise about the Battered Woman Syndrome, it could be argued that a woman accused of killing her husband has had ample opportunity to leave him. This means that there has always been an opportunity to escape, and that therefore *force majeur* does not apply. The critical question then to be decided by the court is whether the psychological evidence about the behaviour of women suffering from the syndrome belongs in the severe pressure variant of *vis compulsiva*. If so, the psychological expertise has found its place within the legal structure and may henceforth be treated as part of, and according to, legal logic.

From a psychological fact it becomes also a legal fact. But what, exactly, is the definition of a psychological fact? How did psychologists discover the Battered Woman Syndrome? Is this perhaps also a preconceived notion, supported by nothing more than logical distinctions or traditional wisdom? Is psychological knowledge also axiomatic and therefore unchallengeable? Could Dr. Lenore Walker, the inventor of the syndrome who testified in the case of Mrs. Ibn Tamas, be wrong? Which methodological criteria have her psychological studies of the syndrome met that now allow that the Battered Woman Syndrome can be presented as a psychological fact, and even be promoted to the status of a legal fact?

Psychology is an empirical science

While one may argue about this, we take the position that psychology is an exclusively empirical science. Anything said by psychologists has the status of a hypothesis as long as it is not yet validated in empirical studies. Consequently, psychology is limited to what is in principle empirically testable. Interesting but unverifiable statements like 'people inherit their character from their existence in previous lives' or 'people's motives for action are largely determined by desires repressed to their subconscious' are outside the field of psychology, for the reason that they are not empirically testable. They are not true or untrue, but irrelevant to empirical science.

Meanwhile, nothing derogatory is said about such claims. Maybe they belong to the most interesting things that can be said about the human condition. But they do not belong to the realm of empirical psychology. Expert testimony in the domain of psychology must not only reflect the latest scientific insights, but also and especially the empirical studies on which these insights are based. In that sense psychology is un-axiomatic: anything can be presented as true (or false), provided that there is empirical support for it. The Battered Woman Syndrome, and the claim that it inevitably leads to a situation in which a woman has no other option than to kill her husband, can be accepted as a fact only if empirical research has demonstrated that such a syndrome exists, and that it is caused by the violent behaviour of a husband (cf. Schuller & Vidmar, 1992).

To many, this point of view may seem uncontroversial. But the problem is that it is easier to speculate about psychology than to run valid and reliable empirical studies. Much of what nowadays is presented as 'research' does not deserve this title, and even serious research may not answer the questions that are disputed in courtrooms. The history of psychology is marred with controversies between various 'schools'. Almost anything that was established before 1950 has been revised or flatly rejected in the 50 years that followed, even though it was based on research that was of high standards according to contemporary methodological criteria.

A considerable degree of reserve or restraint is apparently in order when psychological knowledge is presented as good enough to serve in the context of a legal argument. An extra impediment is that laboratory studies can only rarely reproduce the conditions of a real crime, whereas studies conducted outside the laboratories often lack the controls needed to draw firm conclusions. Thus, if psychological evidence is limited to what is tested under well-controlled conditions, reflecting in full the complexity of situations occurring in real life, and only using methods that have passed the test of time, the field of psychological expertise may become narrow indeed, much narrower than the rich variety of questions posed to us by judges, prosecutors and defence lawyers. As a result, it often happens that psychologists proclaim insights and opinions that really are in dispute or even have already been rejected. There are a large number of topics of this type. As examples we could mention the anatomically correct dolls test, the multiple-personality disorder (MPI, currently also called the dissociative identity disorder, DID), the post-traumatic stress syndrome (PTSS), recovered memories (see chapter 4), statement validity analysis (SVA, including CBCA, see chapter 11), and a good many others. Apparently, research psychologists are not always themselves the best judges of the quality of their research. How then can the courts be protected against unwarranted influences by psychologists?

From science to law in adversarial procedures

The transition from psychological fact to legal fact, which is achieved first by the critical scrutiny and subsequent acceptance of psychological expertise by a court, is a crucial one. But how do courts manage that, given the fact that they themselves are not psychologists, have no special knowledge of the methodology of empirical research, and have no experience with the limitations and pitfalls of laboratory work? In the case of Mrs. Ibn-Tamas and the Battered Woman Syndrome, it appeared to be a difficult process. The trial court excluded Dr. Walker's testimony on the subject, but the court of appeals remanded the case for a new determination of admissibility by a trial court. Associate Judge Nebeker, however, dissented with this judgement, and it is worth looking at his argument.

> As to her method for examining or interviewing Mrs. Ibn-Tamas and analysing her situation, the record reveals only that the expert "had contact" with her. No other indication is made. We learned from the witness that her opinion was going to be based upon a paltry universe of 110 other women who were "researched" by her. We know nothing of these few women other than their apparent claim of being abused. Nothing was said of the techniques for "interviewing", the duration of the interview, the number of times each woman was interviewed or any follow-up. The expert interviewed only the abused women and not their husbands, physicians or family. She even testified that "*we* have talked to" some 60 percent of the abused women referred by others (emphasis added). When questioned by the court, the witness candidly acknowledged that 40 percent of the women apparently were prompted to seek an interview by newspapers, television or radio. No estimated potential margin for error was expressed. The foundation for the testimony is patently inadequate, as there was no indication in the record of what method the expert employed or that the expert's method was generally accepted in the field (Monahan & Walker, 2002, p. 416).

Not bad for a non-expert! But it must be noticed that the crucial objections are really legal rather than methodological. Judge Nebeker refuses to be convinced by stories that came from 110 unidentified women, of whom we cannot know with certainty that they were actually abused. To establish this basic fact, corroboration from other persons should have been obtained and, although this is not expressed in so many words, if possible by way of convictions of accused husbands of the women in the study. In what way, a lawyer would reason, can one study battered women if it has not first been verified that they had been battered at all? Is not the invitation through the media some sort of encouragement for cunning individuals hoping to claim damages, rather than to contribute to a scientific study?

Notice that research psychologists would probably not think it necessary to hear both sides before clients or patients are diagnosed. For them the identity of the 110 women is irrelevant; most subjects in psychological studies remain anonymous. And an invitation through the media to partake in a psychological study is not generally rejected as a way of recruiting experimental subjects. But these objections herald the decision of the trial court, and of the court of appeals. Both refused to accept Dr. Walker's study as a sufficient basis for establishing a legal fact. Judge Gallagher concurred, but for different reasons:

> I believe this proffered testimony on "battered women" is properly considered to be within the category of novel scientific evidence. Consequently, it falls within the underlying doctrine of *Frye v. United States*, 54 App.D.C. 46, 293 F. 1013 (1923). The essence of *Frye* is that there must be a reliable body of scientific opinion supporting a *novel scientific theory* before it is admissible in evidence (Monahan & Walker, 2002, p. 417).

The reference to the Frye criterion is essential in several ways. It requires that scientific information is only presented to a jury if the relevant scientific community recognises it as a virtually indisputable, i.e., generally accepted, fact. But invoking this criterion must be placed in its proper context. We mention three aspects.

In the first place it should be understood that the Frye criterion functions in a context of *adversarial* legal proceedings. In this system two opposing parties argue their case in front of a neutral and (with some exceptions) passive court. Every relevant fact must be presented during the trial, and no facts count that have *not* been presented by either of the two parties. The court does not itself do or order any investigations. The epistemological assumption underlying this is that truth will emerge from a clash of opinions, even if these opinions are not impartial. As a consequence, it is not unusual for parties to seek only experts who will support their side, not because they are paid to do so, not through intentional distortion of the scientific state of affairs, but simply because also in scientific disciplines many things are under discussion. Courts must try to protect themselves against partisan trends in expert testimony, even if it is due to the partisan nature of a scientific dispute. The vehement and sometimes malicious discussions on recovered memories (called the 'Memory Wars'; see chapter 5) are proof of this necessity.

Secondly, it should be realised that in many adversarial proceedings, a judge as well as a jury are involved. It is the jury who decides the ultimate question of guilt or innocence. The judge keeps the order and takes all decisions necessary to ensure a fair trial, such as decisions about the admissibility of evidence. This includes decisions concerning the admissibility of expert testimony, which is done in a separate session where the experts, in the absence of the jury, may explain the content of their testimony. In the Ibn Tamas case, the decisions on the admissibility of testimony on the Battered Woman Syndrome were taken in such sessions and were meant to determine whether or not a jury might become prejudiced or be misled by expert evidence that might be scientifically ill-founded. The judge must make this decision, which is difficult because – as mentioned before – the judge is no expert. To take such decisions, the American legal system has provided trial judges with two sets of criteria: The Frye criterion established in 1923, and the Daubert criteria from 1993. Both these criteria were established by a federal court. State courts are free to apply or to reject them, and in fact do apply the criteria of their own choosing. Hence it may happen that a scientific argument is accepted in one state and rejected in another. However, without entering into the complicated discussions about the relative merits of the two sets of criteria, and even without explaining what precisely the differences are, it should suffice here to stress that the American trial procedure does have criteria for the admissibility of scientific evidence, that is, for the translation of scientific facts into legal facts.

At the same time, it must be admitted that tests like those expressed in Frye and Daubert are, in part, circular. Both tests include the requirement that evidence offered by an expert witness must be 'generally accepted' in the scientific community (cf. Faigman, 1999). General acceptance can mean a variety of things: general acceptance of the proffered facts, general acceptance of the methods that produced the facts, personal recognition of the expert as an authority in the field, publication of those facts in refereed scientific journals, etc. If an entire scientific field fails in critically monitoring its methodology, the courts will be dragged down in their fall. Psychoanalysis is a case in point. The application of psychoanalytic principles in sexual abuse or murder trials have dramatically illustrated this. For this the psychological community has only itself to blame, as empirical psychologists have tolerated psychoanalysts as members in their scientific organisations, as faculty in their universities and other educational programmes, and have rarely protested unequivocally against their appearance as expert witnesses in legal trials.

Also in general we surmise that the psychological community is not the best judge of research quality. Thus, how could the courts know? The systematic testing of the validity of scientific evidence before it is presented to a jury is not an automatic result of adversarial legal proceedings. In the UK, also given to adversarial proceedings, it is less clear which criteria are used in deciding the admissibility of expert evidence.

A third aspect that should be stressed is the principle of precedence. The Frye case was concerned with the admissibility of the polygraph test as proof of the fact that someone was speaking the truth or lying. It was decided in 1923 by the Federal Court of Washington D.C., and has since served as a standard for the evaluation of scientific evidence throughout the United States; since 1993, it continues to do so in more than half of the states. It is not a statutory rule but has the same effect, in that the courts do not need to invent their own criteria all over again. When Judge Gallagher refers to 'Frye', everyone knows what he means, and nobody will challenge the applicability of this criterion. All this may differ drastically if the adversarial system would be exchanged for an alternative class of legal proceedings.

From science to law in inquisitorial systems

The alternative to an adversarial system is the *inquisitorial system*, mostly encountered in continental Europe. Here, the court itself conducts the investigation, not only at the trial, but in some systems right from the beginning, from the moment of discovery of the body, so to say. Often an *examining judge,* who is an extension of the court and has the full power of the court, is in charge of the investigation. At the trial the court is active, asking questions from the prosecution and interrogating the defendant, witnesses and experts. The court decides the guilt or innocence of the defendant and imposes the sentence. The court may also decide to suspend the trial temporarily and order additional investigations. Obviously, such an active role is not very compatible with the system of jury trials, which does not mean that there are no juries in continental Europe; there are some mixed systems in which courts and jury members work together.

In inquisitorial systems there are usually no explicit criteria for the admissibility of expert testimony. Experts are interrogated from the bench, and the bench may decide to ignore the testimony even though it was admitted and therefore presented in court. The case of Bandhu, described in chapter 12, illustrates how a court, without any scrutiny of the qualifications of the experts, accepted expertise about the effectiveness of black magic in Suriname and based its verdict on the rather extravagant claims proffered by two social workers. In the inquisitorial system the role of the prosecution and the defence is to assist the court, not to do battle in front of it. A distinct criticism of the trustworthiness of an expert may be in order, but a direct attack on an expert's expertise might easily be regarded as a double affront: as criticism of the court's ability to select and admit relevant experts, and of the court's ability to weigh the expert testimony itself.

Similarly, it is within the court's power to refuse to hear experts on certain questions, even though the prosecution or the defence argue that such expertise is needed. The court may decide that the expertise is not pertinent to the questions on which a decision is sought, or that the expert will invade the province of the court, i.e., that the court itself has sufficient knowledge of the field, or that the proposed expert is not knowledgeable in the field, or even that the field does not lend itself to expertise.

Such decisions, preliminary to hearing the expert, resemble the admissibility decisions in adversarial systems. But the inquisitorial court has another option: it may listen politely to the expert and only afterwards decide that the expertise must be rejected on one or more of the grounds mentioned above. That decision may be taken implicitly and never be stated, let alone explained publicly. Such a course of affairs could be in conflict, though, with the usual legal obligation of inquisitorial courts to give reasons for their verdicts.

These explanations may be rather succinct, as is often the case in our country, but can also be extensive, as is usual in, for instance, Germany. As a rule such explanations will also refer to the presented expert testimony: why it was accepted as valid evidence, or why it was rejected. Not long ago the Supreme Court in our country decided that a court, when confronted with conflicting expertise proffered by experts who disagree about what their science has to say about the problem at hand, may accept only one of these opinions if it can explain why the different opinion of the other expert must be rejected.[4] Again, such treatment of expert opinion is not unlike the admissibility decisions of adversarial courts, even though under the inquisitorial regime the reason is only given after the court has reached its verdict.

The weakness of the rule that reasons must be given is that it is taken to pertain mainly to reasons supporting a conviction. Convictions must be based on legal evidence, and the verdict must be clear about the legal evidence, presented in court, that convinced the court of the defendant's guilt. However, this is often interpreted to mean that the verdict must list *sufficient* pieces of evidence, not necessarily *all* evidence that contributed to it. Anything more than the required bare minimum of evidence is considered *obiter dicta* (unnecessary additions) and had best be avoided so as not to weaken the verdict and open it up to appeal. It is, therefore, quite possible that an expert opinion significantly contributed to the court's conviction but is not listed under the *sufficient,* i.e., minimally required, pieces of evidence. It may

4 HR 30 March 1999, *NJ* 1999, 451.

therefore happen that a defendant is in fact convicted mainly on the basis of expert evidence without the court even mentioning it, let alone explaining how it interpreted the expertise. In the case of Bandhu (chapter 12), the court decided that the alleged victim Maya was sexually molested after she lost conscious control of her behaviour. The prosecution's story was that Maya lost control through black magic applied by Bandhu. Two experts testified that black magic may indeed have this effect. The court limited its explanation to the fact that Maya lost control, leaving unexplained how this had come about, thereby avoiding any reference to the two experts. But since the prosecution had not offered any alternative reason for Maya's loss of control, we must infer that the court had accepted the expertise.

In such a procedure, the inquisitorial system may embody the worst of two worlds: the preliminary scrutiny of the admissibility of the expertise is avoided, whereas the post hoc explanation of why the expertise was admitted and how it was weighed is omitted as an *obiter dictum*. This is worrisome. Through the court's implicit acceptance as legal evidence, expert testimony is turned into legal fact. The process is risky because the experts are not legal scholars, and the judges are not experts. The transition should be explicit, and subject to public scrutiny. The fifteen chapters of this book abound with examples where scientific expertise is turned into legal fact even though the expertise is debatable or downright mistaken. To illustrate this problem we mention two other examples: the expertise about the 'dissociative amnesia' (chapter 12) that constituted the legal basis for acquitting a man who had strangled his wife, and the 'dragging theory' (chapter 9) explaining how two suspects, after raping the victim, could have left the sperm of a third person on the victim's body, instead of their own.

Conclusion

A critical task of any criminal trial procedure is to turn testimonial evidence into legal fact. In the case of expert testimony; this may be a difficult thing to do because not all expert testimony is reliable, and the courts are not in the best position to select and scrutinise what the experts say. In the case of psychological expertise, this problem is aggravated because there is quite a bit of bogus psychology around, and judges or juries might be insufficiently critical towards a whole body of folk psychology that is accepted in our society, even though there is no scientific support for it or, worse, there is scientific proof to the contrary. Legal discussions about the admissibility of psychological knowledge as evidence have been abundant on a few topics: person identification, false confessions, recovered memories, and some specialised issues in clinical psychology. But the courts, either adversarial or inquisitorial, appear to accept much more psychology without proper discussion of its reliability and validity. These areas we have called 'neglected', not because they do not feature in the courtroom, but because the true state of affairs in the supporting empirical research was not sufficiently taken into consideration. Our suggestion is that courts, judges and juries alike, should be made aware of their implicit use of psychological knowledge and that experts should more often be invited to illuminate the most recent scientific insights, based upon hard empirical research.

Bibliography

American Psychiatric Association (1994). *Diagnostic and Statistical Manual of Mental Disorders, Fourth Edition.* Washington, D.C.: APA.

Anthony, J.C., Le Resche, L., Niaz, U., Von Korff, M.R., & Folstein, M.F. (1982). Limits of the 'Mini-Mental State' as a Screening test for dementia and delirium among hospital patient. *Psychological Medicine, 12,* 397-408.

Aronson, K., & Nilholm, C. (1992). Storytelling as collaborative reasoning: C-narratives in incest accounts. In: M.L. McLaughlin, M.J. Cody & S.J. Read (Eds.), *Explaining One's Self to Others: Reason-Giving in a Social Context.* Hillsdale, N.J.: Erlbaum, 245-260.

Asch, S.E. (1956). Studies in independence and conformity. *Psychological Monographs, 70,* whole no. 416

Baddeley, A.D. (1990). *Human Memory: Theory and Practice.* Hove/Hillsdale: Lawrence Erlbaum Associates.

Bagijn, K. (2000) Getuigen vol afschuw over behandeling van zwerver, *Algemeen Dagblad,* 24 February.

Barbey, I. (1990), Postdeliktische Erinnerungsstörungen: Ergebnisse einer retrospektiven Erhebung, *Blutalkohol, 27,* 258-259.

Barg, J.A. (1997). The automaticity of everyday life. In: R.S. Wyer (ed.), *The Automaticity of everyday life. Advances in Social Cognition, Vol X.* Mahwah, N.J.: Lawrence Erlbaum Associates, 1-61.

Bartlett, F.C. (1932). *Remembering: A Study in Experimental Social Psychology.* London: Cambridge University Press.

Bavelas, J.B., Coates, L., & Johnson, T. (2000). Listeners as co-narrators. *Journal of Personality and Social Psychology, 79,* 941-952.

Bayes, T. (1763). Essay towards solving a problem in the doctrine of chances. *Philosophical Transactions of the Royal Society, 53,* 370-418.

Belli, R.F., Lindsay, D.S., Gales, M.S., & McCarthy, T.T. (1994). Memory impairment and source misattribution in postevent misinformation experiments with short retention intervals. *Memory & Cognition, 22*, 40-54.

Benedek, E.P. & Schetky, D.H. (1987). Problems in validating allegations of sexual abuse. Part 2: Clinical evaluation. *Journal of the American Academy of Child and Adolescent Psychiatry, 26*, 916-921.

Bennett, W.L. (1992). Legal fiction: Telling stories and doing justice. In: M.L. McLaughlin, M.J. Cody & S.J. Read (eds.), *Explaining One's Self to Others: Reason-Giving in Social Context.* Hillsdale, N.J.: Erlbaum, 149-164.

Bennett, W.L., & Feldman, M.S. (1981). *Reconstructing Reality in the Courtroom.* New Brunswick: Rutgers University Press.

Bernstein, E.M. & Putnam, F.W. (1986), Development, reliability, and validity of a dissociation scale, *The Journal of Nervous and Mental Disease, 174*, 727-735.

Blaauw, J.A. (2000). *De Puttense Moordzaak.* Baarn: Fontijn.

Bothwell, R.K., Deffenbacher, K.A., & Brigham, J.C. (1986). Predicting eyewitness accuracy from confidence. *Journal of Applied Psychology, 72*, 691-695.

Bower, G.H. (1981). Mood and memory. *American Psychologist, 36*, 129-148.

Bradford, J. McD., & Smith, S.M. (1979) Amnesia and homicide: The Padola case and a study of thirty cases. *Bulletin of the American Academy of Psychiatry and the Law, 7*, 219-231.

Brilleslijper-Kater, S.N. (2005). *Beyond Words. Between-group differences in the ways sexually abused and nonabused preschool children reveal sexual knowledge.* Amsterdam: Free University. Dissertation.

Brown, R., & Kulik, J. (1977). Flashbulb memories. *Cognition, 5*, 73-99.

Bruck, M., & Ceci, S., *Amicus Brief for the Case NJ v. Michaels, Presented by Committee of Concerned Social Scientists* (unpublished).

Buss, D.M. (1989). Sex differences in human mating preferences: Evolutionary hypotheses tested in 37 cultures. *Behavioral and Brain Sciences, 12*, 1-49.

Candel, I. (2003). *The Truth and Nothing But the Truth: The Accuracy, Completeness, and Consistency of Emotional Memories.* Maastricht: Doctoral Disseration University of Maastricht.

Carlson, E.B. & Putnam, F.W., Ross, C.A., Torem, M., Coons, P., Dill, D.L., Loewenstein, R.J., & Braun, B.G.(1993). Validity of the Dissociative Experiences Scale in screening for Multiple Personality: A multicenter study. *American Journal of Psychiatry, 150*, 1030-1036.

Ceci, S.J., & Bruck, M. (1993). The suggestibility of the child witness: A historical review and synthesis. *Psychological Bulletin, 113*, 403-439.

Centor, A. (1982). Criminals and amnesia: Comment on Bower. *American Psychologist, 37*, 240.

Choi, J.Y., Morris, J.C., & Hsu, C.Y. (1993). Cerebrovascular disease, *Neurological Clinic, 16*, 687-711.

Christianson, S.A., & Merckelbach, H.L.G.J. (in press) Crime related amnesia as a form of deception. In: P.A. Granhag & L.A. Strömwall (Eds.), *Deception in Forensic Contexts.* Cambridge: Cambridge University Press.

Cleiren, C.P.M., & Nijboer, J.F. (2000). *Dutch Criminal Code, Annotated Edition,* Deventer: Kluwer.

Cliffe, M.J. (1992). Symptom-validity testing of feigned sensory or memory deficits: A further elaboration for subjects who understand the rationale. *British Journal of Clinical Psychology, 31,* 207-209.

Cohen, G. (1989). *Memory in the Real World.* London: Lawrence Erlbaum Associates.

Cohen, L.J. (1977). *The Probable and the Provable.* Oxford: Clarendon Press.

Corwin, D.L., & Olafson, E. (1997). Videotaped discovery of a reportedly unrecallable memory of child sexual abuse: Comparison with a childhood interview videotaped 11 years before. *Child Maltreatment, 2,* 91-112.

Crews, F. (1995). *The Memory Wars.* New York: The New York Review of Books.

Critchlow, B. (1986). The powers of John Barleycorn: Beliefs about the effects of alcohol on social behavior. *American Psychologist, 41,* 751-764.

Crombag, H.F.M. (1999). Collaborative storytelling: A hypothesis in need of experimental testing. *Psychology, Crime & Law, 5,* 279-289.

Crombag, H.F.M., & Merckelbach, H.L.G.J. (1996). *Hervonden Herinneringen en Andere Misverstanden.* Amsterdam: Contact.

Crombag, H.F.M., Merckelbach, H.L.G.J., & Elffers, H. (2000). Other people's memory. *Psychology, Crime & Law, 6,* 251-265.

Crombag, H.F.M., Wagenaar, W.A., & Van Koppen, P.J. (1996). Crashing memories and the problem of 'source monitoring'. *Applied Cognitive Psychology, 10,* 95-104.

Crum, R.M., Bassett, S.S. & Folstein, M.F. (1993). Population-based norms for mini-mental state examination by age and educational level, *Journal of the American Medical Association, 269,* 2386-2391.

De Jong, M., Wagenaar, W.A., Wolters, G., & Verstijnen, I.M. (2005). Familiar face recognition as a function of distance and illumination: a practical tool for use in the courtroom. *Psychology, Crime and Law, 11,* 87-97.

De Paulo, B.M. (1994). Spotting lies: Can humans learn to do better? *Current Directions in Psychological Science, 3,* 83-86.

Dekens, K.M.K, & Van der Sleen, J. (1997). *Handleiding het Kind als Getuige.* Amterdam: Elsevier Bedrijfsinformatie.

Denney, R.L. (1996). Symptom validity testing of remote memory in a criminal forensic setting. *Archives of Clinical Neuropsychology, 11,* 589-601.

Dershowitz, A. (1994). *The Abuse Excuse.* New York: Little, Brown & Company.

Ebbinghaus, H. (1885/1966). *Über das Gedächtnis: Untersuchungen zur Experimentellen Psychologie.* Amsterdam: E.J. Bonset (Nachdruck der Ausgabe Leipzig 1885).

Edens, J.F., Otto, R.K., & Dwyer, T. (1999). Utility of the structured inventory of malingered symptomatology in identifying persons motivated to malinger psychopathology. *Journal of the American Academy of Psychiatry and Law, 127*, 387-396.

Edwards, D. & Middleton, D. (1986). Joint remembering: Constructing an account of shared experience through conversational discourse. *Discourse Processes, 9*, 423-459.

Eibl-Eibesfeldt, I. (1971). *Love and Hate.* New York: Holt, Rinehart and Wilson.

Einhorn, H.J., & Hogarth, R.M. (1986). Judging probable cause. *Psychological Bulletin, 99*, 3-19.

Ekman, P. (1988). Lying and nonverbal behavior: Theoretical issues and new findings. *Journal of Nonverbal Behavior, 12*, 163-175.

Ekman, P. & O'Sullivan, M. (1991). Who can catch a liar? *American Psychologist, 46*, 913-920.

Eth, S., & Pynoos, R.S. (1994). Children who witness the homicide of a parent. *Psychiatry, 57*, 287-306.

Evans, B. (1990). *Bias in Human Reasoning: Causes and Consequences.* London: Routledge.

Faigman, D.L. (1999). *The Use And Misuse of Science in the Law.* New York: Freeman.

Festinger, L. (1950). Informal social communication. *Psychological Review, 57*, 271-282.

Festinger, L. (1954). A theory of social comparison processes. *Human Relations, 7*, 117-140.

Festinger, L. (1957). *A Theory of Cognitive Dissonance.* Stanford: Stanford University Press.

Festinger, L., Schachter, S., & Back, K. (1963). *Social Pressures in Informal Groups.* Stanford: Stanford University Press.

Fischhoff, B. (1975). Hindsight ≠ foresight: The effect of outcome knowledge on judgement under uncertainty. *Journal of Experimental Psychology: Human Perception and Performance, 1*, 288-299.

Fitzgerald, J.M. (1996). Intersecting meanings of reminiscence in adult development and aging. In: D.C. Rubin (ed.). *Remembering Our Past: Studies in Autobiographical Memory.* Cambridge: Cambridge University Press.

Fitzpatrick, R.L., & Reynolds, J. (1997). *False Profits. Seeking Financial and Spiritual Deliverance in Multi-Level Marketing and Pyramid Schemes.* Charlott, N.C.: Herald Press.

Fokker, G.A. (1862). *Geschiedenis der Loterijen in de Nederlanden.* Amsterdam: Muller.

Folstein, M.F., Folstein, S.E., & McHugh, P.R. (1975). Mini-mental state: A practical method for grading the state of patients for the clinician. *Journal of Psychiatric Research, 12,* 189-198.

Frederick, R.I., Carter, M., & Powel, J. (1995). Adapting symptom validity testing to evaluate suspicious complaints of amnesia in medicolegal evaluations. *Bulletin of the American Academy of Psychiatry and Law, 23,* 227-233.

Freud. S. (1896). *Zur Aetiologie der Hysterie. Gesammelte Werke, Bd. 1.* London: Imago Publishing Co., 1940-1952.

Friedrich, W.N., Gramsch, P., Broughton, D., Kuiper, J., & Beilke, R.L. (1991). Normative sexual behaviour in children. *Pediatrics, 88,* 456-464.

Fuller, L. The adversary system. In: H.J. Berman (Ed.) (1968). *Talks on American Law.* New York: Vintage, p. 31.

Gambling Impact and Behavior Study: Final Report of the National Gambling Impact Study Commission. University of Chicago: National Opinion Research Center, 18 March 1999.

Garry, M., Manning, C.G., Loftus, E.F., & Sherman, S.J. (1996). Imagination inflation: Imagining a childhood event inflates confidence that it occurred. *Psychonomic Bulletin & Review, 3,* 208-214.

Garven, S., Wood, J.M., & Malpass, R.S. (1998). More than suggestion: The effect of interviewing techniques from the McMartin Preschool case. *Journal of Applied Psychology, 83,* 347-359.

Garven, S., Wood, J.M., & Malpass, R.S. (2000). Allegations of wrongdoing: The effects of reinforcement on children's mundane and fantastic claims. *Journal of Applied Psychology, 85,* 38-49.

Geiselman, R.E., Fisher, R.P., Firstenberg, I., Hutton, L.A., Sullivan, S., Avetissian, I., & Prosk, A. (1984). Enhancement of eyewitness memory: An empirical evaluation of the cognitive interview. *Journal of Police Science and Administration, 12,* 74-80.

Gilbert. N. (1992). Realities and Mythologies of Rape, *Society, 29,* May issue. (Cited by Roiphe.)

Gillie, O. (1976). Crucial data was faked by eminent psychologist. *Sunday Times,* 24 October .

Gilovich, T. (1993). *How We Know It Wasn't so: The Fallibility of Human Reason in Everyday Life.* New York: The Free Press.

Goodchilds, J.D., Zellman, G., Johnson, P.B., & Giarusso, R. (1988). Adolescents and their perceptions of sexual interaction outcomes. In: A.W. Burgess (Ed.), *Sexual Assault, Vol. 2,* New York: Garland, 245-270.

Goodman, D.W. (1995). Alcohol amnesia. *Addiction, 90,* 315-317.

Gordon, B.N., Schroeder, C.S., & Abrams, J.M. (1990). Children's knowledge of sexuality: A comparison of sexually abused and nonabused children. *American Journal of Orthopsychiatry, 60,* 250-257.

Gould, O.N., & Dixon, R.A. (1993). How we spent our vacation: Collaborative storytelling by young and old adults. *Psychology and Aging, 8,* 10-17.

Greenberg, S.A., & Shuman, D.W. (1997). Irreconcilable conflict between therapeutic and forensic roles. *Professional Psychology: Research and Practice, 28,* 50-57.

Groeneweg, J. & Wagenaar, W.A. (1989). *Oorzaken en Achtergronden van Foutieve Geweldsaanwendingen door de Politie.* Leiden: Werkgroep Veiligheid Rijksuniversiteit Leiden, R. 89/30.

Gudjonsson, G.H. (1992). *The Psychology of Interrogations, Confessions and Testimony.* Chichester/New York: John Wiley & Sons.

Hacking, I. (1995). *Rewriting the Soul: Multiple Personality and the Sciences of Memory.* Princeton, N.J.: Princeton University Press.

Hacking, I. (1998). *Mad Travelers: Reflections on the Reality of Transient Mental Illnesses.* London: Free Association Books.

Hannigan, S.L., & Reinitz, M.T. (2001). A demonstration and comparison of two types of inference-based memory errors. *Journal of Experimental Psychology: Learning, Memory, and Cognition, 27,* 931-940.

Hansel, C.E.M. (1989). *The Search for Psychic Power: ESP and Parapsychology Revisited.* Buffalo, N.Y.: Prometheus Books.

Hardin, C.D., & Higgins, E.T. (1996). Shared reality: How social verification makes the subjective objective. In: R.M. Sorrentio & E.T. Higgins (Eds.), *Handbook of Motivation and Cognition, Vol. 3.* New York: The Guilford Press. 28-84.

Hart, P. 't, & Pijnenburg, B. (1989). The Heizel Stadium tragedy. In: U. Rosenthal, M.T. Charles & P. 't Hart (Eds.), *Coping with Crisis: The Management of Disasters, Riots, and Terrorism.* Springfield: C.C. Thomas Publisher.

Hastie, R. (1984). Causes and effects of causal attribution. *Journal of Personality and Social Psychology, 46,* 44-56.

Haworth-Hoeppner, S. (1998). What's gender got to do with it: perceptions of sexual coercion in a university community. *Sex Roles, 38,* 757-779.

Her Majesty's Stationary Office, London, 1992. Hergé (1954). *On a marché sur la lune (Explorers of the Moon).* Bruxelles: Casterman (London: Methuen).

Herman, D.H.J. (1986). Criminal offenses and pleas in mitigation based on amnesia. *Behavioral Sciences and the Law, 4,* 5-26.

Hodges, J.R. (1991). *Transient Amnesia: Clinical and Neuropsychological Aspects.* London: W.B. Saunders Company.

Homans, G.C. (1951), *The Human Group.* London: Routledge & Kegan Paul.

Huffman, M.L., & Ceci, S.J. (1997). *Can Criteria-Based Content Analysis Distinguish True and False Beliefs of Preschoolers? An Exploratory Analysis.* Ithaca, N.Y.: Cornell University. (unpublished manuscript, cited in Ruby & Brigham, 1997).

Hyman, I.E. (1994). Conversational remembering: Story recall with a peer versus for an experimenter. *Applied Cognitive Psychology, 8*, 49-66.

Hynie, M., Schuller, R.A., & Couperthwaite, L. (2003). Perceptions of sexual intent: The impact of condom possession. *Psychology of Women Quarterly, 27*, 75-79.

Israëls, H. (1999). *Der Fall Freud: Die Geburt der Psychonalyse aus der Lüge.* Hamburg: Europäische Verlaganstalt.

Iverson, G.L. (1995). Qualitative aspects of malingered memory deficits. *Brain Injury, 9*, 35-40.

Jackson, J.L., Granhag, P.A. & Otten, D. (1996). *The Truth of Fantasy: The Ability of Barristers and Laypersons to Detect Deception in Children's Testimony.* Leiden: Netherlands Institute for the Study of Criminality and Law Enforcement (Report NSCR WD 96-11).

Johnson, M.K., Hashtroudi, S. & Lindsay, D.S. (1993). Source monitoring. *Psychological Bulletin, 114*, 3-28.

Johnson, M.K. & Raye, C.L. (1981). Reality monitoring. *Psychological Review, 88*, 67-85.

Jones, D.P.H., & McGraw, J.M. (1987). Reliable and fictitious accounts of sexual abuse in children. *Journal of Interpersonal Violence, 2*, 27-45.

Kahneman, D., Slovic, P., & Tversky, A. (1982). *Judgment under Uncertainty: Heuristics and Biases.* Cambridge: Cambridge University Press.

Kamin, L.J. (1974). *The Science and Politics of IQ.* Potomac, M.D.: Erlbaum.

Kebbell, M.R., Johnson, S.D., Froyland, I., & Ainsworth, M. (2002). The influence of belief that a car crashed on witnesses' estimates of civilian and police car speed. *The Journal of Psychology, 36*, 597-607.

Keren, G. & Wagenaar, W.A. (1985). On the psychology of playing blackjack: Normative and descriptive considerations with implications for decision theory. *Journal of Experimental Psychology: General, 114*, 133-158.

Knudson, J.F. (1995). Psychological characteristics of maltreated children: Putative risk factors and consequences. *Annual Review of Psychology, 46*, 401-431.

Koehler, D.J. (1991). Explanation, imagination, and confidence in judgment. *Psychological Bulletin, 110*, 499-519.

Kohnstamm, Ph. (1949). Causaliteit en strafrechts-wetenschap. *Tijdschrift voor Strafrecht, 58*, 201-231.

Kotre, J. (1995). *White Gloves: How We Create Ourselves Through Memory.* New York: The Free Press.

Kraus, R.M. (1987). The role of the listener: Addressee influences on message formulation. *Journal of Language & Social Psychology, 6*, 81-98.

Lakatos, I. (1976). *Proofs and Refutations: The Logic of Mathematical Discovery* (Edited by John Worrall & Elie Zahar). Cambridge: Cambridge University Press.

Landry, K.L., & Brigham, J.C. (1992). The effect of training in Criteria-Based Content Analysis on the ability to detect deception in adults. *Law and Human Behavior, 16*, 663-676.

Larsen, S.F., Thompson, C.P., & Hansen, T. (1996). Time in autobiographical memory. In: D.C. Rubin (Ed.), *Remembering Our Past: Studies in Autobiographical Memory*. Cambridge: Cambridge University Press, pp. 129-156.

LeDoux, J.E. (1996). *The Emotional Brain*. New York: Touchstone.

Leman, P.J. (2003). Who shot the president? Socio-cognitive biases and reasoning about conspiracy theories. Paper presented at the British Psychological Society Conference.

Lesieur, H., & Rosenthal, R. (1991). Pathological gambling: A review of the literature. *Journal of Gambling Studies, 7*, 5-40.

Lief, H.I., & Fetkewicz, J.M. (1995). Retractors of false memories: The evolution of pseudomemories. *The Journal of Psychiatry and Law, 23*, 411-436.

Lindsay, D.S., & Read, D.S. (1994). Psychotherapy and memories of childhood sexual abuse: A cognitive perspective. *Applied Cognitive Psychology, 8*, 281-338.

Linton, M. (1975). Memory for real-world events. In: D.A. Norman & D.E. Rumelhart (Eds.), *Explorations in Cognition*. San Francisco: Freeman, chapter 14.

Linton, M. (1978). Real world memory after six years: An in vivo study of very long term memory. In: M.M. Gruneberg, P.E. Morris & R.N. Sykes (Eds.), *Practical Aspects of Memory*. London/Orlando: Academic Press, pp. 69-76.

Linton, M. (1982). Transformation of memory in everyday life. In: U. Neisser (Ed.), *Memory Observed*. San Francisco: Freeman.

Lochun, S. (1996). *Non-Verbal Behaviours as Indicators of Deception: Are They Useful in A Police Interrogation?* Zoetermeer: Korps Landelijke Politiediensten (Report CRI 70/96).

Loftus, E.F. (1979). *Eyewitness Testimony*. Cambridge, M.A.: Harvard University Press.

Loftus, E.F. (1986). Experimental psychologist as advocate or impartial educator, *Law and Human Behavior, 10*, 63-78.

Loftus, E.F. (1993). The reality of repressed memories. *American Psyxhologist, 48*, 518-537.

Loftus, E.F. (2003). Our changeable memories: Legal and practical implications. *Nature Reviews, Neuroscience, 4*, 231-234.

Loftus, E.F., Coan, J.A., & Pickrell, J.A. (1996). Manufacturing false memories using bits of reality. In: L.M. Reder (Ed.). *Implicit Memory and Metacognition.* Mahwah, N.J.: Lawrence Erlbaum, Associates, 195-220.

Loftus, E.F., Donders, K., Hoffman, H.G., & Schooler, J.W. (1989). Creating new memories that are quickly accessed and confidently held. *Memory & Cognition, 11,* 114-120.

Loftus, E.F., & Guyer, M.J. (2002). Who abused Jane Doe? The hazards of the single case history Part I & II. *Skeptical Inquirer, 26,* May/June and July/August issues.

Loftus, E.F., & Ketcham, K. (1994). *The Myth of Repressed Memories: False Memories and Allegations of Sexual Abuse.* New York: St. Martin's Press.

Loftus, E.F., & Marburger, W. (1983). Since the eruption of Mt. St. Helens, has anyone beaten you up? Improving the accuracy of retrospective reports with landmark events. *Memory & Cognition, 17,* 114-120.

Loftus, E.F., Miller, D.G., & Burns, H.J. (1978). Semantic integration of verbal information into a visual memory. *Journal of Experimental Psychology: Human Learning and Memory, 4,* 19-31.

Loftus, E.F., & Pickrell, J.E. (1995). The formation of false memories. *Psychiatric Annals. 25,* 720-724.

Luria, A.R. (1987). *The Mind of a Mnemonist.* Cambridge, M.A.: Harvard Univesity Press.

Lykken, D.T. (1998). *A Tremor in the Blood: Uses and Abuses of the Lie Detector.* New York: Plenum.

Mack, J.E. (1994). *Abduction: Human Encounters with Aliens.* New York: Ballatine Books.

Mahowald, M.W., & Schenk, C.H. (1995). Complex motor behavior arising during the sleep period: Forensic science implications. *Sleep, 18,* 724-727.

Malmquist, C.P. (1986). Children who witness parental murder: Posttraumatic aspects. *Journal of the American Academy of Child Psychiatry, 25,* 320-325.

Mazzoni, G.A.L., Lombardo, P., Malvagia, S., & Loftus, E.F. (1999). Dream interpretation and false beliefs. *Professional Psychology: Research and Practice, 30,* 45-50.

McCarthy, J.T. (1984). *Trademarks and Unfair Competition.* Rochester, N.Y.: The Lawyers Co-operative Publishing Company (cited by Monahan & Walker, 2002).

McCloskey, M., & Zaragoza, M. (1985). Misleading postevent information and memory for events: Arguments and evidence against the memory impairment hypothesis. *Journal of Experimental Psychology, General, 114,* 3-18.

McGregor, I., & Holmes, J.G. (1999). How storytelling shapes memory and impressions of relationship events over time. *Journal of Personality and Social Psychology, 76,* 403-419.

McNally, R.J. (2003). *Remembering Trauma.* Cambridge, M.A./London: The Belknap Press of Harvard University Press.

Meeter, M. & Murre, J.M.J. (2004). Consideration of long-term memory: Evidence and alternatives. *Psychological Bulletin, 130,* 843-857.

Mehrabian, A. (1972). *Nonviable Communication.* Chicago: Aldine.

Merckelbach, H.L.G.J., Dekkers, Th., Wessel, I., & Roefs, A. (2003). Amnesia, flashbacks, and dissociation in aging concentration camp survivors. *Behavior Research and Therapy, 41,* 351-360.

Merckelbach, H.L.G.J., Hauer, B., & Rassin, E. (2002). Symptom validity testing of feigned dissociative amnesia: A simulation study. *Psychology, Crime and Law, 8,* 311-318.

Merckelbach, H.L.G.J. & Muris, P. (2001). The causal link between self-reported trauma and dissociation: A critical review. *Behavior Research and Therapy, 39,* 245-254.

Michotte, A. (1954). *La Perception de la Causalité.* Louvain: Publications Universitaires de Louvain.

Mill, J.S. (1974/1843). *A System of Logic Ratiocinative and Inductive.* Toronto: The University of Toronto Press.

Moller, J.T., Cluitmans, P., Rasmussen, L.S., Houx, P., Rasmussen, H., *et al.* (1998). Long-term postoperative cognitive dysfunction in the elderly: ISPOCD1 study. *The Lancet, 351,* 857-861.

Monahan, J., & Walker, L. (2002). *Social Science in Law: Cases and Materials* (5th Edition). New York: The Foundation Press.

Moore, M.M. (1985). Nonviable courtship patterns in women: Context and consequences. *Ethology and Sociobiology, 6,* 237-247.

Moore, M.M. (1989). Predictive aspects of nonviable courtship behavior in women, *Semiotica, 76,* 205-215.

Moore, M.M. (1998). Nonviable courtship patterns in women: Rejection signalling – An empirical investigation. *Semiotica, 118,* 201-214.

Nanninga, R. (2001). Verkracht met toverkracht: Haagse rechtbank gelooft in zwarte magie. *Skepter, 14/3,* 8-11.

Nederlands Instituut van Psychologen (1997). *Ruling in the case ABJ v. Wagenaar.*

Nisbett, R.E., & Ross, L. (1980). *Human Inference: Strategies and Shortcomings of Social Judgment.* Englewood Cliffs: Prentice-Hall.

Norman, D.A. (1981). Categorization of action slips. *Psychological Review, 88,* 1-15.

Novick, N.R. (1997). Twice-told tales: Collaborative narration of familiar stories. *Language in Society, 26,* 199-220.

Orbach, Y., Hershkowitz, I., Lamb, M.E., Sternberg, K.J., Esplin, P.W., & Horowitz, D. (2000). Assessing the value of structured protocols for forensic interviews of alleged child abuse victims. *Child Abuse & Neglect, 24,* 733-572.

Paddock, J.R., Noel, M., Teraanova, S., Eber, H.W., Manning, C.G. & Loftus, E.F. (1999). Imagination inflation and the perils of Guided Visualisation. *The Journal of Psychology, 133,* 581-595.

Parkin, A.J. (1998). *Memory and Amnesia: An Introduction.* Oxford: Blackwell.

Parwatikar, S.D., Holmcomb, W.R., & Menninger, K.A. (1985). The detection of malingered amnesia in accused murderers. *Bulletin of the American Academy of Psychiatry, 13,* 97-103.

Pasupathi, M. (2001). The social construction of the personal past and its implication for adult development. *Psychological Bulletin, 127,* 651-672.

Pennington, N., & Hastie, R. (1986). Evidence evaluation in complex decision making. *Journal of Personality and Social Psychology, 51,* 242-258.

Pennington, N., & Hastie, R. (1988). Explanation-based decision making: Effects of memory structure on judgment. *Journal of Experimental Psychology: Learning, Memory, and Cognition, 14,* 521-533.

Pennington, N., & Hastie, R. (1993). The story model of juror decision making. In: R. Hastie (Ed.), *Inside the Jury: The Psychology of Juror Decision Making.* Cambridge: Cambridge University Press.

Perper, T. (1985). *Sex Signals: The Biology of Love.* Philadelphia: ISDI Press.

Petersen, R.C., Smith, G.E., Waring, S.C., Ivnik, R.J., Tangalos, E.G., & Kokmen, E. (1999). Mild cognitive impairment: Clinical characterization and outcome. *Archives of Neurology, 56,* 303-308.

Picknett, L., Prince, C., & Prior, S. (2001). *Double Standards: The Rudolf Hess Cover-Up.* London: Little, Brown & Company.

Poole, D.A., & Lamb, M.E. (1998). *Investigative Interviews of Children: A Guide for Helping Professionals.* Washington, D.C.: American Psychological Association.

Pynoos, R.S., & Nader, K. (1988). Children who witness sexual assaults of their mothers. *Journal of the American Academy of Child and Adolescent Psychiatry, 27,* 567-572.

Rabinowitz, C., A darkness in Massachusetts. *Wall Street Journal,* 30-1-1995.

Rasmussen, J. (1983). Skills, rules, and knowledge signals: Signals, signs, and symbols, and other distinctions in human performance models. *IEEE Transactions on Systems, Man, and Cybernetics, 3,* 257-268.

Read, J.D., & Lindsay, D.S. (1997). (Eds.) *Recollections of Trauma: Scientific Evidence and Clinical Practice.* New York: Plenum Press

Read, S.J. (1987). Constructing causal scenarios: A knowledge structure approach to causal reasoning. *Journal of Personality and Social Psychology, 52,* 288-302.

Reason, J.T. (1984). Absent-mindedness and cognitive control. In: J.E. Harris & P.E. Morris (Eds.), *Everyday Memory, Actions and Absentmindedness.* London: Academic Press.

Reason, J.T. (1990), *Human Error.* Cambridge: Cambridge University Press.
Remijn, C. (2004). *The major-event major-cause heuristic: The effect of post-event information on causal reasoning.* Maastricht: Unpublished Master's Thesis, Faculty of Psychology, Maastricht University.
Remoff, H.T. (1984). *Sexual Choice: A Woman's Decision.* New York: Dutton/Lewis Publishing.
Riley, K.C. (1988). Measurement of dissociation. *Journal of Nervous and Mental Disease, 176,* 149-150.
Roediger, H.L., Meade, M.L., & Bergman, E.T. (2001). Social contagion of memory. *Psychonomic Bulletin & Review, 8,* 365-371.
Roiphe, K. (1993). *The Morning After: Sex, Fear, and Feminism.* London: Hamish Hamilton.
Rompen, C., Meek, M.F., & Van Nadel, M.V. (2000), A cause célèbre: The so-called 'Ballpoint murder'. *Journal of Forensic Science, 1126-1129.*
Ross, C.A., Joshi, S., & Currie, R. (1991). Dissociative experiences in the general population: A factor analysis. *Hospital and Community Psychiatry, 42,* 297-301.
Ruby, C.L. & Brigham, J.C. (1997). The usefulness if the criteria-based content analysis technique in distinguishing between truthful and fabricated allegations. *Psychology, Public Policy, and Law, 3,* 705-737.

Schacter, D.L. (1986a). Amnesia and crime: How much do we really know. *American Psychologist, 41,* 286-295.
Schacter, D.L. (1986b). Feeling-of-knowing ratings distinguish between genuine and simulated forgetting. *Journal of Experimental Psychology: Learning, Memory, and Cognition, 12,* 30-41.
Schacter, D.L. (1996). *Searching for Memory: The Brain, the Mind, and the Past.* New York: Basic Books.
Schacter, D.L. (2001). *The Seven Sins of Memory: How the Mind Forgets and Remembers.* Boston: Houghton Mifflin Company.
Schooler, J.W., Ambadar, Z., & Bendiksen, M. (1997a). A cognitive corroborative case study approach for investigating discovered memories of sexual abuse. In: J.D. Read & D.S. Lindsey (Eds.), *Recollections of Trauma.* New York: Plenum Press, pp. 379-387.
Schooler, J.W., Bendiksen, M., & Ambadar, Z. (1997b). Taking the middle line: Can we accommodate both fabricated and recovered memories of sexual abuse? In: M.A. Conway (Ed.), *Recovered Memories and False Memories.* Oxford: Oxford University Press, pp. 251-291.
Schreiber, F.R. (1973). *Sybil.* Chicago: Henry Regnery.
Schuller, R.A., & Vidmar, N.J. (1992). Battered woman syndrome evidence in the courtroom. *Law & Human Behavior, 16,* 273-291.

Shesgreen, S. (1973). *Engravings by Hogarth.* New York: Dover Publications.

Sims, G.F. (1883). In the Signal Box. In: *The Life Boat and Other Poems.* London: Vernon and Co.

Skinner, B.F. (1972). *Beyond Freedom and Dignity.* New York: Knopf.

Slovic, P., Fischhoff, B., & Lichtenstein, S. (1982). Facts versus fears: Understanding perceived risk. In: D. Kahneman, P. Slovic & A. Tversky (Eds.), *Judgment under Uncertainty: Heuristics and Biases.* Cambridge: Cambridge University Press, 463-489.

Smith, G.P. (1997). Assessment of malingering with self-report instruments. In: R. Rogers (Ed.), *Clinical Assessment of Malingering and Deception.* New York: Guilford Press, 351-370.

Smith, G.P., & Burger, G.K. (1997). Detection of malingering: Validation of the Structured Inventory of Malingered Symptomatology (SIMS). *Journal of the American Academy of Psychiatry and Law, 25,* 180-183.

Snowdon, D.A., Greiner, L.H., Mortimer, J.A., Riley, K.P., Greiner, P.A., & Markesbery, W.R. (1997). Brain infarction and the clinical expression of Alzheimer disease. *Journal of the American Medical Association, 277,* 813-817.

Spanos, N.P. (1996). *Multiple Identities & False Memories: A Sociocognitive Perspective.* Washington, D.C.: American Psychological Association.

Sporer, S.L., Penrod, S.D., Read, J.D., & Cutler, B.L. (1995). Choosing, confidence, and accuracy: A meta-analysis of the confidence-accuracy relation in eyewitness identification studies. *Psychological Bulletin, 118,* 315-327.

Swihart, G., Yuille, J., & Porter, S. (1991). The role of state-dependent memory in red-outs. *International Journal of Law and Psychiatry, 22,* 199-212.

Taylor, P.J., & Kopelman, M.D. (1984). Amnesia for criminal offenses. *Psychological Medicine, 14,* 581-588.

Thoennes, N. &Tjaden, P.G. (1990). The extent, nature, and validity of sexual abuse allegations in custody/visitation disputes. *Child Abuse & Neglect, 14,* 151-163.

Thoennes, N., & Pearson, J. (1988). Summary of findings from the sexual abuse allegations project. In: E.B. Nicholson (Ed.), *Sexual Abuse Allegations in Custody and Visitation Cases.* Washington, D.C.: American Bar Association.

Thorp, E. (1966). *Beat the Dealer.* New York: Vintage.

Tversky, A. & Kahneman, D. (1973). Availability: A heuristic for judging frequency probability. *Cognitive Psychology, 4,* 207-232.

Tversky, A. & Kahneman, D. (1974). Judgment under uncertainty: Heuristics and biases. *Science, 185,* 453-458.

Tversky, H.L., & Marsh, E.J. (2000). Biased retelling of events yield biased memories. *Cognitive Psychology, 40,* 1-38.

Usher, J.A., & Neisser, U. (1993). Childhood amnesia and the beginnings of memory for four early life events. *Journal of Experimental Psychology: General, 122,* 155-165.

Van Eck, C. (2001). *Door Bloed Gezuiverd: Eerwraak bij Turken in Nederland.* Amsterdam: Uitgeverij Bert Bakker.

Van Koppen, P.J. (2000), *Report on the Interrogations in the So-called Putten Murder Case.* Letter to defence counsel, personal communication.

Van Mancius, E., (1994). *Implanted memories: No difference between real and false memories,* Unpublished Master's Thesis, Department of Experimental Psychology, Leiden University.

Vanderlinden, J. *et al.* (1991). Dissociative experiences in the general population in the Netherlands: A study with the Dissociative Questionnaire (DIS-Q). *Dissociation, 4,* 189-184.

Van 't Veer, A., Moerland, H., & Fijnaut, C. (1993). *Gokken in drievoud; Facetten van deelname, aanbod en regulering.* Arnhem: Gouda Quint.

Verkade, D.W.F., & Wagenaar, W.A. (2002). Onderscheidend vermogen en verwarring van merken. In : P.J. van Koppen, D.J. Hessing, H.L.G.J. Meckelbach & H.F.M. Crombag (Eds), *Het Recht van Binnen.* Deventer: Kluwer, 59-84.

Victor, J.S. (1993). *Satanic Panic: The Creation of a Contemporary Legend.* Chicago: Open Court.

Von Kries, J. (1889). *Über die Begriffe der Wahrscheinlichkeit und Möglichkeit und ihre Bedeutung in Strafrecht,* Quoted by: H.L.A. Hart & A.M. Honoré (1959), *Causation in the Law.* Oxford: Clarendon, p. 415.

Vrij, A. (1995). Behavioral correlates of deception in a simulated police interview. *The Journal of Psychology: Interdisciplinary and Applied, 129,* 15-29.

Vrij, A. (2000). *Detecting Lies and Deceit: The Psychology of Lying and Its Implications for Professional Practice.* Chicester: Wiley.

Vrij, A., & Semin, G.R. (1996). The experts' beliefs about nonverbal indicators of deception. *Journal of Nonverbal Behavior, 20,* 65-80.

Wagenaar, W.A. (1970). Appreciation of conditional probabilities in binary sequences. *Acta Psychologica, 34,* 348-356.

Wagenaar, W.A. (1986). My memory: A study of autobiographical memory over six years. *Cognitive Psychology, 18,* 225-252.

Wagenaar, W.A. (1988a). The proper seat: A discussion of the position of the expert witness. *Law and Human Behavior, 12,* 499-510.

Wagenaar, W.A. (1988b). *Identifying Ivan.* London: Harvester Wheatsheaf.

Wagenaar, W.A. (1988c). *Paradoxes of Gambling Behaviour.* Hove and London: Lawrence Erlbaum Associates.

Wagenaar, W.A. (1988d). People and places in my memory: A study on cue specificity and retrieval from autobiographical memory. In: M.M. Gruneberg, P.E. Morris & R.N. Sykes (Eds.), *Practical Aspects of Memory: Current Research and Issues, Volume I.* Chichester/New York: John Wiley & Sons, pp. 228-233.

Wagenaar, W.A. (1996a). Autobiographical memory in court. In: D.C. Rubin (Ed.), *Remembering the Past: Studies in Autobiographical Memory.* Cambridge: Cambridge University Press.

Wagenaar, W.A. (1996b). Profiling crisis management. *Journal of Contingencies and Crisis Management, 4,* 169-174.

Wagenaar, W.A. & Groeneweg, J. (1987). Accidents at sea: Multiple causes and impossible consequences. *International Journal of Man Machine Studies, 27,* 587-598.

Wagenaar, W.A., & Groeneweg, J. (1990). The memory of concentration camp survivors. *Applied Cognitive Psychology, 4,* 77-87.

Wagenaar, W.A., & Keren, G. (1988). Chance and Luck are not the same. *Journal of Behavioral Decision Making, 1,* 65-75.

Wagenaar, W.A., & Loftus, E.F. (1990). Ten cases of eyewitness identification: Logical and procedural problems. *Journal of Criminal Justice, 18,* 291-319.

Wagenaar, W.A., & Van der Schrier, J.H. (1996). Face recognition as a function of distance and illumination: A practical tool for use in the courtroom. *Psychology, Crime & Law, 2,* 321-332.

Wagenaar, W.A., Van Koppen, P.J., & Crombag, H.F.M. (1993). *Anchored Narratives: The Psychology of Criminal Evidence.* Hemel Hempstead: Harvester Wheatsheaf.

Wagenaar, W.A., & Veefkind, N. (1992). Comparison of one-person and many-person lineups: A warning against unsafe practices. In: F. Lösel, D. Bender & T. Bliesener (Eds.), *Psychology and Law.* Berlin/New York: Walter de Gruyter, pp. 275-285.

Walker, L.E.A. (1979). *The Battered Woman.* New York: Harper & Row.

Wason, P.C., & Johson-Laird, P.N. (1972). *Psychology of Reasoning: Structure and Content.* London: Batsford.

Wegner, D.M. (2002). *The Illusion of Conscious Will.* Cambridge, MA/London: The MIT Press.

Weiner, B. (1985). 'Spontaneous' causal thinking. *Psychological Bulletin, 97,* 74-84.

Weldon, M.S., & Bellinger, K.D. (1997). Collective memory: Collaborative and individual process in remembering. *Journal of Experimental Psychology: Learning, Memory, and Cognition, 23,* 1160-1175.

Wilkins, A.J., & Baddeley, A.D. (1978). Remembering to recall in everyday life: An approach to absentmindedness. In: M.M. Gruneberg, P.E. Morris & R.N. Sykes (Eds.), *Practical Aspects of Memory.* London/Orlando: Academic Press, pp. 27-34.

Williams, L.M., (1994). Recall of childhood trauma: A prospective study of women's memories of child sexual abuse. *Journal of Consulting and Clinical, Psychology, 62,* 1167-1176.
Wilson, T.D. (2002). *Strangers to Ourselves: Discovering the Adaptive Unconscious.* Cambridge, MA: The Belknap Press of Harvard University Press.
Woodruff, D. (1957). *The Tichborne Claimant.* London: Hollis & Charter.

Zajonc, R.B. (1980). Feeling and thinking: Preferences need no inferences. *American Psychologist, 35,* 151-175.
Zaparnik, J., Yuille, J.C., & Taylor, S. (1995). Assessing the credibility of true and false statements. *International Journal of Law and Psychiatry, 18,* 343-352.

Name Index

Ambadar, Z. 75ff, 153
Anthony, J.C. 67
Aronson, K. 168
Asch, S.E. 166

Back, K. 166
Baddeley, A.D. 71, 126, 131
Bagijn, K. 27
Barbey, I. 204
Barg, J.A. 212
Bartlett, F.C. 83
Bavelas, J.B. 175
Bayes, Th. 118
Belli, R.F. 140
Bellinger, K.D. 175
Bendiksen, M. 75ff, 153
Benedek, E.P. 182ff, 189
Bennett, W.L. 78, 93, 119, 175
Bernstein, E. 198
Blaauw, J.A. 145, 146
Bothwell, R.K. 129
Bower, G.H. 201
Bradford, J. McD. 202
Brigham, J.C. 113, 189, 191
Brilleslijper-Kater, S.N. 184
Brown, R. 204
Bruck, M. 169, 181
Burger, G.K. 208, 209
Burns, H.J. 138
Burt, C. 73
Buss, D.M. 241

Candel, I.E.L. 82
Carlson, E. 197ff
Ceci, S.J. 169, 181, 191
Centor, A. 201
Choi, J.Y. 59
Christianson, S.A. 199
Cleiren, C.P.M. 251
Cliffe, M.J. 210
Coan, J.A. 144
Coates, L. 175
Cohen, G. 131
Cohen, L.J. 80, 93
Corwin, D.L. 72
Crews, F. 73, 153
Crichton, M. 239
Critchlow, B. 200
Crombag, H.F.M. 75, 79, 93, 126, 135, 138, 150, 153, 174, 191, 196, 205, 230
Crum, R.M. 59, 66

De Jong, M. 229
De Paulo, B.M. 192
Dekens, K.M.K. 180
Demjanjuk, J. 123
Denney, R.L. 209
Dershowitz, A. 183

Dixon, R.A. 175

Ebbinghaus, H. 123
Edens, J.F. 209
Edwards, D. 175
Eibl-Eibesfeldt, I. 236
Einhorn, H.J. 29, 36
Ekman, P. 192
Elffers, H. 138
Eth, S. 153
Evans, B. 114

Faigman, D.L. 257
Feldman, M.S. 78, 93, 119
Festinger, L. 166, 167
Fetkewicz, J.M. 157
Fischhoff, B.F. 241
Fitzgerald, J.M. 124
Fitzpatrick, R.L. 16
Fokker, G.A. 11, 12
Folstein, M.F. 58
Frederick, R.I. 209
Freud, S. 71, 73
Friedrich, W.N. 184
Fuller, L. 61

Garry, M. 155
Garven, S. 172
Geiselman, R.E. 126
Gilbert, N. 242
Gillie, O. 73
Gilovich, T. 114
Goodchilds, J.D. 237
Goodman, D.W. 200
Gordon, B.N. 184
Gould, O.N. 175
Greenberg, S.A. 181
Groeneweg, J. 39, 90, 153, 204, 222
Gudjonsson, G.H. 143
Guyer, M.J. 72, 154

Hacking, I. 171, 196ff
Hannigan, S.L. 31
Hansel, C.E.M. 74
Hardin, C.D. 169
Hart, P. 't 223
Hastie, R. 30, 78
Hauer, B. 209
Haworth-Hoeppner, S. 238
Hergé 89
Herman, D.H.J. 203
Hess, R. 205
Higgins, E.T. 169
Hodges, J.R. 197, 200
Hogarth, R.M. 29, 36
Hogarth, W. 11
Holmes, J.G. 175
Homans, G.C. 115
Huffman, M.L. 191
Hyman, I.E. 168
Hynie, M. 237

Israëls, H. 71
Iverson, G.L. 208

Jackson, J.L. 181, 190
Jelicic, M. 205
Johnson, M.K. 136, 138
Johnson, T. 175
Johnson-Laird, P.N. 115
Jones, D.P.H. 183

Kahneman, D. 60, 114, 125, 126
Kamin, L.J. 73
Kebbell, M.R. 35
Kelly Michaels, M. 169
Keren, G. 10, 21
Ketcham, K. 89
Knudson, J.F. 171
Koehler, D.J. 115
Kohnstamm, Ph. 30

Kopelman, M.D. 202
Kotre, J. 129, 167
Kraus, R.M. 175
Kulik, J. 204

Lakatos, I. 72
Lamb, M.E. 186
Landry, K.L. 113
Larsen, S.F. 128
LeDoux, J.E. 34
Leman, P.J. 35
Lesieur, H. 12
Lief, H.I. 157
Lindsay, D.S. 75, 153
Linton, M. 127, 129
Lochun, S. 192
Loftus, E.F. 61, 68, 72, 75, 89, 128, 135, 138, 139, 144, 153, 154, 155, 166, 204
Luria, A.R. 71
Lykken, D. 68

Mack, J.E. 75
Mahowald, M.W. 200
Malmquist, C.P. 153
Mamet, D. 239
Manning, C.G. 155
Marburger, W. 128
Marsh, E.J. 175
Mazzoni, G.A.L. 156
McCarthy, J.T. 46
McCloskey, M. 139
McGraw, J.M. 183
McGregor, I. 175
McNally, R.J. 153, 201ff
Meek, M.F. 119
Meeter, M. 200
Mehrabian, A. 236
Merckelbach, H.L.G.J. 75, 138, 153, 196, 199, 204, 209
Michotte, A. 31
Middleton, D. 175
Mill, J.S. 31
Miller, D.G. 138
Moller, J.T. 65
Monahan, J. 43, 253ff
Moore, M.M. 236ff
Muris, P. 199
Murre, J.M.J. 200

Nader, K. 153
Nanninga, R. 207
Neisser, U. 153
Nijboer, J.F. 251
Nilholm, C. 168
Nisbett, R.E. 31, 36, 114
Norman, D.A. 214
Novick, N.R. 175

O'Sullivan, M. 192
Olafson, E. 72
Orbach, Y. 186

Paddock, J.R. 155
Parkin, A.J. 196, 201, 208
Parwatikar, S.D. 201
Pasupathi, M. 168
Pavlov, I. 212
Pearce, H. 73, 74
Pearson, J. 182
Pennington, N. 78
Perper, T. 240
Petersen, R.C. 63
Picknett, L. 205
Pickrell, J.E. 144
Pijnenburg, B. 223
Ponzi, P. 14
Poole, D.A. 186
Popper, K. 114
Pratt, J.G. 73, 74
Putnam, F.W. 198

Pynoos, R.S. 153

Rabinowitz, D. 169
Rasmussen, J. 214
Rassin, E. 209
Raye, C.L. 136
Read, J.D. 75, 153
Read, S.J. 30
Reason, J.T. 47, 130, 214, 216ff
Reinitz, M.T. 31
Remijn, C. 32
Remoff, H.T. 240
Reynolds, J. 16
Rhine, J.B. 73
Riley, K.C. 198
Roediger, H.L. 168
Roiphe, K. 242ff
Rompen, J.C. 119
Rosenthal, R. 12
Ross, C.A. 197
Ross, L. 31, 36
Ruby, C.L. 189, 191

Schachter, S. 166
Schacter, D.L. 131, 197, 201, 203, 208
Schenk, C.H. 200
Schetky, D.H. 182ff, 189
Schooler, J.W. 75ff, 153
Schreiber, F.R. 71
Schuller, R.A. 113, 254
Semin, G.R. 192
Sherman, S.J. 155
Shesgreen, S. 11
Shuman, D.W. 181
Sims, G. F. 211, 252
Skinner, B.F. 212
Slovic, P. 60, 182
Smith, G.P. 208, 209
Smith, S.M. 202
Snowdon, D.A. 63
Spanos, N.P. 196
Sporer, S.L. 129
Swihart, G. 201

Taylor, P.J. 202
Thoennes, N. 177, 182ff
Thorndike, E. 212
Thorp, E. 10
Tjaden, P.G. 177, 182ff
Tolstoy, L. 201
Tversky, A. 60, 114, 125, 126
Tversky, H.L. 175

Usher, J.A. 153

Van 't Veer, A. 12
Van der Schrier, J.H. 66, 229
Van der Sleen, J. 180
Van Eck, C. 106
Van Koppen, P.J. 79, 93, 135, 150, 151, 158, 160, 191, 230
Van Mancius, E. 154
Van Nadel, M.V. 119
Vanderlinden, J. 198
Veefkind, N. 135
Verkade, D.W.F. 43
Victor, J.S. 166
Vidmar, N.J. 113, 254
Von Kries, J. 30
Vrij, A. 82, 192

Wagenaar, W.A. 10, 13, 21, 22, 39, 43, 61, 66, 68, 71, 79, 90, 93, 123, 126, 127, 135, 150, 153, 154, 187, 191, 204, 222, 223, 229, 230
Walker, L. 43, 253ff
Walker, L.E.A. 113, 253
Wason, P.C. 115
Wegner, D.M. 30, 203, 204
Weiner, B. 30

Weldon, M.S. 175
Wilkins, A.J. 131
Williams, L.M. 90, 153
Wilson, T.D. 30, 211, 212
Woodruff, D. 71
Zajonc, R. 34
Zaparnik, J. 190
Zaragoza, M. 139

Subject Index

Accident scenarios 222ff
Advanced courtship behaviour 237ff
Adversarial law 255
Alcohol blackout 200
Alcohol intoxication 200
Alternative scenarios 118, 181
Alzheimer's disease 59
Amnesia and cognitive control 203ff
Amway 15
Anchored narratives 78ff, 93ff
Artificial shop method 46
Autobiographical memory 125, 143
Automated behaviour 212
Average individual 57ff

Bandhu case 207ff, 260
Battered woman syndrome 113, 253
Bayesian methodology 77, 118
Blackjack 10ff

Car recognition 230
Card counting 10ff
Case histories 71ff
Cat recognition 231
Causa proxima 219
Causal explanation 29ff
Causal fields 29
CBCA 113, 189ff
Chain letters 13
Chance and luck 21ff
Child abuse 177ff
Chocomel 47
Coerced confessions 143
Coercion 238
Cognitive dissonance 166
Cognitive interview 126
Coincidence 29
Collaborative storytelling 166ff
Concentration camp survivors 90, 153
Conditioned reflex 212
Condom possession 237
Confessions 143ff
Confirmation bias 114
Conformity 166
Consistency with established theories 74
Consumer confusion 43ff
Conversational remembering 168
Courtship behaviour 235ff
Criteria-Based Content Analysis 113, 189ff
Criteria for responsibility for multiple-cause events 39
Criteria for scientific evidence 72ff

Date retrieval 127
Date-rape 242

Daubert criterion 257
Decay theory of forgetting 126
Deception 149ff, 192
Demand characteristics 74
Dementia 58ff
DES 197ff
Detecting malingering 206ff
Diagnostic and Statistical Manual of Mental Disorders 196
DID 196ff
DIS-Q 198
Dissociation 197ff
Dissociative amnesia 196
Dissociative disorders 196ff
Dissociative Experiences Scale 197ff
Dissociative Identity Disorder 196ff
Dissociative Questionnaire 198
Double-capture slips 217
Dress signals 238
DSM 196
Dyas criteria 46

Exit study 44

Face recognition 228ff
False accusations of sexual abuse 182ff
False memories 152
Federal Trade Commission 15
Feigned amnesia 202ff
Fells Acre case 169
Flashbulb memories 204
Flirting 236
Force majeur 211, 251ff
Forgetting 123ff
Free will 224ff
Frye criterion 256ff
Fugue 196ff

Gambler's fallacy 22ff
Gambling 9ff
GEMS-model 214ff
Generalisability 73
Goodness of narratives 78ff
Great effect-great cause hypothesis 31ff
Guess the maker method 46
Gut Springenheide 44

Heizel Stadium 223
Herald of Free Enterprise 38, 222
Hindsight 241ff
Hypothetical speak 150

Ibn Tamas case 253
ID & T 48
Illumination 229
Imagination inflation 155
Imagining 155
Inquisitorial law 258
Interference errors 217
Interference theory of forgetting 127
Interrogation 143ff
Interviewing children, rules 186ff
Intuitive theory of mechanics 31ff

Jane Doe 72, 154
Justification and exculpation 252

Knowledge-based behaviour 215ff

Lapses 215ff
Lay's Mediterrãneas 51ff
Legal precedent 71
Lineup tests 134ff
Luck and chance 21ff

Malingered amnesia 202ff
Malingering 206
Market leader effect 47

McMartin Preschool case 169, 172
Memory wars 153ff, 257
Metamemory 86, 138
MID 59
Mini Mental State Examination 58ff
Miranda rights 71
MMSE 58ff
Monstra 72
MPD 196ff
Multi-infarct dementia 59
Multilevel Marketing 15ff
Multiple causation 38
Multiple Personality Disorder 196ff
Mutual reinforcement learning 167

Namous 106
Nonverbal communication 191ff
Nun study 63
Nuremberg trial and Rudolf Hess 204

Occam's razor 224
Onus probandi 62
Operant conditioning 212
Organic amnesia 200ff

Parapsychology 73
Pearle 49
Plausibility of underlying symptoms 73
Police trickery 149ff
Ponzi schemes 14
Post-event information 135ff
Present sense impressions 56
Presumption of innocence 114
Probable cause 114
Proces-product distinction 185ff
Proof of existence 72
Psychoanalysis 257
Psychogenic amnesia 195ff
Public control 72
Pyramid schemes 13ff

QED 198
Questionnaire for Experiences of Dissociation 198
Questionnaire method 47

Reality monitoring 131
Recovered memories 75ff, 124, 152
Red-out 201
Reflexes 211ff
Reminiscence 124
Replicability 73
Resolution of the eye 229
Retrieval cues 125
Retrograde amnesia 203
Retrospective trauma 243
Rule-based behaviour 215ff

Self defence 211
Shopping list method 45
SIMS 208
Skill-based behaviour 214ff
Slips 215ff
Smiths Food Group 51ff
Social comparison 166
Somnambulism 203
Source awareness 138ff
Source awareness 150
Specsavers 49
Story grammar 93
Structured Inventory of Malingered Symptomatology 208
Studio interviews 185ff
SVT 209
Symptom Validity Testing 209

T-Mobile 48
Trademarks 43ff

Traffic accidents 220ff
Transgenerational hypothesis of sexual abuse 170
Trattoria Chips 51ff
Trickery 149ff

Updating of memory 128

Victim studies 153
Vis absoluta 251ff
Vis compulsiva 251ff
Visual acuity 228ff
Visualisation 155

Yolanda 154

Zippo cigarette lighters 44, 55